CHILDREN UNDER STRESS

by Sula Wolff

Allen Lane The Penguin Press
London 1969

First published in 1969

Allen Lane The Penguin Press
Vigo Street, London W1

Penguin Books Inc.
7110 Ambassador Road
Baltimore
Maryland 21207

SBN 7139 0037 7
Library of Congress Catalog Card Number
70–78187

Printed in Great Britain by
The Bowering Press, Plymouth

Contents

Foreword

Dr Wolff has a double qualification for the task she has undertaken in this book. She writes, firstly, from a very full experience of clinical work in paediatrics and in child psychiatry. In addition to her clinical practice, however, she has devoted a number of years to research into child development and into the behaviour disorders of childhood.

Her own researches have added significantly to our knowledge of medical, social and environmental factors which contribute to the appearance, and to the recognition, of emotional disturbance in the early years. In the past, child psychiatrists have sometimes been noted more for their therapeutic zeal than for their scientific rigour. The list of well-authenticated studies in this field is not very long: Dr Wolff has drawn upon all the best scientific papers in her field published in Britain and America, and has also culled the European literature. As a result, her review of childhood psychiatric disturbances, and what causes them, is backed by solid research findings: and because of her familiarity with research, she conveys a sense of the limits, as well as the extent, of knowledge in her field.

At the same time, the author emphasizes the need to use one's imagination in order to see the world, and particularly the important people in the small world of the family, through the eyes of her child patients. Both in her text, and in the numerous case-histories which illustrate it, she reveals a rare understanding of the child's point of view. Clearly, this is someone with whom children can feel at home, an adult to whom they can talk freely because she really seems to know what they are talking about.

The themes dealt with in this book are of practical interest to all those engaged in the professions concerned with young children – to teachers, nurses, social workers and child-care officers, as well as to family doctors and child therapists. But this does not exhaust her potential audience, because these are topics of concern to all parents. There must be few fathers and mothers who have not wondered, at some time, whether they have handled minor crises in their children's upbringing as wisely as they might have; and fewer still who have not known moments of anxiety about their children's behaviour. Without ever indulging in preaching about how we ought to treat our children, Dr Wolff has here presented a clear account of how normal children weather the storms of growing up, and has mapped out some of the commonest sources of trouble. Because she gives full recognition to the great range of innate differences between individual children (and individual parents) she makes it easier for us to know when *not* to worry, as well as helping us to recognize the signs that a child really is in distress and in need of help.

Because of the width of her own training and experience, Dr Wolff's survey gives due importance to each of the potential sources of trouble, including genetic factors, physical illness, bereavement, parental illness or parental discord, and harmful features in the child's material and social environment. In doing so, she makes it plain that it is possible to get the measure of each of these noxious influences and to learn how to counteract them. Above all, she abundantly illustrates the remarkable capacity for recuperation and renewed emotional development displayed by children who have been under stress; and it is surely this which makes working with, and for, such children so peculiarly rewarding.

G. M. CARSTAIRS

Author's Note

The case-histories in this book are taken from my clinical notes. All names are fictitious and family circumstances have been disguised as far as this was possible without doing violence to the psychological reality of the patient and his family. When children and parents are quoted, they are quoted verbatim, because no amount of paraphrasing can equal the individual verbal gifts people display when they describe their personal life experiences.

To the patients and their families I am grateful for helping me to increase my understanding.

Introduction

With rare exceptions, problem children are no different from other children. They react with normal psychological mechanisms to their life experiences. All children in the course of growing up encounter minor stresses: accidents and illnesses, the birth of a new baby, a move of house and school, the inevitable demands for increasing maturity and self-control. Most children at some time react to these stresses with temporary behaviour disorders, such as nightmares, bed-wetting, temper tantrums or excessive fears. Parents usually know almost intuitively what these symptoms mean and they respond by lessening the pressures on the child. Serious difficulties arise only when the stresses are overwhelming or when the adults are too preoccupied to attend to the child's signals of distress. Skilled psychological help is then necessary, although the reactions of the child are 'normal' in the sense that any child under these conditions would react similarly.

There are two indications that psychological appraisal and skilled help are needed for a child. The first is the occurrence of a critical life situation. The second is severe or persistent disturbance of behaviour. A crisis such as admission to hospital, bereavement or the break-up of a family is generally recognized as stressful. Most people are concerned about the possible effects on children of such events, and evidence is accumulating that expert help at these times can prevent psychological disturbances in later life.

In known situations of crisis children's disturbed behaviour is often overshadowed by the events themselves. Some outward signs of distress are expected and when they occur they are as a rule tolerated and understood. Many children, however, are identified as in need of special help not because of the life situation in which they are caught but because of the behaviour disturbances they display. Children for example who draw attention to themselves because they steal repeatedly or because they soil themselves, are children suffering from unrecognized, hidden stress and this is often aggravated by the adverse responses which their difficult behaviour elicits from other people.

Whether a situation is stressful for a child varies with the developmental level he has reached. The disappearance of his mother into hospital, for example, is not noticed by a baby under three months because he is not yet aware of people and objects as distinct from himself. After seven months of age there is clear evidence that a baby misses his mother. But the nature of the anxieties aroused by her departure and the ways in which the child copes with his upset differ according to his maturity. At eighteen months he may think his mother has gone forever because he cannot imagine a future and his understanding of language is too poor for him to be consoled by explanations and reassurances. At four, when the child is egocentric and regards himself as the originator of everything that happens around him, and when he views all bad events as, magically, caused by some failure on his part, he may explain his mother's illness as due to his own misdeeds. To understand the impact of adverse events and circumstances on children, we need to know how at different stages of their development they perceive and think about the world, that is, we must know something about their *intellectual development*.

The child's intellectual level determines how he experiences his environment. His *social and emotional development* has to do with what he experiences. This, of course, is determined in large measure by the culture in which he grows up. Parental attitudes and child rearing practices are part of this culture and so are the provisions made for children in the wider world. Social and emotional development also occurs in recognized stages. These are however less universal than the stages of intellectual growth, and their characteristics as outlined by psychoanalysts hold with any certainty only for children in our Western culture. A major contribution of the psychoanalysts has been to show that at each stage of social and emotional development the child is concerned with particular aspects of his relationship with the people in his environment; that each stage presents its own problems to be solved; that different sources of anxiety exist at different stages; and that with increasing maturity the child's responses to excessive stress undergo progressive changes.

A second and equally important psychoanalytic contribution is Erikson's proposition that each stage of childhood sets a unique and permanent stamp on future personality.[47] The experiences of childhood are not lost. When they are favourable the individual reaches maturity with his potentialities for human relationships, for work and for happiness unimpaired. He responds to his environment in a realistic way and he can adapt to changing circumstances. When childhood experiences are overwhelmingly stressful, arrest of personality occurs and a pattern of repetitive maladaptive behaviour may be set in train, which like an ill fate prevents the individual from ever achieving his full potentialities in adult life. A child for example who was deserted by her mother in childhood may be unable to master this event satisfactorily at the time. It often happens that such a person continues even in adult life to seek for a loving mother and in so doing makes inordinate and inappropriate demands on other people such as her husband, or even her employer. When these other people realize they cannot meet the demands made upon them, they turn away, once more abandoning the crippled individual just as her mother had abandoned her in the past.

Help for children under stress fulfils a double purpose: the relief of present anxieties and the prevention of personality defects in later life.

Adverse events are harmful for children when they arouse more anxiety than the child can cope with. A knowledge of intellectual and emotional development helps us to understand the impact and the consequences of such events. But circumstances can be harmful for children not through commission but through omission: they can deprive the child of essential learning experiences. Children separated from their mothers and reared in orphanages during their first two years of life may be permanently handicapped in their emotional relationships with other people. Children from culturally deprived homes often do not achieve their full educational potential in later life. Just as physical growth is stunted by nutritional deficiency in childhood so personality growth also is impaired if the environment does not satisfy the child's psychological needs.

The first chapter will present an outline of intellectual and emotional development in childhood and will also describe the effects on later personality of emotional and social deprivation.

Part I
CHILD DEVELOPMENT AND SYMPTOM FORMATION

1. Personality Development

Intellectual growth depends largely on innate biological processes which set limits to achievement. Although an unsatisfactory environment can prevent a child from attaining his maximum potential, extra stimulation and teaching cannot help him to grasp ideas and relationships for which he is not yet ready.

Children differ from each other in their rates of development and in their levels of intelligence at any given age, but the sequence of developmental stages from birth to maturity, the order in which one step follows another, is the same for all children, from the very dull to the exceptionally clever.

As a result, it is possible to predict within limits how at different stages environmental events will be perceived by children and what measures are best suited to help them in the face of adverse circumstances. It is not the event itself, but the child's experience of it that is important and one major determinant of experience is the child's level of intellectual functioning.

Before the child begins to speak he cannot convey his experiences; all knowledge about his mental life must rest on inference. In the past such inferences were based on the communications of older children and the recollections of adults undergoing psychoanalytic treatment. It is only in the last thirty years that inferences about early experiences have been based on actual observations of infant behaviour.

Piaget's systematic studies of children of all ages,[124, 125, 126,] Spitz' work on the infant's smiling response,[156] Schaffer's more recent observations of attachment behaviour in infancy[143, 144, 145,] are among the major research contributions to our knowledge of the intellectual aspects of infantile experience.

The First Stage from 0 to 2 Years: from Adualism to Dualism

At birth the baby's senses are fully developed but he has no capacity to recognize objects and people as such, nor is he aware of himself as a separate person. He lives in a state of adualism in which he cannot distinguish between his inner and his outer world, between 'me' and 'not me'. This state lasts until he is between three and six months old and until then the disappearance of people from his life and the substitution of one caretaker by another go unrecognized.

At just over three weeks infants begin to make eye-to-eye contact with other people and between six and twelve weeks they will smile regularly and indiscriminately at all human faces, even at life-sized cut-outs or models, provided the faces are seen in full front view and are moving. *The smiling response* is the child's first act of social behaviour and it seems to be innate, depending solely on biological maturation. Between three and six months stereotyped smiling changes into selective smiling at familiar people: the child now 'recognizes' his parents. This indicates that he is beginning to have inner images of familiar people against which he can match the faces that enter his life. Babies reared in institutions by a succession of different caretakers, all equally unfamiliar, do not develop *discriminatory smiling*. This more sophisticated social response which occurs during the second quarter of the first year of life already depends in part on the environment. At about seven months babies not only smile selectively at familiar people, they also cry when their mothers leave them and display clinging behaviour when reunited with their mothers after brief separations.

Shortly after this the *stranger response* first manifests; the baby becomes fearful and resists approaches from strangers.

During the second half of the first year of life the baby becomes increasingly aware of people and objects as distinct from himself. He now reacts to separation from his mother, and, if this has been short, he reacts also to being reunited with her. There is other evidence that memory traces begin to be laid down at this time. Under six months babies who have had an inoculation earlier do not react with anticipatory cries to a second injection. Over six months they increasingly display 'memory cries' especially when the interval between injections has been brief.[100] While at first infants will reach out only for toys they can see and cease to pay attention when the object is covered up, towards the end of their first year of life they pursue hidden objects, clearly being aware now that even things that are not seen still exist.

Piaget considers that the main intellectual gains in the first two years of life are the step from adualism to dualism and the building up within the child's mind of inner images of the practical, outer world of people and things. By the age of two the child is mobile and on his feet. He has learnt by experiment what the effects of his own activities are on the objects around him. He can feed himself and he plays with all sorts of objects in his environment.

From our point of view the important discoveries about the child's first stage of intellectual development are that separations are not perceived and traumatic experiences not remembered below the age of three to six months, but that after this time both separations and other traumata can be shown to have quite definite effects on subsequent behaviour.

The Second Stage from 2 to 7 Years: Animism

The importance of the second stage of intellectual development is that although the child now rapidly acquires an increasing vocabulary and changes from a creature of action to one with words and thoughts, his thinking and his reasoning are quite different from those of adults. As a result he misinterprets his environment. These misinterpretations can cause profound anxiety especially when they go unrecognized by the adults who care for the child, and they lay the foundations for the irrational components of adult personality that persist to a greater or lesser degree in us all.

On the basis of his systematic experiments and observations of thousands of Geneva children, Piaget has described four principal characteristics of this stage: egocentrism, animism, precausality and an authoritarian morality.

Under the age of seven children live in an *egocentric* world. They talk more when with each other but there are few shared topics. Each child talks only of what concerns himself. Piaget has called such an interchange a 'collective monologue'.[125] It is evidence that children at this stage believe that what concerns them must of course also be uppermost in other people's minds and that they cannot imagine anyone else's point of view. The child sees himself literally as the centre of the universe. When he notices that as he walks along the street the sun by day and the moon by night seem to move in the same direction, he believes they follow *him*. When he is asked why this should be he gives explanations such as 'to hear what we're saying' or 'when we're looking nice he (the sun) looks at us'.[124]

His explanations for the events in the physical world are *animistic*. Everything is alive and has feelings and thoughts just as he does. There are no impartial, natural causes for events. All explanations are psychological in terms of motivation and every event occurs by intent. The wind blows because it wants to; the table against which the four-year-old bumps his head is 'naughty'. At this stage children believe in magic and words are as powerful as actions. Children cannot yet dissociate the word from the object it names nor the thought from the things thought about. The psychological and the physical world are one. Dreams really happen and good or bad wishes can quite possibly come true.

Logic at this stage is *precausal*, that is, non-scientific. Children do not reason from their observations but on the basis of an internal model of the world. They are insensible of contradictions and will accept false explanations without question, whether they spring from their parents or from their own inspirations: 'you have to have an operation' to get a baby, although mother clearly has no scar. The fact that at Christmas time he meets a different man dressed in red in every department store does not shake the under-seven's belief in a single Father Christmas. He is not worried, as is the older child, by calculations that the old man could never get round to all the children in the world in the time available.

6

If of two identical balls of plasticine one is rolled out to form a sausage, it becomes 'bigger, because it's longer'. The animistic child's world is not so different from the world of Alice in Wonderland and magic is a frequent explanatory concept.

A child patient aged seven had during a treatment session spilt some wet sand on his blazer. He became very anxious in case it should turn into cement. He had recently been watching the concrete mixer at the bottom of his street with fascination: 'When you mix sand and water,' he said, 'it makes cement.' Reassurances that, when dry, the sand would brush off easily did not convince him. He was beginning to take note of observed phenomena. However, the statement that '*this* sand' would not set hard evoked the response 'is it magic sand then?'

His investigations of how children play marbles led Piaget to formulate his views on the *authoritarian morality* of the under-sevens.[126] Rules for them are sacrosanct. They may not know what the rules are, but the rules cannot be changed; they have always been the same; if anyone made them it was God. Likewise, children may not always do what their parents tell them, but there is no question in their minds that the parents are right. Only in the next stage can children conceive of democratic co-operation and of mutual modification of rules in which they too have an active role to play. An integral part of authoritarian morality is 'the idea of immanent justice', that the crime begets the punishment. If a five-year-old disobeys his mother by running into the street and then falls over, he fell *because* he was naughty.

An awareness of the characteristics of this animistic stage of life helps one to make sense of the child's reactions to upsetting events. Anything bad that happens is likely to be seen as a punishment and, because he lives in an egocentric world, a punishment for something *he* has done wrong. If his parents quarrel he cannot conceive that they argue about anything other than himself. If he is ill and homesick for his mother in hospital, the explanation that he must have been naughty and she cross with him comes to him readily. His authoritarian and magical view of the world leads him to suppose that had she really wanted to, she could have saved him from his illness.

The Third Stage from 7 to 16 Years: Realism

After the age of seven, the child gradually loses his egocentrism, his animism, his precausal logic and his authoritarian morality. He begins to be aware of words, thoughts and rules as separate from the concrete objects and activities of the world. In his social relationships a democratic, co-operative attitude is possible. In his reasoning he takes account of what he observes; in his explanations for physical events he uses concepts of time, of mechanical forces and finally of true logic. Between seven and twelve years of age he uses *concrete operational logic*. He can draw the right conclusions about physical events when he is actually watching an ongoing operation. He can now work out that because two pieces of plasticine were the same size initially, they remain equal in size although the shape of one has been changed. But until he is about twelve years old he can make this deduction only if he has the plasticine before him.

After the age of twelve, *abstract logic* develops. Increasingly the child can now perform logical operations in his head. He no longer needs two actual pieces of plasticine in order to work out the solution to the problem. His thoughts alone are enough.

SOCIAL AND EMOTIONAL DEVELOPMENT

We have seen that the child begins life with a fragmentary view of himself and his environment. He then passes through a stage at which he is extremely gullible and prey to anxieties aroused by his own fantastic beliefs about the nature of the world. Not until he is seven or eight years old does he become a rational human being. Yet during the first seven years of his life the child experiences a series of crucial relationships with other people: with his parents and his brothers and sisters. Throughout this time he is dependent on a very imperfect mental apparatus. It is not surprising that much of his experience is distorted and that only exceptionally fortunate individuals escape without temporary manifestations of distress and without at least minor residues, persisting into adult life, of unrealistic fears and irrational behaviour.

Social behaviour and emotional development also follow a regular sequence of stages, confirmed repeatedly by everyday observations of children and by the clinical experience of psychologists and psychiatrists. It is the psychoanalysts, however, who have helped us most to organize our observations into significant patterns. Childhood behaviour has become understandable and we are better able to assess the emotional needs of children of different ages and also the risks attached to environmental hazards at each stage.

Anxiety, the great disorganizer of behaviour, springs from different sources as the child grows up and this too psychoanalysts have helped us to understand.

The First Year of Life: the Oral Stage

The newborn infant sleeps most of the time. His conscious awareness is almost entirely confined to feeding experiences: hunger, sucking, satiation and internal rumblings. That is why this stage is called the oral stage. Mouth activities are all important as a source of initial satisfactions. A second feature of the emotional life of the infant is that he is helpless and entirely dependent on his mother. Without someone to look after him, he would die. He cannot get about; he cannot feed himself; all he can do is signal distress by crying. Unpleasant emotions arise when some pressing biological need such as thirst or hunger is not being met and this is the origin of the child's first experiences of *anxiety*: *the absence of vital supplies*.

People do not exist in the infant's earliest experiences. Parts of people, their faces, their warmth, their comforting then appear, to be forgotten as soon as they vanish from the baby's immediate experience. Gradually parents are recognized and assume some permanence in the infant's mind. Even so when he is with one person he forgets everyone else. His relationship is strictly one-to-one, and its chief characteristic is that he is dependent on the other for food, but also, once he is a little older, for stimulation and excitement. His parents in turn make no demands on him at all. His mother is quite satisfied so long as he is healthy, grows and develops according to her expectations.

9

The Second Year of Life: the Anal Stage

By the beginning of his second year of life the child has turned into a different kind of person. He is now on his feet and able to get about. He can not only do some things for himself, like eat a biscuit, he can also have an effect on his environment by, for example, emptying the coal bucket. His main relationship is still with one person, his mother, and he follows her about wherever she goes. But she now begins to teach him how society will expect him to behave. She begins to inculcate social rules. 'No', she says as he attempts to scatter the contents of her handbag and this marks a profound change in their relationship. He must not only be well; he must be good.

Symbolic of the altered relationship between the child and his mother is the process of toilet training, from which this stage derives its name. The child now has formed stools and he can decide whether to hold on or to let go. To this extent he has acquired some autonomy.

The child's main task at this stage is to learn to co-operate with a more powerful person and this brings with it a host of new experiences, of satisfactions and of anxieties. *Anxiety now springs from shame and from the disapproval of others.* If the toddler exerts his will over his mother, refusing, for example, to use his pot, she signals disapproval; when he wets his trousers she conveys disgust at his dirtiness. If he complies with her wishes, she praises him and he feels pride in achievement. The 'potting couple' is quite different from the 'nursing couple'.

The Third Stage from 2 to 6 Years: the Genital Stage

The child's social life now undergoes a third major change. More and more of his time is spent not as one of a pair but as *one of a group*: with both his parents after father is home from work; with his mother and the new baby; in play with other children; in a nursery group.

Here he has his first encounters with triangular situations, which present a new set of social demands and a new range of emotions. Jealousy and rivalry arise for the first time and their mastery depends on the child's capacity to postpone for the future the immediate fulfilment of his wishes. This the toddler, the anal stage child, cannot do. He cannot yet conceive of a future so that to be told to wait is meaningless. When he is frustrated he cannot control his impulses and has a temper tantrum. But he can be diverted. In the genital stage the child is no longer entirely dependent on concrete objects: he can think and talk about them and his inner world extends beyond the present into the future. He can wait until 'later' or until 'tomorrow' or even until 'I grow up'. This is the stage at which children view themselves as becoming grown-ups: 'When I grow up, I'll be a policeman', or 'a nurse', or 'just like Daddy'. It is the stage of 'primary identification' when children begin to compare themselves in size, age and sex with others, when they become aware of their own sexual identity and begin to model themselves on the parent of the same sex. It is the stage at which children explore their bodies including their sex organs and when they first develop erotic feelings for the parent of the opposite sex, and longings for an exclusive relationship with that parent. This feature of the stage has given it its name.

Freud's theory about the oedipus complex is borne out by everyday observations of children. The boy, in love with his mother, has death wishes towards the father he regards as a rival and fears castration as a punishment. The girl, in love with her father, wants her mother away and sees herself as already wounded in some way because she has no penis. When a three-year-old drew 'a wigwam with me and Daddy in it' and said to her father 'Mummy and Michael haven't been born yet', the father knew at once that this was a declaration of love, a demand that her relationship with him should exclude all others.

Children between two and six are full of questions. Most of their questions are answered by their parents with uniform frankness. Parents expect to teach their child about the world. Only questions about sexuality and about babies are not answered in this same instructive way. In public places the child is hushed and even at home such questions are still often countered with evasive and even false replies. As a consequence the biological facts of life attain an air of mystery and the child often comes to regard his questions as 'naughty'. Curiosity becomes sharpened and goes underground.

If we remember that the genital stage child is an animistic child operating with precausal logic we are not surprised when he misinterprets his observations and the information his parents give him. A five-year-old, whose younger brother had recently been circumcised, asked his mother 'But what do they do in the hospital when they cut it off?' And before she could reply he said 'They save it for the babies that are coming out of the hospitals.' The fact that in their joint nightly bath he could see his brother still had his penis did not influence his theory. The three-year-old brother himself said, 'It's growing again.' All too often adults reinforce such childish fantasies. 'I'll get your wee mouse' was a frequent joke made by an auntie as she tickled her small nephew.

As he attains a sense of his own future, of his identity as a person and of the sexual ties existing between parents, the child develops *a third, new and powerful source of anxiety: his conscience*. In the anal stage children can inhibit forbidden impulses only in the actual presence of someone who threatens disapproval. Now, in the genital stage they can remember their parents' probihitions whenever a forbidden impulse arises in their mind. They have acquired a voice of conscience. The guilt this can arouse in the animistic stage of childhood, when thoughts are as powerful as deeds, when morality is harsh and authoritarian, when crime begets punishment and the *lex talionis*, the law of an-eye-for-an-eye, operates, is immense. If one remembers this, then children's fantasies of their own destructiveness and of gory mutilations befalling them in turn, will cease to be astonishing.

The Concepts of Fixation and Regression

Many behaviour disorders of childhood can be understood in developmental terms, once one has sufficient information about the individual child's life experiences. The concept that is most useful here is that of *regression*. When a child is exposed to circumstances that arouse in him more anxiety than he can cope with, one possible psychological mechanism available to him is to give up behaviour patterns appropriate to his age and revert to behaviour that gratified him in the past. A toddler under stress, for example, may abandon his strivings for autonomy and independence and revert to infantile clinging. Another common example is that of a three- or four-year-old, whose expressions of hostility towards his baby sister are met by his mother not with understanding but reproof. The older child's position as the well-loved child in the family is now threatened not only by his younger sister but by his mother's crossness. He may regress to anal stage behaviour and start to wet and soil himself again, or to oral behaviour demanding to be fed and nursed just like the baby. The mother may then at last pick up the cues and work out for herself what is bothering her older child. She now offers the comfort and reassurance he needed and he becomes 'a big boy' once more. Occasionally, however, a mother may be insensitive even to such gross hints of discomfort, or too harassed to respond in the way she really wants to. It is then that difficulties can arise. Regressive symptoms may persist and the child can suffer a partial *arrest of development* with constriction of his personality. He may, for example, have lifelong, irrational fears of his own destructiveness whenever he is in a situation of rivalry with another person.

The level to which a child regresses is thought to be determined by the actual experiences he has had during this earlier stage, at which he is said to be *fixated*. Anything that makes a stage memorable, excessive anxiety or excessive pleasure, can lead to, in the one case negative, in the other positive fixation. The first three stages of social and emotional development result in negative fixation much more commonly than later stages, presumably because the child's prelogical reasoning at that time is an obstacle to his mastery of anxiety.

The Fourth Stage from 6 to 12 Years: Latency

When the nursery child becomes a school child, he experiences a further transformation of his social life. His energies become diverted from the intimate relationships within his family and are invested in two main activities: peer relationships and learning. Psychoanalysts use the word latency to describe this stage because in it the erotic longings of early childhood, its jealousies and its fears, become hidden until the psychological and social changes of puberty bring them to life once more.

The child now for the first time discovers how he stands amongst a group of his equals, how clever, how popular, how energetic he is compared with others of his age.

The Fifth Stage from 12 to 25 Years: Puberty and Adolescence

The adolescent has to face the physiological changes in his own body on the one hand and his family's and society's altered expectations of him on the other. The biological changes and the arousal of sexual feelings lead to a re-awakening of many experiences of the genital and even of earlier stages. Unresolved conflicts of the prelatency era surface once more; and because of this return of earlier experience, adolescence is commonly thought of as offering the individual a second chance to solve unsettled problems remaining from previous stages of development. We all know of teenagers who refuse to wash and whose bedrooms are islands of chaos in an otherwise orderly household. This is the time too when 'puppy fat' can turn into obesity because solace is sought in food.

Erikson, who has made a profound contribution to our understanding of adolescence, describes the main task to be completed then as identity formation.[48] This has four components: (1) The definition of a working role; (2) The acquisition of social attitudes and opinions; (3) Separation from parents emotionally and in fact; and (4) The definition of a sexual role. In all these areas final choices are not made at once. The adolescent experiments with jobs; with ideologies and allegiances to different groups and movements; and with different sexual partners. Clothes and specifically teenage activities help both adolescents and their parents towards a changed way of relating to each other. Mutual turning away from each other may be a necessary step towards independence and maturity. Adolescent rebellion against parents is often exaggerated in children with excessive dependency needs stemming from much earlier feelings of insecurity. Parents who are inadequate and unsure of themselves are threatened by any independent views on the part of their children and often try to insist on continued conformity to their own standards. The children of such parents are frequently driven into extremes of adolescent rebellion.

THE CONTRIBUTION OF EARLY STAGES OF DEVELOPMENT TO LATER PERSONALITY

The notions that infantile experiences in the oral stage colour later attitudes to food and drink; that anal stage experiences affect all subsequent reactions to excreta, to dirt in general, to orderliness and to money; that genital stage experiences play a vital part in determining adult sexual adjustment, are not new. Erikson, however, has drawn attention to more general links between childhood experience and adult personality.[48] He sees each stage as posing a particular problem in human relationships; the outcome of each stage, that is whether the problem is resolved satisfactorily or not, depends on the actual life experiences of the child at the time.

In the oral stage, for example, the crucial experience is that of dependency, and the way in which the individual baby experienced this first dependent relationship with his mother will determine his future attitudes to all situations in which he is dependent on someone else. His first solutions become enduring solutions. A satisfactory infancy engenders *trust*; an infancy in which the child's needs are inadequately met results in pessimism and *mistrust*. People positively fixated to the oral stage crave dependency throughout their lives. Negatively fixated people resist all later dependency situations. If they are ill, for example, they struggle vigorously to maintain their upright posture and autonomy: they refuse to go to bed even with a fever. They are so anxious at the idea of giving up work and accepting nursing care, that is, of symbolically returning to a stage of helpless infancy, that they become awkward patients.

In the anal stage the crucial experience is a co-operative relationship with a more powerful other person. A satisfactory toddler stage engenders *autonomy* and confidence in one's own capacities to satisfy others, while a stressful anal stage leads to *doubt and shame*, that is, to fear of exposure. Excessive compliance in adult life, or alternatively, irrational obstinacy find their roots in adverse experiences associated with the earliest social training in childhood.

The genital stage, during which the child has his first experiences of life in a family group and during which he becomes aware of sexual roles and sexual urges, presents him with a choice between *initiative and a lively curiosity* on the one hand, and *anxious, inhibited withdrawal* on the other.

During latency permanent attitudes towards work, working colleagues and friendship groups begin to be laid down. If latency experiences bring with them too much anxiety then the child may grow up with feelings of *inferiority* about his abilities and his standing among his peers. If on the other hand he had a relatively trouble-free time during his primary school years, he is likely to grow up highly motivated towards *industry* and co-operation with his fellows.

A satisfactory adolescence is completed when the individual has attained *a firm sense of his own identity* and is satisfied with the choices he has made. When adolescence is too stressful, identity formation is impaired. The individual remains without a firm sense of who he is and what he wants from life. He gets by through aligning himself temporarily with others as if he felt one of them, and often he participates in mutually conflicting activities. Nothing he does seems either right or wrong to him; nothing is inevitable; his satisfactions are always incomplete. This state Erikson has called *role diffusion*.[48]

CHILDHOOD DEPRIVATION

So far we have been concerned with the developmental processes that determine whether particular events are likely to be anxiety-inducing in children of different age-levels. We have also explored very briefly some of the later effects on personality of too much anxiety or stress at a particular stage of life.

We shall now look at what is known about the environmental ingredients that are basic necessities for normal personality development, ingredients without which the individual remains partly stunted in personality growth even if the actual stresses he has to cope with in childhood are not overwhelming.

For centuries the development of children reared under grossly abnormal circumstances has aroused curiosity and interest. Experiments were done by kings and emperors on children brought up from birth in an environment in which no word was ever spoken to see whether language, which was thought to be the basic expression of the human soul, was acquired or innate.[24]

Educationalists of the late eighteenth and early nineteenth century studied children found wandering in the countryside, who had supposedly been reared by wolves. Such children rarely acquired normal social skills and their speech remained rudimentary. Psychologists in Victorian times observed illegitimate children found hidden by their mothers in dark attics, cut off from human contact. Their subsequent development also often remained stunted.

Modern work on the effects of emotional and social deprivation on children began with studies in orphanages in the 1940s. Lowrey, an American child psychiatrist, was the first to describe a clinical syndrome of self-centredness and inability to give and receive affection, together with aggressive behaviour and speech impairments in children who had spent their first three years of life in an orphanage.[105] This behaviour pattern was never found in children who had entered the orphanage after the age of two or three.

Lowrey's observations were confirmed by a classical study by another American psychiatrist: Goldfarb.[62] He investigated fifteen children who lived in an orphanage from the age of about four months to three years and were then fostered out. He also studied a control group of children who had arrived at the orphanage at the same age but who had been fostered out at once. The group deprived of family life in early childhood were inferior to those reared by foster parents in many aspects of personality. They were less intelligent, their memory was poorer and they showed marked impairment of language development and of school adjustment.

In another classical study it was shown that children reared by their mothers during the first year of life, even in a grossly unfavourable setting (a women's prison), made better intellectual progress and were also physically healthier than babies cared for hygienically but in the emotionally sterile atmosphere that existed in foundling homes in the nineteen forties.[157]

There has been much discussion whether these results of orphanage child-rearing described twenty years ago were due

17

to the lack of continuous mothering in the early years of life, as has been suggested by Bowlby,[20] or whether the monotony, the lack of stimulation, and the absence of facilities for play in those stringently hygienic institutions were responsible for the loss of intellectual and of social capacities in the deprived children.

More recent work has shown that even in a good, up-to-date institution babies automatically get more social and verbal stimulation when they are looked after by a single mother-figure rather than by a succession of different nurses.[130] Even if the period of continuous mothering is brief it has clear-cut effects both immediate and enduring. Babies given special mothering by a single person for eight weeks were socially more responsive and more vocal than a control group, and even at twenty months they were superior in their language skills. On the other hand, supplementary, impersonal, verbal stimulation has no effect on the language development of institution-reared infants.[29]

Dr Kellmer Pringle found that the language skills of four-year-olds reared in a residential nursery were inferior to those of matched control children living at home and attending nursery schools.[88] In her study both groups of children came from socially and culturally deprived families. She concluded that children in residential care, who spend most of the day in each other's company, are retarded in their language development because of their lack of contact with adults.

All these studies indicate that during their very early years children need more than a stimulating environment and opportunities for exploration and play. They also need a continuous relationship with a mothering person who can respond to them according to their individual needs and who can act as a source of continuity of experience which, as we saw earlier, is the basis for those permanent inner images of outer people and things which the child builds up in the course of his first two years of life.

Important clues about the developmental needs of human infants and children come from studies of animal behaviour. Harlow investigated the behaviour of rhesus monkeys under different conditions of infant rearing.[69] He found that when monkeys are deprived of their mothers from birth, they react to surrogate wire mothers but only if these are covered with terry cloth. It is 'contact comfort' and not food that stimulates the young monkeys to cling to the artificial mother substitute and to go to her for shelter in distress. But, even in the company of such substitutes, monkeys will show defects in their adult personality if they are reared apart from their mothers and from other infant monkeys during a particular period of early childhood. Such deprived monkeys in later life failed to establish the usual social hierarchy with other monkeys. They were solitary and aggressive. They failed to develop normal sexual behaviour, and, if the females did become pregnant, they were unprotective and unmaternal to their offspring, refusing even to let them suckle. Monkeys need to be exposed to certain social learning experiences in infancy in order to develop appropriate patterns of social, sexual and parental behaviour in adult life. If deprived of these essential experiences during a *critical period* in their early childhood, they cannot make up for this later on.

In human beings the findings are less clear. Some individuals, grossly deprived of affectionate care in early childhood, develop into apparently normal and even gifted adults. Constitutional differences in temperament have been postulated to explain this. Schaffer has shown that babies who are constitutionally very active and mobile suffer less from a period of under-stimulation in hospital than less active babies.[145] Constitutional factors have also been adduced to explain the fact that some individuals who show the lack of emotional responsiveness and poor verbal facility that is often found in people reared in institutions during their first three years of life, do not have a clear-cut past history of such gross maternal deprivation. Moreover, the effects of maternal deprivation may to some extent be remediable, and the concept of *sensitive periods* is more appropriate in the field of human learning.

In summary we can say that between six months and three years of life, the baby depends for his future emotional and intellectual development on stimulation and affectionate care from people he knows well and who know him as an individual. Whether such needs can be met in the absence of a

19

continuous mother figure is not yet known. What is known is that loss of the mother, especially if followed by care in an impersonal institution, is likely to have long-lasting and perhaps permanent, adverse effects.

2. The Origin of Symptoms

Disturbed behaviour arousing alarm or anger in other people may be the first indication that a child is struggling with an emotional problem. Persistent night terrors, stealing, bed-wetting, refusal to go to school often occur long before the stresses to which the child is reacting become apparent. Most usually these stresses come from the environment, occasionally they are the result of unrecognized constitutional handicaps. In this and the following chapter we shall examine how behaviour disturbances in children come about, how common they are and how they are identified.

To say that disturbed behaviour is *maladaptive* may at first appear tautological. In fact, however, this formulation carries us a step further in understanding behaviour difficulties. When an insecure four-year-old clings to her mother, refusing to stay in her nursery class unless the mother stays too, repeatedly climbing into her parents' bed at night and screaming whenever her mother goes out of the house, the response she will evoke, especially in public where such babyish behaviour is likely to make her mother feel ashamed, is one of rejection. The mother strenuously discourages clinging, pushes the child forward, indicates she is 'too big' now for such behaviour. But the more the mother pushes, the more the child clings. Deadlock is reached. The child's disturbed behaviour makes it difficult for the mother to respond with approval and confident support. Yet without these the child cannot manage to conduct herself better. Her disturbed behaviour, arising from feelings of insecurity, evokes responses from others which make her feel even less secure. To this extent it is maladaptive.

Psychiatrists regard repetitive maladaptive behaviour as a *symptom*. This second label makes a further contribution to our understanding of behaviour disturbances. When a patient comes to the doctor complaining of a pain in his stomach it is the doctor's business to find out what this pain means. He startes from the premise that if the patient has a pain then there is something wrong with him to cause it. The doctor's job is to find this cause, and, if possible, to remedy it. In the case of physical illnesses the symptoms, supplemented by a physical examination, lead the doctor to discover which body part or system is affected by illness. In the case of psychological disturbances symptoms, supplemented by detailed observations of behaviour, alert the doctor to the life difficulties and conflicts the patient is struggling with. In both situations *the symptom is a communication*. It tells one something about underlying disturbances. In both cases the message is not an obvious one. It needs to be carefully interpreted taking many other circumstances into account. The symptom is a message in disguise.

Symptoms do not have any general meaning. Their significance is personal and specific for each individual. The act of stealing, for example, can carry a host of different meanings. To understand the particular meaning of a symptom it is necessary to explore the individual's past and present life situations and to listen to what he has to tell us about his thoughts and feelings. Although there is no general code for deciphering the meaning of individual symptoms, certain theoretical formulations about the origins of symptoms have general applicability.

Behaviour disorders in children can be usefully classified into two main groups: (1) *neurotic behaviour disorders* due to excessive anxiety; and (2) *disturbances resulting from defective socialization*.

NEUROTIC SYMPTOMS AND THE MECHANISMS OF DEFENCE

Psychoanalysis has provided us with a very satisfactory theoretical framework for the understanding of neurotic symptoms. Neurotic behaviour disorders in children are very common. They are not due to any lack of essential early life experiences. The children affected have not characteristically suffered major deprivations in infancy or early childhood. Their parents are not on the whole either neglectful or themselves delinquent but have tried to bring up their children in conformity with accepted standards of social behaviour.

The key to the understanding of neurotic symptoms is *anxiety*. We have seen that anxiety can spring from three different sources which become effective at different developmental stages:

(1) Primary anxiety, a fear of dissolution, resulting from conflict between inner needs and inadequate environmental supplies and beginning as early as the oral stage;

(2) Anxiety related to shame and loss of self-esteem, resulting from conflict between primitive impulses and their prohibition from without and arising during the anal stage;

(3) Anxiety due to guilt, stemming from conflict between primitive impulses and the dictates of conscience, which begins during the genital stage.

Anxiety occurs when there is a *conflict* either between inner wishes and impulses on the one hand and the external world on the other, or between inner urges and one's own conscience. When anxiety becomes overwhelming, certain psychological processes come into play to protect the individual from total disorganization of behaviour. These protective devices are called the *mechanisms of defence*.[53] The basic mechanism is that of *repression*. Here the wish or impulse, unable to attain satisfaction or, alternatively, not tolerated either by the environment or by the individual's conscience, is repressed into the *unconscious*. The unconscious is a hypothetical layer of the mind whose contents are not accessible to the individual. Material that has been repressed cannot be attended to. A repressed thought ceases to exist within conscious awareness. It is a characteristic of repressed wishes and impulses that, although unconscious, they are not lost. They continue to strive for and in fact to find expression in various indirect ways.

Psychological concepts become meaningful only in relation to actual human behaviour. Let us look at a clinical case to see what we can learn about the nature of maladaptive behaviour, symptom formation, the sources of anxiety and the defence mechanism of repression.

23

John, aged seven, had a very mild cerebral palsy which made him clumsy and exposed him to constant urgings at school and at home to improve his handwriting. The parents and the teacher knew that he had a special muscular difficulty, but he did not. He was aware only of his poor performance and of criticism from others and he was anxious because his self-esteem was low. Every morning when it was time to go to school he complained of feeling sick. He came to dislike writing and put off doing his homework. This led to increased supervision and pressuring from the parents. When other children were out playing he was still sitting over his lessons. Instead of showing resentment, as some other child might have done, John now began to take small toys belonging to other children at school and to display these quite openly. His teacher was particularly distressed by the fact that he showed no remorse when confronted with his misdeeds. Both teacher and parents reacted at first by impressing on the child how very bad and wrong it was to 'steal'. John clearly understood this since his games now consisted entirely of police and robbers. The stealing however continued. The more he stole the more disapproval he gained from others, and the more he sensed this the more he stole. Finally the parents sought psychiatric help. The stealing, in this case a reaction to disapproval and excessive pressure from others, resulted only in making matters worse for him. It was an example of maladaptive behaviour and did not fulfil its aim of making him feel better. Moreover, it was not improved by ordinary social pressures but persisted in a repetitive, stereotyped way. It had become a symptom.

Two questions required to be answered in this case. Firstly, why was John unable to express resentment at the excessive parental pressures he experienced; why did he need to repress his anger and develop a symptom instead? Secondly, why were his parents compelled to be so hard on him? The first question is answered readily. John was an adopted child and his mother suffered from a chronic medical illness which prevented her having children of her own and constituted a threat to her life span. John knew this. Every afternoon she had to rest, she could never play running-about games with him and often, as he left for work, his father would say to John, 'Look after Mummy.' John was in the animistic stage of intellectual development so that for him his mother's health depended on his own goodness and badness. He was never angry with her and he was very solicitous whenever she felt tired or unwell. To express anger or frustration with his mother was impossible for this child because it carried the threat that as a result his mother might become ill and die and he would once more have no one to look after him. Angry feelings aroused by his physical handicap, by his frustrations at school and by his parents' strictness evoked not only shame but overwhelming anxiety that he might lose his mother, and he reacted to this by repressing all anger. He never felt cross. His initial symptom of sickness in the morning, to escape the situation in which his self-esteem was reduced, went unheeded and the next step was that his repressed feelings of anger and of unfairness ('Other people get more than I do') found expression in the form of stealing. When he was blamed for this, the guilt aroused served only to increase his anxiety which was already more than he could cope with. His defences became stronger, guilt feelings too were repressed and, although in his play he was always on the side of law and order, he continued to steal.

Before we examine why John's parents were so strict with him let us define some common defence mechanisms.

(1) *Repression*. This, as we have been, is the basic protective device against overwhelming anxiety. A number of others are recognized.

(2) *Regression*. This, as we saw in Chapter 1, is one of the commonest defence mechanisms in children, the child reverting to behaviour characteristic of an earlier developmental stage to which he had become fixated. A child who is falling behind at school for example but who had a happy oral stage may repress her anxieties in the classroom, instead sitting, apparently blissfully sucking her thumb. Many children already toilet trained regress to anal behaviour, bed-wetting, when an acute illness forces a hospital admission.

(3) *Denial*. This is also common in children, experience being falsified for the sake of mental comfort. The sudden death of an important person in the child's life may be ignored altogether: the child behaves as if the event had not occurred. A more common example is that of the child who steals and vigorously denies this in the face of abundant proof. The diminution of self-esteem and his overwhelming guilt make it impossible for him to face up to his own actions. The more

forcefully he is confronted with his misdeeds, the greater his anxiety and the firmer his denial. Only when the grown-ups take active steps to reduce the child's anxiety and guilt will he be able to give up his defensive manoeuvre and to look at his own behaviour squarely.

(4) *Displacement*. Here feelings and impulses directed against one person become shifted to another. For example a child may feel too guilty to express hatred openly towards his younger brother; instead he becomes provocative and belligerent with his classmates.

(5) *Reaction formation*. Unwelcome feelings and urges are turned into their opposite. John was never angry when his mother frustrated him. Instead he was a rather 'goody-goody' boy, over-solicitous about her welfare and, for a seven-year-old, rather too helpful when she was ill. Another example is that of a nine-year-old girl who finds herself over-restricted by the mother and grandmother with whom she lives. Every minor ailment is scrupulously attended to and her good manners are a source of pride to the mother. For a mild stoop she is made to sleep in a plaster shell at night. 'She's my little masterpiece,' the mother explained, 'she's got to be right.' This child is obsessed by fears that her mother will die. Whenever the mother leaves the house the girl becomes panicky and has visions of her mother meeting with an accident. Although keen to go to school camp she has to return home after only a day away because of overwhelming fears that in her absence the mother might be harmed. As a child the mother suffered from exactly similar fears. The underlying hostility which these symptoms served to disguise became clear when she said, 'I used to pray that my mother wouldn't die. Well, I've had my prayers answered. I can't get rid of her now.' Excessive concern and solicitude were a reaction formation against hostile feelings in both mother and child.

(6) *Projection*. This means that one's own unacceptable impulses are attributable to others; for example, a boy who feels angry and rebellious towards his father may repress these feelings and instead, unrealistically, regard his father as hostile and punitive.

(7) *Isolation*. When the emotion attached to an experience is split off, when feelings and experiences are compartmentalized,

we speak of isolation. A child may, for example, be over-fastidious about cleanliness, disgusted by minor unpleasant experiences but completely oblivious of the smell and mess that he carries with him when he has soiled his pants.

(8) *Flight into fantasy*, (9) *Intellectualization* or *rationalization* and (10) *Ritualistic behaviour* are other defensive manoeuvres used to ward off anxiety. All involve some degree of repression of unwelcome impulses.

(11) *Sublimation* is the only defence mechanism which allows full and creative use of primitive impulses. Here urges in conflict with the environment or conscience are translated into effective social action. Sexual curiosity in a five-year-old, for instance, finds expression in general curiosity about the world. The sexual drive is transformed into an urge to learn. The resultant behaviour is not maladaptive but on the contrary highly adaptive and rewarded with consequent diminution of guilt and increase in self-esteem. Similarly, unwelcome aggressive urges can become transformed into socially accepted leadership behaviour.

None of the defence mechanisms described is in itself abnormal. All are used by children and adults to cope with the anxieties and fears associated with the common conflicts that everyone has to master. When in childhood anxiety is overwhelming and defensive manoeuvres are resorted to in a massive way, symptoms may develop and adult behaviour may to some extent become maladaptive.

Let us return to John's parents.

Because of the mother's illness they felt that they could not 'guarantee' for a healthy, normal child, so that they offered themselves as parents for a handicapped child they thought would find no home elsewhere. For the father this was of especial significance. He had had an intelligent, domineering mother and a weak and feeble father. Throughout his childhood he had supported his father and rebelled against his mother without ever being aware of the slightest anger against the father for not coping better. He repressed his feelings of resentment and became instead a champion of the weak. This reaction formation was not however entirely successful and he found that his support of the underdog was always mixed with critical feelings which distressed him. As a child he had felt too guilty to face his critical feelings towards his father. In later life he could express critical feelings only towards people he was in fact benefiting. He displaced resentment meant for his father on to these other people. He married an ailing wife and was aware of resenting the extra domestic chores this imposed on him. He adopted a handicapped child and found himself, against his better judgement, constantly urging the boy to do better. He even engaged a crippled housekeeper at one stage and then became very irritated indeed by her appeals for sympathy and understanding. The mother provided a further clue to the father's repetitious pattern of behaviour towards his child: 'Perhaps you feel', she said to him during one of their interviews, 'that you must be strict with John because you don't want ever to be like your father.'

This neurotic pattern of the father, in other ways a highly competent man, went some way to explain the excessive pressures he imposed on his child.

Graham was six years old when he was referred to a child psychiatrist because of persistent soiling. He was the younger of two boys and had always been a little slower in his development than his older brother. As a baby he was constipated and his mother had delayed toilet training until he was nearly two because she felt that up to then he did not really understand what was required of him. When she began to train him, he vigorously resisted sitting on the pot. She had high standards of cleanliness and stormy scenes ensued. When he was three he was at length clean. He was at this stage a very active and rather aggressive child who had frequently to be restrained from attacking other children. Six months later, at three-and-a-half, a marked change occurred. He became shy and quiet, refused to go out to play and at the same time he began to dirty his pants once more. The only precipitating event that the mother recalled was that he had been frightened by a large dog who had pounced on him. In addition to his soiling and inhibited behaviour Graham had developed a fear of dogs. No amount of admonition, shaming and retraining made any difference to the soiling and the mother found it quite impossible to follow her doctor's initial advice which had been to 'ignore it'. When he was five Graham started school. He was extremely quiet in class and made poor progress, especially compared with his older brother. At this stage the mother became even more upset and infuriated by the soiling. Her father was ill and her older sister who lived with the grandparents was left with the full responsibility of running the grandfather's business. This the mother felt she could not allow. She had always had some guilt towards her sister because she, the mother, had been her father's favourite and felt she had a happier life. She felt she owed it to her sister to help her out and she began to work in the business daily. Meanwhile, the grandmother came to look after the two boys. It was she who had to change Graham when he returned soiled from school each day. This was mortifying for the mother, increasing her annoyance at the extra burden she had undertaken for her sister. Because of her special feelings for this sister she felt guilty about her anger and displaced this on to Graham's soiling which she now could tolerate no longer.

The final link in the chain of events which made this little boy's symptoms understandable was provided by Graham himself. He was rolling out plasticine with his hands one day and as he did so he said, 'It's magic. If you touch it you die.' He spoke little and to a number of queries as to what it was that he had made he responded only with vigorous shakes of his head. The final interpretation, 'You think that if you touch your wee-wee you die', however, evoked a firm 'yes'. His brother had told him this. When his fears about touching his penis were discussed with the parents they suddenly recalled that just before the onset of the soiling, at three-and-a-half, Graham had had a painful infection of his penis for which he had been taken to the doctor. The doctor at the time had said something about 'dirty hands' causing the trouble.

Now we are in a position to reconstruct the sequence of events more meaningfully. Graham had experienced a difficult anal stage. The acquisition of bowel control had been associated with a series of battles between him and his mother. At three-and-a-half he had just emerged from this stage a rather aggressive, belligerent child. He was often reprimanded for his hostile attacks on other children and he began to be aware that his brother was not only more competent but also gained more approval than he did. It was at the onset of his genital stage of development, just at the time when his sexual curiosity, sexual exploration and masturbatory activities were beginning, that he developed the painful infection of his penis. At this age he would naturally try to link this up with some forbidden activity of his own. The doctor's remark about 'dirty hands' and his brother's ominous pronouncement served to strengthen his belief that masturbation and his sexual curiosity were responsible for his ailment and might even cause him to die. He reacted by repressing many genital stage activities including his aggressive play with other children.

Instead he regressed to anal behaviour, to which the struggles he had had with his mother over the pot had predisposed him. He was now a quiet, docile, uncurious child who showed no sexual interests and did not get cross with others. He merely enraged his mother by soiling regularly several times a day. He had no control over this symptom, which only served to diminish his self-esteem. When he entered school and found he was not managing as well as the others he became even more quiet and withdrawn. Graham's symptoms disappeared dramatically in the course of treatment and he once more became an active and assertive boy (pp. 203–5). The change in him coincided in time with his mother's decision to give up the work in her father's shop. Both were able simultaneously to relinquish their defensive manoeuvres and to allow themselves direct expression of their feelings.

These two case-histories provide examples of how defence mechanisms operate in childhood. They also illustrate the fact that when children's symptoms persist obstinately the parents are often found to have some difficulty of their own that prevents them from reacting to their children in a more helpful way. John's father was strict and excessively critical of his handicapped child for reasons that had to do with his feelings towards his own father in childhood. Graham's mother became more intolerant of his symptom when her guilt towards her sister forced her to take on greater responsibilities than she really cared to have.

Whenever defence mechanisms are used to ward off anxiety the feelings that are repressed are no longer available to reality testing and to modification with age and maturity. The repressed part of the personality remains infantile and is no longer accessible to learning. Whenever childhood conflict is repressed rather than resolved by means of sublimation, some distortion of personality takes place. All of us are exposed to this process to a greater or lesser extent. If, during childhood, social pressures are excessive, if the individual has to use defensive manoeuvres in a massive way to ward off anxiety, then a large part of his personality remains infantile. Excessive use of defence mechanisms in childhood predisposes the person to the development of neurosis in later life so that he may then react to relatively minor stresses by becoming ill.

DEFECTIVE SOCIALIZATION AS A CAUSE FOR SYMPTOMS

Two investigations into children's behaviour disorders have demonstrated very clearly that what may on the surface look like the same symptom can in fact be brought about by two quite different sets of circumstances: excessive social pressures on the one hand, inadequate socialization on the other.

E. J. Anthony studied children aged between four and fifteen years who presented with soiling.[4] He distinguished between children who had never achieved bowel control, the 'continuous' group, and those in whom toilet training had been successful but who began to soil again later on, the 'discontinuous' group. He explored the type of toilet training the children had had. He found that at one extreme were mothers whose methods had been coercive. They had started potting early and enforced their demands rigorously. They had high aspirations, expecting their children to achieve bowel control early and if they failed with one child they increased their expectations with the second. They tended to misinterpret cues given by their toddlers and to offer the pot on all occasions. These coercive mothers were on the whole self-confident, in step with their culture and they tended to come from skilled working and middle class families. At the other extreme were mothers who had exerted unusually low toilet training pressures. They had deferred training until their children were over two years old, their aspirations for bowel control were low and if they failed with one child they lowered their expectations still further with the next. These mothers lacked assurance and lived in neglected homes. They were slovenly and tended to come from unskilled working class families. Often other children in the family also suffered from bed-wetting and soiling. Anthony found that on the whole children with the 'discontinuous' type of soiling had been exposed to high training pressures, while those with 'continuous' soiling had experienced unusually low training pressures.

He went on to study the children themselves. This he did by observing their 'disgust reactions' in a number of test situations. In one of these the child had to put his finger into a series of pots containing substances ranging in consistency from water to sticky materials. In another the child was presented with a series of smells from pleasant perfumes to putrid, faecal smells. In a third the child was given a series of colours to look at from pastel hues to dark greens, yellows and browns. He presented the children with a word association test in which lavatory words were mixed up with neutral words and finally he made them look at pictures of children at toilet. He measured the physical manifestations of anxiety during these tests by means of a galvanometer measuring skin resistance. (This is affected by the amount of sweating that occurs on the palm of the hand.) He found that sticky substances, putrid smells, faecal colours, lavatory words and lavatory pictures tended to elicit physical manifestations of anxiety in one group of children, the 'discontinuous' soilers, but not in the other. His experimental finding was in line with a more general observation: children who had been rigorously toilet trained and who had once achieved bowel control but had broken down later tended to be very fastidious and meticulous in their general demeanour. These were the children who showed marked disgust reactions in the test situation. Their symptom, soiling, was out of step with the rest of their behaviour. Children who had never achieved bowel control and who had usually been rather haphazardly trained were less particular about dirt in general and showed no special disgust reactions. Their symptom was in line with their greater tolerance of mess and disorder. Anthony concludes that in the first, the 'discontinuous', group soiling was a neurotic symptom, the children requiring skilled psychological treatment, while in the second, 'continuous', group the symptom was due to defective socialization and usually responded to patient and systematic toilet training.

Hersov studied quite a different symptom: non-attendance at school.[71, 72] He distinguished between school refusal and truanting and found that although from the school's point of view the symptoms looked alike, there were in fact marked differences between children who refused to leave home for school each morning and those who set off for school regularly but either never arrived there or else went into school and then took off again. In cases of school refusal, the parents always knew where the child was: he was at home. Parents of truanters often knew nothing about their child's difficulties until the attendance officer called at their house.

When the home backgrounds of the two groups of children were compared, it was found that the truanters tended to come from lower social class families, which were more often disrupted by broken marriages and in which the parents had lower educational levels and aspirations. Parents of truanters were more often negligent and rejecting in their attitudes to their child while mothers of school refusers tended to be overprotective. Clear differences between the children themselves also emerged. Truanters often manifested antisocial behaviour such as lying and stealing and a number had appeared in court. Children with school refusal tended to be 'model' children. They frequently suffered from excessive shyness, fears and physical symptoms, especially abdominal pain and vomiting in the morning when it was time to go to school. Whereas truanters were often educationally retarded and as a result did not enjoy school, school refusers tended to be good scholars and to like being at school once they got there. The paradox is that they want to be in school but cannot bring themselves to go. A detailed clinical analysis of a series of cases showed that school refusal was a neurotic symptom, whose basis usually was anxiety about the mother.[72] The child could not leave the mother in case some harm befell her while he was away, and often what he feared most of all was the potentially damaging effect of his own hostile impulses towards her. Truanters on the whole have no such internal, neurotic conflicts. Psychologically they are a much more normal group, their behaviour conforming to the standards of their own particular families and neighbourhoods. The conflict here is rather between their own social sub-culture and the standards of society at large with which they cannot identify. Socialization has been inadequate.

In a study of 500 records of children referred to a Child Guidance Clinic in Illinois, Hewitt and Jenkins found that the symptoms presented by the children clustered to form three syndromes which correlated statistically with recognizable situational patterns.[73]

(1) The first syndrome of *unsocialized aggressive* behaviour consists of delinquency, aggression, solitariness and isolation.

It was found in children whose background was one of *parental rejection* characterized by such features as illegitimacy, overt rejection and open hostility.

(2) The second syndrome of *well-adjusted aggressive* behaviour, consisting of delinquent and aggressive gang activities in children who got on well with their peers, was found associated with a background of *parental neglect and delinquency in the family*. These children characteristically lived in delinquent neighbourhoods but they had normal relationships with their families and friends.

(3) The third syndrome of *over-inhibited* behaviour is related to one of two situations: *family repression*, consisting of a hypercritical, inconsistent father, a dominating mother and lack of sociability in either parent; or *chronic physical defect or ailment* in the child.

Despite a recent critical reappraisal, Hewitt's and Jenkin's work has found support from a number of other investigators [102, 137] and it remains a landmark in child psychiatric research.

In summary, behaviour disturbances in children can arise as a consequence of two kinds of circumstances. Firstly they may spring from deficiencies in the process of socialization to which all children are normally exposed. Such deficiencies can be due to absence of essential early life experiences, in particular of a continuous relationship with the mother during the first two or three years of life. They can also arise when the child is reared in a sub-culture whose standards differ from those of the society as a whole, into which he has to fit as he gets older. Such 'socialized aggressive' children usually know very well what the generally accepted standards are. Their own behaviour, however, built up from early childhood identifications with their parents, is different; the standards of society remain 'out there'; they have not been incorporated and the individual himself is often painfully aware of this.

Secondly, behaviour symptoms can arise when the child is under excessive pressure so that he has to use massive defensive manoeuvres to cope with his anxiety. Such pressures can stem from illness, physical handicap or poor intellectual endowment, that is, from factors within the child himself, or, alternatively, from adverse environmental circumstances of the kind with which we will be dealing at some length later on in this book.

3. Disturbed Children in the Community

HOW COMMON ARE BEHAVIOUR DISORDERS
IN CHILDREN?

Three decades of research into the prevalence of behaviour disorders in childhood have established the following facts:[91, 102, 115, 130, 163]

(1) many behaviour disorders are very common;

(2) some symptoms have two age periods of incidence;

(3) boys differ from girls in the kind of problem behaviour they commonly display; and

(4) children behave differently at home and at school.

(1) Studies of the prevalence of behaviour disorders have established for example that in the primary school age group bed-wetting occurs in 15% of children, nail-biting in 30% and stealing in 5%.

(2) Timidity, over-sensitivity, temper tantrums, negativism and food fads are especially common during the pre-school years and then again at puberty. The genital stage of emotional development and later on, adolescence, are times of stress for many children and it is at these times that behaviour disorders occur most often.

(3) A pioneer study, although one that would hardly satisfy present day scientific standards, was done by the eminent child psychologist, Susan Isaacs, in 1932.[79] Her material consisted of nearly 600 letters sent to her correspondence column in a weekly magazine by middle class mothers and nannies. The children reported on in these letters came from comfortable homes and most of them 'enjoyed modern methods of upbringing'. A third of the letters described educational problems; the rest neurotic disorders. Among these, naughtiness,

35

temper tantrums and other difficulties in relation to authority occurred most often, fears were next in frequency. While rebellious behaviour was commoner in boys, fears predominated among girls. Despite its scientific shortcomings, this early work demonstrated two facts, confirmed repeatedly by later, more rigorous studies. The first is that parents worry more when their children are troublesome and aggressive than when they are quiet and fearful. The second is that while boys tend to have more acting-out, aggressive and delinquent behaviour disorders, girls are more often inhibited and fearful.

One of the landmarks in research on childhood behaviour disorders is the long-term follow-up study of a one-in-three sample of all children born in Berkeley, California, between January 1928 and June 1929.[109] This study too demonstrated clear sex differences. Both boys and girls were outwardly aggressive at the age of two and three years. In girls, however, this behaviour was shortlived, while in boys it continued into the early school years. Girls thus lead boys in social learning and in the exercise of social controls. Their more frequent fearfulness, timidity and depression in later years indicates that they tend to internalize aggressive feelings which boys more often continue to express outwardly. Such sex differences in behaviour, the Berkeley workers suggested, are not due to any inherent biological differences between the sexes but to the differing social roles allotted to boys and girls in Western society.

How such behavioural differences can be induced even in early infancy has been shown by Caudill in a comparative study of American and Japanese mothers and their babies.[31] American mothers often leave their babies on their own, but when they are with them, they stimulate and activate them very much. This is in marked contrast to Japanese mothers who generally have their babies with them but play with them, handle them and talk to them very much less. American babies in turn are more active and more noisy than Japanese babies. While the Japanese mother treats her male and female children alike, the American mother is more stimulating to her infant sons than to her daughters. Even at this early age, Western mothers behave differently to children of different sexes.

Others have shown that in Western society boys are in more conflict than girls over their aggressive impulses. The reasons are not far to seek. A boy is expected to be assertive, fearless and able to stand up for himself. Dependency is not encouraged after the infant years. Most of his early upbringing, however, is by women, his mother and his primary school teachers. He cannot use them as role models. They cannot say to him, 'Be like us.' He must be different. Yet this difference is often not at all well tolerated by the very people who try to engender it.

Douglas, who followed up a national sample of British children, showed that girls excel in school subjects taught by women such as reading, writing and spelling, while boys excel in subjects generally taught by male teachers such as arithmetic, geography and science.[38] Children did well in subjects taught by people who could serve as role models for them. In addition, the teachers' evaluation of the children contributed to their progress. Positive evaluation stimulates effort and achievement; negative evaluation had the opposite effects.

In the primary schools, most teachers are women, and Douglas found that they underestimated boys' abilities and were more critical of boys than of girls, both as regards their work and their behaviour. While intelligence tests showed no difference between the sexes, boys performed less well than girls on tests of achievement and the performance, especially of working class boys, declined relative to that of girls in the course of their primary school years.

Douglas's conclusion is that primary school teachers tend to be out of sympathy with the aggressive behaviour of working class boys and that this unfavourable attitude on the part of women teachers adversely affects the boys' classroom behaviour and also their attitudes to school subjects.

In part the teachers' bias against boys may be due to the fact that both physically and socially boys mature more slowly than girls and women teachers may set their standards by the social achievements of girls.

Similar conclusions were derived from the National Child Development study, in which a second national cohort of children was examined. These were born in 1958 and re-investigated in 1964 to provide evidence for the Plowden

Committee. Streaming in schools favoured girls. They got into the upper streams more often than the boys and, once there, they did well, while boys swelled the lower streams of classes and tended to deteriorate in their school performance as the years went by.[34]

Studies such as these indicate that boys are more susceptible than girls not only, as is well known, to the physical complications of birth and to organic illnesses, but also to other environmental influences. It is always found that many more boys than girls are referred to psychiatrists, especially during the school years.

(4) In a recent survey of all 10- and 11-year-old children living on the Isle of Wight teachers and parents were asked to rate their children on checklists of behaviour disorders.[141] Two psychiatrists then independently examined a proportion of the children. Agreement between the psychiatrists on the severity of psychiatric disturbance was very good. Agreement was also good between the psychiatric ratings of disturbance and the behaviour scores obtained either on the parent or the teacher scales. But there was very little agreement indeed between the ratings accorded to each child by parent and teacher. Children judged to be disturbed by psychiatrists, had been identified as disturbed either in the school setting or by their mothers at home, but rarely in both situations. The same was found in a recent study of Edinburgh primary school children.[177, 178, 179] There was no association between symptom counts based on teachers' rating scales and symptom counts based on mothers' reports. Mothers and teachers agreed on the presence of easily recognized symptoms like stammering, other speech difficulties, nail-biting and tics, school refusal, stealing and lying. They also agreed on whether the child had poor concentration or attention and on whether he fought a lot. Presumably these are behaviour characteristics occurring both at home and at school to which teachers and mothers are equally sensitive.

Mothers and teachers did not agree in their estimate of the presence of sadness, withdrawal, solitariness, obsessionality, over-activity, disobedience and bullying. This means either that mothers and teachers differ in their sensitivity to these particular types of behaviour or that these symptoms are situationally determined, some children being unhappy and inhibited at home but not at school, some children being obedient and easy to manage at home, but rebellious and difficult in the school setting.

ARE SYMPTOMS THE SAME AS ILLNESS?

So far we have concerned ourselves only with the prevalence of various behaviour symptoms in boys and girls of different ages. Symptoms can be reliably estimated and counted, and several surveys of children in the community have now been done in order to establish norms.[97, 109, 152, 177] It has been argued that if we know, for example, that over one third of children still wet their bed at the age of two years, then the complaint of bed-wetting at this age is not a serious one. At least the symptom is not statistically abnormal.

We now know what types of behaviour are statistically normal and abnormal for boys and girls at different ages. But because a boy of eight still wets his bed at night when most boys of his age do not, this does not necessarily mean that he is emotionally disturbed or needs to see a psychiatrist. A number of other factors must be known about a child before he can be identified as sick and in need of treatment. Some of these factors relate less to his symptoms, but instead are associated with his life situation.

For example, if the eight-year-old comes from a stable family in which other members have also been enuretic, and if his mother confidently expects him to 'outgrow' his symptom as the other children have done, the problem is an entirely different one from that of a boy, previously dry, who begins to wet his bed again during a hospital admission for a burn and whose mother reacts by punishing him because she finds the symptom more than she can tolerate.

TWO COMMON MEASURES OF PSYCHIATRIC DISORDER IN CHILDHOOD: SYMPTOM COUNTS AND GLOBAL ASSESSMENTS OF DISTURBANCE

When one looks at large populations of children it is true to say that the numbers of symptoms reported for a child, by his mother or by his teacher, correlate with other measures of psychological disturbance. On the whole, children who have been referred to a psychiatrist have higher symptom counts than non-referred children. Overall judgements by teachers, parents and psychiatrists about whether or not a child is emotionally disturbed also correlate with symptom counts. But the fit is never perfect. Some children judged to be disturbed have very low symptom counts (for example, a child with a disabling single symptom such as psychogenic vomiting); other children, with high symptom counts, do not obtrude as problem children to their parents or their teachers.

In practice, children are identified as emotionally disturbed by their parents and their teachers not on the basis of symptom counts but on the basis of overall, global judgements. These are of course greatly influenced by the tolerance on the part of the parents and teachers of various kinds of deviant behaviour in children. As Leon Eisenberg, the eminent American child psychiatrist, has put it: 'The possibility exists that the difference between the child who appears at the clinic and the one who does not may lie less in the child than in the threshold for discomfort or in the diagnostic perception of his parents or teachers.'[43] Agreement can usually be reached about whether a child displays a certain type of behaviour or not, whether he steals for example, or is unduly shy. Opinion is, however, often divided about the implications of such behaviour and what, if anything, needs to be done about it.

DIFFERENCES IN TOLERANCE OF BEHAVIOUR
DISORDERS IN CHILDHOOD

The first person to study the differing perceptions of children's behaviour disorders by teachers on the one hand and psychiatrists on the other was Wickman in America in 1928.[173] He asked teachers to rate the children in their classes on a checklist of troublesome behaviour. Teachers were also asked to assess the children globally as well-adjusted, or as having minor emotional problems, or as having serious problems. Teachers identified 10% of the boys and 3% of the girls in their classes as seriously maladjusted. These children were characterized by their acting-out and difficult behaviour. Next, Wickman asked teachers and also psychiatric clinic staff to rank a number of behaviour disorders according to their seriousness. No agreement at all was found between the teachers and the psychiatric clinic staff in what symptoms were judged to have serious implications for future mental health. Teachers singled out sexual behaviour, disobedience and failure to learn as harmful symptoms; psychiatric clinic workers on the other hand stressed the seriousness of withdrawal, anxiety and unsociability.

Over the years, professional opinions about children's emotional disturbances have changed, so that the views of teachers and psychiatrists have come to be more alike. Several recent studies have shown that teachers are more sensitive to the difficulties of shy and withdrawn children, while psychiatrists and psychiatric social workers now regard acting-out, aggressive behaviour as more ominous than they did in the past, no longer believing that uninhibited expression of feelings and impulses is necessarily a healthy reaction to stress.[166]

The change in teachers' attitudes can perhaps be credited to the more widespread acceptance of psychoanalytic views that excessive repression and inhibition has a crippling effect on personality development. The psychiatrists have learnt perhaps from the failure of their own treatment methods with delinquents and from follow-up studies which showed aggressive and delinquent children to have a worse outcome in adult life than inhibited, neurotic children.[133]

The attitudes of teachers and psychiatrists to different kinds of behaviour disorders in children are now in more agreement, but there are still marked differences in assessments by parents and by teachers of the children they both know. These discrepancies, as we have seen, are probably at least in part due to real differences in the behaviour of children at home and in the school setting.

What conclusions can we draw from these findings?

First, there is no universally applicable definition of emotional disturbance or psychiatric illness in children. Such an ideal concept of illness is erroneous and it is erroneous not merely in the case of childhood emotional disorders. In general medicine too, the question of 'what is a case?' does not always have a clear-cut answer. One person tolerates a chronic cough for years without considering himself ill;

another with the same symptom presents himself to the doctor, is diagnosed as having chronic bronchitis and receives treatment for this condition. There is no ideal definition of psychiatric illness in childhood. But this does not mean that we cannot assess the presence of illness in a common-sense way. It merely means that we must be critical of the measures we use, that we must know their limitations, and that we must be aware of the biases that exist in our judgements about illness.

The second point is that if we want to find out how common psychiatric disturbances are in children, it is not any good asking only teachers or only mothers. We must ask both.

In view of all the difficulties, it is perhaps surprising that there is so much uniformity in the numerical estimates of psychiatric disturbances among school children. Surveys invariably show that between 5% and 10% of school children have serious psychiatric disorders. This is about ten times the number of children who actually get referred to a psychiatrist.

HOW DOES SOCIETY REACT TO PSYCHOLOGICALLY DISTURBED CHILDREN?

Psychological disturbance in childhood is not a purely private matter. Although the people who first notice a child's difficulties are usually his parents, and the first professional person to be consulted is often the family doctor, many children are identified as disturbed by public agencies.

Two quite distinct systems of public identification and treatment of children with behaviour disorders have developed over the years in this country. Disturbed children may be identified at school or they may be brought before the courts. The school's function is to educate the child; the main responsibility of the courts is the protection of society and, with the help of the children's departments, to safeguard the child.

There is an obligation on local education authorities to provide schooling for all children who can benefit from it, and to provide special schooling for all children who, because of some physical, mental or psychological handicap, cannot benefit from education in ordinary school classes. One such group consists of 'maladjusted pupils'. These were defined in the Handicapped Pupils and School Health Service Regulations, 1945, as 'pupils who show evidence of emotional instability or psychological disturbance and require special educational treatment in order to effect their personal, social or education re-adjustment'. The concept of '*maladjustment*', a word which defies definition except in pragmatic terms, is an educational one. The 1955 Committee on Maladjusted Children described such children as 'insecure and unhappy in that they fail in their personal relationships . . . At the same time, they are not readily capable of improvement by ordinary discipline . . .'.[113] The Committee stated further that 'Maladjustment does not always show itself in aggressive or troublesome conduct; indeed, quiet and passive behaviour may overlay deep emotional disturbance. Maladjustment may, however, be linked with bad behaviour or delinquency. . . . Insecurity and anxiety are closely associated with maladjustment.' Educational child guidance clinics were set up to help such children and their parents, and with the advent of the National Health Service, links grew up between these educational clinics and hospital psychiatric services for children. Special day and residential schools were established for maladjusted children who required teaching in smaller classes, or who were thought likely to benefit from special residential care and treatment away from home.

Children who draw attention to themselves by disturbing the public order outside their own homes or schools meet with very different reactions.

Over the age of ten, children are liable to prosecution if they break the law. '*Delinquency*', unlike 'maladjustment', is not a vague concept. It can be defined precisely in terms of court conviction for offences specified in law.[171] Although attitudes to offenders and to juvenile offenders in particular have changed considerably since the beginning of this century, the general approach to delinquent children is one which, if not frankly punitive, still stresses discipline and training above all else. Detention centres, attendance centres and most approved schools exemplify such an approach, which contrasts with the approach to 'maladjusted' children who, as the Underwood report pointed out, do not as a rule respond to 'ordinary discipline' and are thought to require special treatment and educational techniques.[113]

These two different approaches, psychological understanding and treatment for maladjusted children, discipline for delinquents, may seem to be the counterparts of the two main mechanisms which, as we saw in the last chapter, can cause behaviour disorders in children: excessive stress on the one hand, inadequate socialization on the other. Superficially the different administrative practices seem appropriate. Children exposed to excessive stresses become maladjusted and require a psychological treatment approach. Deprived and inadequately socialized children display delinquent behaviour and require social training. Such notions, however, do not correspond with the facts. We have already seen that exactly the same symptom, for example stealing, can spring from excessive anxiety *or* from inadequate socialization. Yet it is the symptom, the actual behaviour, and not its underlying mechanisms, that often determines whether a child will be referred by his teacher to a child guidance clinic or will be charged by a policeman and appear in court. Behaviour alone is not a good indicator of the underlying disturbance. Moreover, the individual psychologically disturbed child has very often experienced both kinds of harmful circumstances: inadequate socialization *and* exposure to excessive stresses. Usually it is not a question of either/or, but rather of how much of each.

In a recent study comparisons were made between a group of boys awaiting admission to approved schools and a group awaiting placement in maladjusted schools.[6] There were behavioural differences between the two groups but also many similarities. The school behaviour of the maladjusted group was worse than that of the approved school group and the former had more often been seen at child guidance clinics. Thus, maladjusted boys, unlike approved school boys, tended to draw attention to themselves at school. In addition another public agency was frequently alerted to their difficulties: proportionally more of them lived in children's homes and were therefore known to local authority children's departments. Marital disharmony, separation and divorce were equally common among the parents of both groups of children, but court appearances of other members of the family had occurred more often in the approved school group. The conclusions to be drawn from this study are that while differences exist both in background and behaviour between the two groups of boys (the maladjusted tending to show disturbances within their homes and schools, approved school boys in the community outside home and school) there is also considerable overlap between them. Whether a child is sent to an approved school or to a maladjusted school may depend on circumstances that have nothing to do with the nature of his difficulties or of his past life experiences.

All comparisons between delinquent and non-delinquent children indicate that the former tend to come from lower socio-economic classes and from deteriorated urban areas.[42] In part this may reflect real differences in the behaviour of children from different sections of the community. Nevertheless, the class difference between children who appear at court and other disturbed children is exaggerated by selective methods of identification and referral to other agencies. Police patrols are more active in deteriorated urban areas than in sedate suburbs and slum children who commit delinquent acts are more likely to be found out than children who live in middle class areas. More important are the differences in the reactions of parents in different social classes.

When middle class children engage in delinquent behaviour, their parents and teachers tend to take the initiative in seeking medical or educational advice before the coercive agencies such as the police, the children's department or the N.S.P.C.C. step in. Class differences in the identification and treatment of illness have been found for all types of deviant behaviour. In the case of adult mental illness, Hollingshead and Redlich, working in Newhaven, U.S.A., found that upper and middle class psychiatric patients tended to be referred to psychiatrists by private physicians while lower class patients were more often referred by social agencies, the police and the courts.[75] Stein and Susser, working in Lancashire county and Salford city, showed that middle and upper working class mentally defective children were usually taken by their parents to child guidance or mental health department clinics for diagnosis and advice. In lower working class families a defective child's difficulties were often not recognized until he was at school and sometimes not until an act of delinquent behaviour brought him in conflict with the law. The diagnosis of mental deficiency in these lower working class, disorganized families was often made by child care and N.S.P.C.C. workers involved with the families.[159]

A recent study of all Edinburgh teenagers seen by psychiatrists during the course of one year showed that the adolescents who were referred to hospital psychiatric departments, usually by general practitioners, tended to come from middle class areas of the city.[107] Teenagers seen by psychiatrists in other settings, mainly in approved schools or in the general hospital after a suicide attempt, came from the socially disorganized areas of the city.

All these studies show that when middle class children are disturbed, it is their parents who generally identify the disorder and mobilize help. They go to their doctor. Disturbed working class children on the other hand are more often identified by public and coercive agencies. The treatment approach of these agencies is different from that offered to children whose parents take them to the doctor.

However, there is now a growing recognition in this country that children who come forward because their parents are worried about them often have quite similar problems to children identified as 'maladjusted' in the school setting or as 'delinquent' by the courts. From the point of view of helping the child towards a better adjustment in society it may be irrelevant whether he appears first at a psychiatric clinic or in a court of law, and current reforms of the law relating to juvenile offenders and proposals, for the treatment of delinquents and their families reflect such a view. This is a matter to which we shall return in later chapters of this book.

IDENTIFICATION OF EMOTIONALLY DISTURBED
    CHILDREN – TO WHAT END?

It has often been said that if only we can identify psychiatric disorders in children earlier, we should be able to prevent more serious illnesses in later life; that if we can know in advance which children will become delinquent, we shall be able to take prophylactic action. Yet it seems to me that the argument for ever earlier and more sensitive identification of psychiatric disorders in children requires to be seriously questioned. In particular, we must be clear what we are identifying children for. If it is to improve parents' and teachers' understanding of children, so that the child's apparently senseless and aggravating behaviour becomes meaningful, and if it leads to more sensitive and helpful handling of children at home and in the school, then the recognition of problems is beneficial. If, on the other hand, it leads parents and teachers to an anxious giving up of responsibility and a feeling that only experts in special settings can cope, if it leads to the exclusion of more and more children from ordinary care in the home and at school, then deliberate efforts to recognize emotionally disturbed children are of questionable value.

Emotionally disturbed children are not handicapped in the usual sense. Most of them have no permanent psychological defect for which allowances must be made. They are, as a rule, children reacting with normal psychological mechanisms to excessive stresses in their lives, and their behaviour disorders require to be understood in the light of these stresses. To treat emotionally disturbed children as if they were essentially different from other children may be harmful. When adults fear for a child's future, these anxieties are communicated to the child. They may undermine his self-confidence and may actually contribute to bring about the feared consequences.

The recognition of emotional disturbances for research purposes is quite a different matter. We need to find out how we can improve the environment for children as a whole so that fewer emotional disturbances occur. We must identify situations that are potentially harmful and prevent them from happening or, if that is not possible, we must learn how to help children in stressful circumstances in order to prevent later psychological difficulties. In this way we shall achieve more than if we expend our energies identifying and labelling children as problem children or even trying to predict who might develop problem behaviour in the future.

Part II
STRESSFUL SITUATIONS AND VULNERABLE CHILDREN

4. Illness and Going to Hospital

A universal stress in childhood is illness. Many children have accidents and operations and by the time they are grown up most will have had some contact with a hospital. It may come as a surprise therefore to find that there are few systematic studies of the emotional effects of illness and hospitalization on children, and that recommendations for improving the psychological care of sick children are more often based on humanitarian beliefs than on scientific evidence.[114] Why should this be so?

PROFESSIONAL DENIAL OF THE STRESS OF ILLNESS

Many illnesses in childhood are of course mild; they are experienced as a passing interlude of relative inactivity, concentrated parental concern and spoiling in the midst of otherwise busy lives. Often parents cope with such illnesses without any professional help or else with just one or two visits from the family doctor. For the professionals, the doctors and the nurses, however, the picture is different. They spend most of their time looking after more seriously ill children. They encounter many children who are unhappy, some who are in pain and not a few who suffer from disfiguring, crippling or even fatal illnesses. Often they are called upon to carry out procedures which add to the child's distress. Such experiences are upsetting, especially in hospitals where children, unlike adults, are completely dependent on the medical and nursing staff who look after them. Doctors and nurses have somehow to deal with their own anxieties in the face of suffering, since their feelings of distress may actually interfere with their professional tasks. Anxiety and guilt are commonly felt by people who care for ill children. They do not make for effective functioning.

Without special help to deal with their own anxieties, doctors and nurses commonly resort to methods of coping which preserve their efficiency, but at a cost. The most common solution is to adopt an attitude of clinical detachment: to split off the emotional aspects of illness and its treatment as they affect both the patient and oneself. The patient and his illness are treated objectively; subjective feelings and impulses are repressed. The fact that serious illness has equally serious emotional implications is denied and the psychological consequences of illness, of physical handicap and of hospitalization are not faced.

It is this massive denial on the part of professionals – necessary because without special training they have no other way of coping with the distressing experiences of their everyday lives – which has in my view delayed the scientific exploration of the effects of illness on children's emotional development. We have been afraid to look in case what we see is more than we can bear. Yet our fears may be to a large extent irrational. Human beings, especially children, are resilient. They have capacities for coping with adversity that often surprise us. But unless we look, we shall not know what these strengths are nor how best to help children to make the most effective use of them.

I propose to look first of all at the psychological implications of being ill; to examine children's reactions to hospitalization; next to explore the impact of some major stresses such as operations and burns; then to consider children's reactions to chronic illness; and finally to describe what doctors and nurses can do to enable children to cope better with illness and being in hospital.

THE PSYCHOLOGICAL IMPLICATIONS OF BEING ILL

Illness generally involves going to bed and being looked after. For the adult this invites regression to a situation of dependency. Many people readily permit themselves this agreeable experience, which can act as a sort of recompense for being ill and out of circulation. Anna Freud has shown us that, unlike adults, young children do not return to infancy with such pleasurable abandon. Some children, for whom the mastery of independent eating, washing and toileting was accomplished in the face of great longings for dependency and passivity, do not give up these achievements easily: they become difficult and intractable patients. Other young children lapse readily into a state of helpless infancy from which they had only just emerged and may have to re-learn many of their social skills during convalescence. Restriction of movement can be even more upsetting for the child than the experience of being nursed. We have all seen what Anna Freud describes: 'Young toddlers, who have only recently learned to walk. . . stand up stubbornly in their beds for the whole course of even a severe illness (for instance measles) . . .'[54]

An added stress in many illnesses is physical restraint imposed, for example, by prolonged immobilization in plaster casts for orthopaedic conditions or by chronic medical illnesses such as tuberculosis and rheumatic fever, which necessitate weeks or even months of rest in bed. In general motor restraint increases expressions of aggressive feelings both in toddlers and older children. There is more verbal aggression but also more restlessness and irritability. Sometimes children tolerate actual physical restraint surprisingly well only to react to minor additional discomforts with outbursts of rage and temper. Children in plaster casts often believe that once the cast is off they will at once, as if by magic, be completely well. If unprepared for the reality which faces them, their disappointment may find expression in unexpected ways such as regressive behaviour, e.g. infantile demands for attention, bed-wetting and even soiling.

Moreover, parents change when their child is ill. In their anxiety for their child to recover and their gratitude to the doctor or the nurse for what is being done to help the child, they are only too ready to overlook what they know to be temporary misery. They too operate with denial mechanisms. They know the illness will pass but often they do not face their child's anxieties. *He* may not know that he will soon be well again.

Anna Freud has pointed out that parents undergo a change

of attitude when their children become ill. They behave to them quite differently from usual. In their efforts to get the child to eat, they may adopt methods of force feeding; to keep him at rest they restrain him physically; and to avoid non-cooperation over essential medical or nursing procedures even the most scrupulously truthful parent may resort to deception.

Children in the animistic stage of development are dependent on adults to help them to make sense of their illness. These children suffer when their parents and doctors are themselves so worried and preoccupied that they cannot listen to their childish fears and provide truthful and rational explanations.

Mark, a little boy of six, was admitted to hospital with an infectious osteomyelitis, affecting his thigh and the bones of his face. He bore weeks of hospitalization and immobilization in plaster stoically. Then he was moved to a convalescent home which he knew to be farther away from his home than the hospital. Here he refused his food and began to vomit. Extensive investigations failed to reveal a physical cause for his eating disturbance and the nurses and his parents became worried. 'You must eat to get better,' they said. But he refused. From being a favourite patient, easy to nurse, he became a problem. The more the nurses and his parents worried about him, the more pressure they put on the child. They were cross with him; they reasoned with him and they urged him to eat. When they asked him to explain why he would not eat, all he could say was 'I don't like the peas.'

At this stage outside help was summoned and I went to see Mark in his hospital bed. As an outsider, not directly responsible for his nursing care, and not therefore preoccupied with fears that unless I could persuade him to eat he would lose weight and go downhill, I was free to attend to what he had to say. When I asked him, 'What is the matter with your face, why is it swollen?', he replied in matter-of-fact tones, 'It's because I bite my nails.' It was clear he accepted responsibility for his illness, thinking he had caused it by doing something naughty. The parents confirmed that he was a nail-biter and that they had often told him it was a 'dirty habit'. They also remembered the doctor saying that perhaps the infection had been caused by dirt getting into his mouth. They were shocked however to think that their son was blaming himself for being ill: *that* connexion, between a naughty habit and his illness, was made by Mark himself. He had always been exceptionally 'good' in the ward. His parents used to praise him and say that if he was good and did what the nurses told him, he would get better more quickly, a remark designed to reinforce the notions, magical and egocentric, that he already had about his own responsibility for his illness. When he was moved to the convalescent home against his will, he could not afford to protest openly, to make a fuss, to be 'naughty'. Instead he developed symptoms: food refusal and vomiting, over which he had no control.

It was now clear what had to be done. Rather than increase his sense of responsibility for his illness, by stressing that he must do his part to get better and demanding good behaviour, we had to get across to him that nail-biting or indeed naughtiness of any kind did not cause illness; that illnesses happen 'by accident' and it was the business of the doctors and nurses to get him well whatever he did. We had to convey to him that we understood that he refused the hospital food because he was angry with the doctors and nurses for sending him far away; that we did not mind him being cross because we knew that all children who are ill and in hospital sometimes feel cross; and that this would not interfere with his getting better.

Animistic explanations for illnesses are usual in children between three and seven or eight years of age. In an article written nearly twenty years ago children are quoted as explaining their diabetes 'because I ate too much sugar' and their rheumatic fever 'because I ran too much'.[96] If one is alert to such childish misconstructions, it is not difficult to know what one can do to diminish the anxieties caused to children by illness at this stage of life.

CHILDREN'S REACTIONS TO HOSPITALIZATION

It is often difficult to disentangle the effects of being in hospital and away from home from the effects of the illness itself and its treatment. A number of research workers have focused on the effects of separation from parents in hospital, choosing as their subjects children who did not feel particularly ill and who were not exposed to operations and other major treatment procedures.

In general one can say that whether a child is emotionally disturbed during or after an admission to hospital depends on three factors: (1) his age; (2) his personality and past life experiences; (3) what actually happens to him in hospital.

55

(1) *The Effect of Age*

Schaffer has shown that *under seven months* babies do not fret in hospital. They tend to be rather quiet and they cry more than when they are at home, but they respond to the strange nurses who look after them just as they do to their own mothers at visiting times and, when their mothers leave, they do not protest. On coming home these very young babies at first remain subdued and quiet. But in addition they display extreme preoccupation with their surroundings, staring at the objects in their environment and craning their necks to get a better view. Toys and people cannot distract them and their mothers can make no contact with them. Schaffer called this behaviour 'the global syndrome'. He describes it as lasting from a few hours up to three days and he attributes it to the perceptual monotony to which the children are exposed in hospital and to acute awareness of new sensations in new surroundings when this monotony is interrupted.[143]

In some hospitals special efforts are now made to prevent sensory deprivation of very young infants. The babies are provided with interesting toys dangling before their eyes; they are propped up to get a view of the ward activities; and nurses are encouraged to talk to and play with them whenever they undertake nursing procedures. Frequent visiting by parents and social approaches from bigger children who are up and about can contribute to prevent the 'global syndrome' from developing.

Under seven months, babies do not react with anxiety to brief separations. But what about their mothers? For the very young infant his mother does not yet exist as a person. But she too may not have loving and cherishing feelings for him from the moment of his birth. Maternal feelings are often delayed and develop after continual proximity during the first few days and even weeks of the baby's life. If a mother has to part from her child before she has experienced loving feelings for him she may be handicapped later in establishing a close bond with him. Moreover her confidence in handling him when he comes home from hospital may be undermined if she has not been able to do anything for him during his illness. The more seriously ill he was, the more vulnerable he now appears to her and the more reluctant she is to touch him too much. She may even be afraid to allow herself to love him if she still has some fears that he will be taken from her again.

Without close contact with her sick baby, the mother may not be able to identify with him when he is well again. In her anxiety to do the right thing she may copy what she has seen the nurses do in hospital. When she baths and feeds him her handling of the child is at first detached and clinical and it may take her a long time to respond to the baby as an individual, to get to know his likes and dislikes and to establish a mutually satisfactory relationship with him. One mother, whose daughter was in a children's hospital for many months after her birth, developed a closer attachment to the ward sister, whom she got to know very well, than to her own child for whom she had done little throughout a prolonged illness. The child had difficulties in her social adjustment for many years and the mother continued to find her hard to understand.

The only real solution is for nurses to involve mothers actively in the care of their babies in hospital, and to admit mothers to hospital with their babies whenever possible.

After seven months of age, babies fret in hospital. Like younger infants, they cry a lot and 'talk' very little. But unlike younger babies, they react with anxiety whenever a strange nurse approaches them and they cling to their mothers at visiting time, protesting loudly when the mothers leave. In hospital fretting reactions last from one to eight days and then they stop. The children now cry less and move about and babble more. They become more responsive to strangers but never as responsive as younger babies. They continue to cling to their mothers and to cry whenever the mothers leave. After discharge home these older babies show a syndrome of 'over-dependence', which lasts about two weeks. During this time, they cling to their mother and cry whenever she disappears from view.

In Schaffer's series only nine out of seventy-six children under the age of one year showed no untoward reactions at all to a brief hospitalization and of these four were under two months on admission and one had been in hospital for only four days.

Schaffer has shown us that the lower age limit at which

children begin to show signs of suffering as a result of separation from their mothers is seven months. What about the upper age limit? Until what age are children vulnerable to hospital separations from their mothers?

A group of Boston psychiatrists, to whose work we shall refer again later, have shown that no matter how excellent the medical and nursing care of children in hospital, no matter how sensitive their handling from an emotional point of view, *children under the age of four years* remain manifestly disturbed while in hospital and have many more behaviour disorders after discharge than do older children.[128] Three weeks after discharge half the under-fours still showed severe reactions and of those given special nursing care a third were then still severely disturbed. While in hospital behaviour is most disturbed in children aged between two and four years. In this age group screaming and panic attacks are common, outbursts of anger occur whenever parents leave and some children become depressed, withdrawn and develop eating and sleeping disturbances. If confined to bed, rocking and thumb sucking are common. This last type of behaviour is not seen in children who are up and about in the ward and it also occurs less often when children receive a great deal of individual attention.

Between seven months and about four years of age the emotional effects of separation and of illness and its treatment are at their maximum. None of the changes in hospital practice designed to counteract anxiety in children have been effective in the under-fours admitted to hospital on their own. There is evidence, although not of a statistical kind, that when mothers are admitted to hospital together with their children, sickness, pain and frightening medical procedures can be tolerated with only temporary upsets and without the later disturbances found in children admitted alone. It is not the mother's explanations and reassurances that work but her actual presence. Anna Freud considers the parent in this situation to fulfil the functions of a substitute ego. Alone the child cannot master his anxieties. He may have fears of overwhelming attack and destruction because with his limited capacities he cannot understand what is going on. When his mother or father are present he leaves all this to them. He trusts them to put things right.

(2) *The Effects of Personality and Past Life Experiences*

The Boston study of children in hospital demonstrated clearly that children who had been exposed to traumatic experiences prior to their hospitalization reacted with greater distress.[128] The same was true of children whose previous personality adjustment and relationships with their parents were poor. This often comes as a surprise to laymen, and even to nurses. They feel that if a child has not been happy at home then he should not mind so much if he has to leave his home temporarily. In fact, of course, the reverse is true. The insecurity of a rejected child, for example, impairs his chances of an independent adjustment away from home. He does not carry with him the firm inner image of a loving mother which can reassure him while he is parted from her.

(3) *The Impact of Actual Hospital Experiences*

Some twenty years ago David Levy observed that there were many young children in whom fears, anxieties and nightmares followed closely on an operation.[101] Symptoms were particularly severe when the operation occurred between the ages of one and three years and when the genital organs were involved, as for example in circumcision. When one operation followed another, the second intensified the child's fears if these were still present, but had no extra effect if they had already subsided. Levy advised postponing surgery if possible until after the age of three and putting off a second operation until the disturbances following the first have gone.

A more recent study in a London teaching hospital was concerned with children undergoing eye operations for squint.[167] Here children under four were found to react particularly badly and to be unresponsive to special help to allay their fears.

An experimental group and a control group of children matched for age, sex and intelligence, were selected. The control children underwent the normal ward routine while the experimental group were interviewed by a psychiatrist on their first, third and fifth hospital days. The interviews were aimed firstly at helping the child to express his feelings and his views about being in hospital and about his operation and, secondly, to correct his misperceptions and mistaken ideas. Many children cried as soon as these topics were broached in the first interview but then seemed relieved and settled well. They revealed highly unrealistic fantasies about their operation, often thinking that their eyes were to be removed and put back. One boy said, 'I was one of the lucky ones, I got my own eye back.'

While in hospital just over half the experimental group showed disturbed behaviour and less than half the control group were disturbed. One week after discharge, however, the situation was reversed: only a third of the experimental group were still disturbed compared with two-thirds of the controls. Six months after discharge only three of the twenty experimental children showed disturbances compared with eleven of the controls. Often children who were disturbed while in hospital settled down quickly once they were at home again, while those who showed few outward manifestations of distress in hospital frequently became quite disturbed on returning to the safe and familiar environment of their own families.

The improvement in the children given special help during their stay in hospital was confined to those over four. It is disquieting to note that every single child under four years of age was still disturbed six months after his hospital admission for what was after all a routine, although perhaps a particularly frightening, operation.

The Boston study too showed that hospital stresses such as operations and other procedures necessitating an anaesthetic added to the children's emotional disturbances both in hospital and after discharge.[128] Children under six reacted particularly badly and children under four failed to respond to improvements in nursing techniques (see pp. 70, 71).

It is not surprising that operation is especially stressful for children under six years of age. During the genital stage of emotional development (between the third and the sixth year of life) children are preoccupied with their bodily intactness and castration anxieties are readily stimulated. This emotional stage coincides with the intellectual stage of animism in which children tend to misconstrue the nature of their ailments and of the treatment they are getting. Illnesses are explained in moralistic terms; painful procedures are viewed as punishment and arouse more guilt and anxiety than at any later stage of life.

One of the lessons to be learnt is that non-urgent operations should be postponed until children are over four years old and that no operation should be performed without a very good reason. It may seem superfluous to point this out, but some surgical interventions are still occasionally done for what can only be described as magical reasons. Examples are operations for so-called 'tongue-tie', performed on children with poor speech, exactly at an age (3 or 4 years) at which surgery is most upsetting. The operation itself is minor, but the symbolic implications are profound. This is even more true of circumcision, an operation rarely thought necessary by paediatricians these days, but still frequently suggested by parents, recommended by general practitioners and carried out by surgeons.

A little boy, whose father had died before his birth, was becoming more boisterous and assertive during his third year of life and somewhat of a handful for his elderly mother. She found it difficult to answer his questions about his daddy and his great enthusiasm for all grown-up men was an embarrassment to her. She was often checking him, although this made her feel guilty. He began to masturbate and she checked him for this also. Then he started to wet his bed again and she consulted the doctor. He retracted the foreskin which he thought might be too tight and the child screamed. The doctor advised the mother to perform this manoeuvre daily but she could not bring herself to do it. The bed-wetting continued. The doctor then suggested that perhaps a circumcision was indicated, but at the same time he referred mother and child to a child guidance clinic.

This child did not have a circumcision. His bed-wetting cleared up when the mother was given the opportunity to discuss her own unresolved difficulties and then decided to start him at a nursery school and to take a part-time job. Many children in similar situations will not be spared this operation, often suggested for reasons that predetermine its traumatic effect: masturbation guilt and castration anxieties are reinforced. Although no systematic study of a group of toddlers and older children undergoing circumcision has been done, the accounts of fears and night terrors, over-inhibited behaviour and regressive symptoms following this operation are numerous.

The Long-Term Effects of Hospitalization

The Boston workers demonstrated that hospital admission, even if brief and not associated with particularly stressful events such as surgery, can lead to emotional disturbances lasting six months or more especially in children under four.[128]

Bowlby and his co-workers at the Tavistock Institute have shown however that long-term effects even of a prolonged stay in hospital in early life, are not as great as was at one time feared.[22] Bowlby followed up a group of children who had been in hospital for some months with tuberculosis under the age of four and who had not been exposed to such extra stresses as operation. He compared these children several years later with a group of their school fellows who had not been in hospital. He found slightly more behaviour disorders among the ex-patients, but their general school adjustment and their educational progress were not impaired in comparison with the control group. It is important to note that all assessments of the children were based only on the reports of teachers and we know that such reports do not provide a complete picture of a child's functioning. We know too from the work of Hewitt and Jenkins[73] that the type of difficulties to be expected as a result of chronic physical illness are neurotic disturbances: anxiety, fears, nightmares and over-inhibited behaviour and that these are exactly the kinds of symptoms which teachers do not pick up as easily as difficult, aggressive and antisocial behaviour.

Hospital Experiences of Emotionally Disturbed Children

Despite the infrequency of long-term emotional difficulties following hospitalization, when children with known psychiatric disorders are compared with normal controls we find that disturbed children have been in hospital much more often and for much longer than other children in the community. In the author's study of primary school children with behaviour disorders, a third of the clinic attenders had never been in hospital, a third had been admitted once and another third had been admitted two or more times. Among the non-disturbed control group two thirds had never been in hospital, a quarter had been once, and less than one-sixth had been admitted on two or more occasions. While 26 of the 100 clinic attenders had spent three or more weeks of their lives in hospital, only 7 of the non-disturbed children had been in hospital that long.

Although the association between hospitalization and emotional disorder is clear, this study does not help us to decide whether hospitalization causes psychiatric illness or whether both admission to hospital and psychiatric illness depend on a third factor common to both. All one can say is that children admitted to hospital repeatedly are vulnerable children, who are in special need of skilled help in coping with the anxieties aroused by their illnesses.

THE IMPACT OF MAJOR STRESSES: BURNS

Even relatively minor surgical interventions can have serious psychological implications, depending on the age of the child and the nature of the operation. What about the effects of really serious surgical emergencies in childhood?

One of the most distressing events in paediatric practice, and one that illustrates well the problems facing all families with a seriously injured child, is that of a severe burn. To those concerned, the event is more than an accident: it is a disaster. Until recently the problems of treating the general bodily effects of shock following extensive burns, of preventing infection and of skin grafting areas of deep burning had fully occupied medical and surgical attention. Parents and children were left to cope with the feelings aroused by the accident, the distress of dressings, operations and other medical procedures and the aftermath of scarring – a permanent reminder of what had happened – as best they could.

The idea that if his mother had been a better mother and had loved him more she would have prevented the accident is a common one in children during the stage of magical thinking. In this period of their development nothing happens fortuitously and grown-ups are seen as all-powerful. Such ideas occur not only to the children involved in serious accidents, they occur also to parents and to hospital staff.

Burns and scalds are most common in large families living in over-crowded homes, conditions under which accident prevention may become almost impossible. Despite this, mothers feel profoundly guilty and lose their confidence in themselves as good mothers. Doctors and nurses tend to attribute the accident to carelessness especially when, as is so often the case, the family belongs to that socio-economic group with which middle class hospital staff have least in common. Their critical attitudes and their inability to identify with the family tend to reinforce the parents' feelings of guilt and inadequacy.

Woodward and Jackson investigated the emotional sequelae of burns and scalds in children treated at the Birmingham Accident Hospital before and after a change of regime. Before the experiment no special regard had been paid to the specific emotional effects of the accident and its treatment. The organization of the Burns Unit had been aimed primarily at providing the most effective and the most efficient treatment for the burn. Visiting time was limited and in the case of babies and toddlers parents were allowed only to look at their children through the glass walls of their wards. Joan Woodward followed up 198 children treated under these conditions one year after their discharge from hospital.[181] She found that over eighty per cent had emotional disturbances compared with only seven per cent of their unburned brothers and sisters. The most common symptoms were specific fears and anxiety, difficulties of management, such as negativism and aggressiveness, eating and sleep disorders and bed-wetting. Over half of the mothers of burned children complained about their own nerves and one in six had had medical treatment for a 'nervous breakdown'.

Two changes were then made in the unit. The first was to institute daily visiting for all children and the second to engage a psychiatric social worker. Her task was to interview all mothers during the child's admission to hospital and to maintain contact with them following discharge. Each mother, in her meetings with the social worker, was able to relieve herself of her feelings of distress and guilt and to report on her child's reactions. Formerly mothers were often so overwhelmed with guilt and anxiety that they had to repress these feelings. Instead they often displayed irrational behaviour towards their children: unreasonable anger, for example, or restrictive over-solicitousness. Now that they were given help to face and cope with their own feelings, they were better able to perceive and to respond to their children's needs. Children's accusations and their aggressive behaviour are hard to tolerate by a mother already burdened with self-blame. They become understandable and manageable for a mother who has been helped to cope with her own distress and is given continued support until her child has fully recovered both physically and psychologically. Of seventy-one children who were visited frequently and whose mothers received this special counselling, only twenty per cent manifested emotional disturbances one year after discharge from hospital.

REACTIONS TO CHRONIC ILLNESSES

Advances in paediatric knowledge and in the medical and surgical treatment of children, especially of children with congenital abnormalities, have led to the survival of many children who would have died even ten years ago. Children born with abnormalities of the heart or of the spine or of their kidneys now survive with treatment, and their physical condition and expectations of life may be excellent. However, all these children have been exposed to prolonged hospitalization and often to major surgery usually very early in their lives; their parents have at one time faced the possibility that their child may die; and many such children carry with them into later life some outward signs of their illness. They may be stunted in growth; at the very least they have a large scar. How such children and their parents adapt emotionally to these physical abnormalities would make a fascinating study and one long overdue.

One chronic condition in childhood, diabetes, presents a special problem not only because it is a life-long illness but because its treatment demands self-restraint on the part of the patient. Diabetic children are generally subjected to a routine of daily injections of insulin, many must in addition keep to a diet and limit their intake especially of sweets, the foods which symbolize comfort and having a treat. Most children come to accept the daily injection and learn to give it to themselves. Dietary restrictions are more often a problem especially as puberty approaches. At this time children become acutely aware of the implications of their illness for the future and they resent the fact of being different from other people. Magical notions of why *they* were singled out by this disease are commonly revived. Guilt feelings especially in relation to the parents arise and are defended against vigorously. Reaction formation is a common defence mechanism: the more anxious the child is about his illness and his future and the more guilty he feels, the more he is likely to throw caution to the winds, to flaunt all dietary restrictions and to be aggressively obstinate with his parents and the doctor when they remonstrate with him.

Unless doctors, nurses and parents are aware of the anxieties underlying such behaviour, a fruitless struggle may ensue between them and the adolescent patient. The common-sense approach is to reason with the child, to point out the necessity of keeping to the dietary rules in order to maintain control of the illness and even to stress the seriousness of the situation. This approach only serves to reinforce the anxieties and guilt feelings with which the adolescent is already struggling. Such a frontal attack is likely to fail. A more successful approach is temporarily to by-pass the issue of what the child does about treating his illness and to focus instead on how he feels about being a diabetic; to explore with him his views of how he came to be ill, his ideas of how this illness is affecting his family and what the implications are for his own future. Such a process of exploration frequently uncovers surprising errors and misperceptions, the correction of which brings relief. One twelve-year-old boy thought his mother's worry about his diabetes had caused her own serious illness. He refused to go to school, preferring to hang about at home and do small errands for her. The more pressure was put on him by his parents and the school the more guilty he felt and the more he dug his heels in. In such a situation only a reduction of anxiety will help the patient to give up his struggle against his illness and to resume its treatment. The main difficulty about many chronic illnesses is that the patient cannot be merely a passive recipient of medical care: he must himself cooperate actively in the management of his disease. This is often difficult, especially for adolescents, unless the psychological aspects of the illness are also understood and dealt with.

HOW CAN HOSPITAL CARE BE MADE LESS STRESSFUL?

The emotional well-being of children in hospital has been the concern of a few notable paediatricians for many years.

Sir James Spence in the forties admitted mothers together with children under three years of age to the Newcastle Children's hospitals. He advocated this 'not on sentimental grounds but on the practical grounds of efficiency and necessity'.[154] He found it advantageous for the child, the mother and the nurse who, he felt, could learn much from the mother. Older children in the ward benefited because nurses now had more time available for them since babies and toddlers were largely cared for by their own mothers. For medical students the situation was valuable because it made them familiar with the circumstances they were likely to meet in their later practice: mothers caring for sick children. Older fears that when mothers move into a hospital ward or visit freely the risks of cross-infection will be increased, have been proved false. American paediatricians supported this move to humanize children's wards. They began to describe the 'loneliness' of infants[9] and to recommend that nurses should cut out many 'useless' procedures, such as four-hourly pulse and temperature recordings for children who are clearly not suffering from feverish illnesses, and should instead devote more time to fondling the babies and playing with the older children in their care. It was not then known that between seven months and three or four years of age children do not respond to the kindly overtures of a succession of strange people in a way that would make such nursing assignments effective.

The arguments of the pioneers in the process of humanizing children's hospitals were not however persuasive enough to penetrate the defences of doctors and nurses working in hospitals, and little research was then available to back up their innovations.

Even when the Platt Committee reported in 1959 on the care of children in hospital,[114] its recommendations (which included free visiting, admissions of mothers together with very young children, individual care of each child by a single nurse and careful preparation of children and their parents prior to admission) were based on opinion rather than on scientific proof. The impetus for this report derived in part from the writings of James Robertson[132] and from a film he made in 1952. This film was able to penetrate the protective barrier of hospital personnel as no publication of more systematic work has done. *A Two-year-old Goes to Hospital* showed paediatricians and nurses precisely what was before their eyes throughout each working day. But the frame of the camera distanced the subject of the film, two-year-old Laura in her hospital cot, from the viewer, and the result was that phenomena usually ignored were seen for the first time.

The film was effective in two ways. It demonstrated the typical reactions of a two-year-old to going to hospital and it also showed a number of what were then traditional hospital routines, to be not only useless but actually harmful.

Laura and her mother walk into the ward confidently and are received by a friendly nurse. Then comes the first jolt for the viewer: the ritual bath. Laura has clearly been washed and dressed by her mother for the occasion, yet she must be bathed all over again and not by her mother, who waits anxiously in the office, but by a strange nurse. The response is predictable. Laura resists mildly and then cries. What chance has a nurse assigned the task of bathing a child, aged two-and-a-half on admission, of making a friendly relationship with the new-comer? If this is to be her first contact with the child, how can she win her confidence and trust?

When this film was discussed not long ago with a group of nurses working in a children's hospital, they made it clear that the message of the film accorded with their personal experi-ence. They did not have to be persuaded that separation from parents is frightening for a child. They had been taught to use their first contact with a child to make friends with him. Yet at the same time their instructions were also to undress and bath him. These two instructions are conflicting. They cannot both be carried out. The junior nurse however does not know this. She feels incompetent when her ministrations evoke tears. Unrealistically she thinks that a more skilled person could do the task without upsetting the child. She may not know that the response she is getting is inevitable and inherent in the situation. She is left to protect herself as best she can against the impact of the child's tears and her own feelings of inadequacy and humiliation, increased by the knowledge that the mother in the next room, her senior colleagues in the ward and all the other children can hear what the result of her first contact with the new child has been. No wonder that in this situation, which she cannot alter, without the opportunity to discuss her own feelings with anyone, the nurse will sometimes try by whatever means she can think of to stop the crying, for the child's sake as much as for her own. When she learns that she cannot succeed, she will in time cease to attend to the child's expression of distress, concentrating instead on the task in hand.

In this situation the mother's first knowledge of the nurse is that she makes her child cry. Some mothers may accept this as a necessary routine in order for their child to get better. The magical belief that the worse the medicine the better the cure is still common. Other mothers relieve their feelings by indirect hostility towards the nurse, perhaps commenting that the hospital clothes put on her child do not fit him. But at times the nurse has to meet direct aggression. One student nurse told that as she undressed a child, who was extremely upset, weeping as he refused to let his clothes go and clinging to each garment when she took it off, the father became upset too. He was deterred from removing the child only by the mother's remark: 'You can't take him out. We don't even know what's wrong with him.' The nurse felt that although the parents were divided about removing the boy from hospital, they were together in their disapproval of her. The stage is set for the relationship between parents and nurse to develop into one of distrust, mutual criticism and defensiveness. A common way out in this dilemma is for parents and nurses to have as little to do with each other as possible.

Under the age of four only the mother's actual presence in hospital can alleviate the child's anxiety. If one has a choice, admission to hospital should always be postponed until the child is older. For this reason new hospital techniques have been developed. For example young children often have routine operations done as day patients, returning to their own homes the same night. Convalescence is no longer thought to have anything to offer pre-school children, unless it takes the form of a holiday with mother.

For children *over four years of age*, who are already accustomed to cope in many situations without their parents, separation from home may be less important than the illness itself, especially if the child's relationship with his parents had previously been satisfactory. A number of studies have shown that changes in ward routines, based on awareness of the sources of distress for children in this age-group, can do much to alleviate anxiety during their hospitalization.

Prugh and his co-workers in Boston studied two groups of children nursed under different ward conditions.[128] The first, or 'experimental', group had special psychological preparation for admission and a special admission procedure designed to minimize anxiety. They were visited by their parents daily and a special play programme was provided for them. They also received preparation for and extra comforting during medical and nursing procedures, and particularly nervous children were allotted to a single nurse who did everything for them ('case assignment'). A paediatrician with psychiatric training directed a weekly ward management conference for all the staff in which psychological problems of children and of staff in relation to the children could be discussed.

The second, or 'control', group of children were nursed according to traditional ward routine. They had weekly visiting, and nursing was organized in the conventional way whereby nurses of different degrees of seniority perform different tasks in the ward ('task assignment'). Under this arrangement a child may, for example, be washed and fed by a nursing orderly, have his pulse and temperature taken by a junior nurse and get his injections from a more senior nurse. No nurse is *his* nurse and no nurse gets to know him really well.

A comparison of the behaviour of the two groups of children while still in hospital and after their discharge home showed that in children over four years of age the experimental programme cut down the incidence of emotional disturbances considerably.

The hospital practices found to be helpful in preventing lasting emotional disturbances after discharge in children between four and twelve years of age, often increase outward manifestations of distress while the child is still in hospital. Frequent visiting leads to tears when the parents leave; encouragement to come out with feelings about, for example, 'needles', makes for noisier injection times; free discussion of being ill and in hospital may stimulate outbursts of anger and frustration directed both at the nursing staff and at the parents.

That such techniques are however beneficial in the long run and make for a more realistic adjustment to illness was shown by Boverman in a study carried out in Chicago in a unit for the long-term treatment of children with rheumatic fever.[19, 131] All children were visited frequently, they were nursed by their individual nurses whom they got to know well, they were prepared in advance for all medical procedures and their parents had discussion groups to learn about their child's illness. School and play were important ingredients in each child's hospital day. Even in this excellent ward environment a psychotherapeutic experience was shown to make an additional contribution.

The experiment consisted of dividing the children into three groups. One had no extra treatment. The second took part in three weekly classes in which they were taught about their illness. The third group were also seen three times at weekly intervals. They were given no information but they had psychotherapeutic group sessions in which their anxieties were explored by a psychiatrist. He began the session by telling the children he knew they were worried about being ill and in hospital, and inviting them to talk about their upset feelings and how they coped with these.

All three groups of children were re-examined at the end of the three weeks and then at intervals up to two years. It was found that at three weeks the children who had been encouraged to talk about their worries (the 'treated' group) were still as anxious as on admission, while the other two groups were less anxious. By the end of two years, however, the situation had been reversed and the treated group was now less anxious than the other two. After three weeks the 'taught' group knew more about their illness than the 'untreated' group. But the 'treated' group knew as much. After two years the 'taught' group had forgotten what they had learnt but the 'treated' group were still well informed.

The conclusion of this experiment is that to encourage children to talk about their worries prevents the early repression of anxiety that normally occurs in hospital but also leads to a better long-term adaptation to illness: these children are less anxious later on than children not given this extra help and they spontaneously learn more about their illness. The most helpful intervention is to let the children talk rather than to give them explanations and instructions: teaching is ineffective in the long run.

Such a psychotherapeutic programme can be carried out by all nurses and doctors provided they are given some special training and have continued psychiatric support. It is the only way in which children's personality development can be safeguarded while they are exposed to the considerable stresses of being in hospital. Without such active prophylactic intervention, many children, especially those exposed to long-term or to particularly stressful experiences in hospital, regress temporarily and a few sustain some permanent inpairment of their personality. For them the subjective meaning of the illness has become more disabling than the illness itself.[19, 131]

To train nurses and doctors to recognize psychological aspects of illness and their importance for personality development is important for a second reason. When a child's symptoms are not due to a physical illness, but are psychologically determined, doctors trained only to deal with organic illness may find that nothing they know of makes the situation any better. They have examined the patient and found nothing organically wrong but the complaint is still there. In this unsatisfactory situation drastic measures are sometimes resorted to. When bed-wetting or soiling in children does not respond to pills, regular toileting and encouragement, a period in hospital is still often recommended and many children are subjected to enemas and purgatives with only temporary improvement. Many children with abdominal pain due to anxiety have numerous physical investigations done because no explanation for the symptoms can be found on physical examination. In such a dilemma, the surgeon is often called in more readily than the psychiatrist and the child has an exploratory operation before his emotional state and his life history are examined. Such intensive physical investigations are likely to confirm the child's and the parents' view that there may be something physically wrong or, if not, that 'nothing' is wrong. There is 'no reason' for the child to do what he does. 'Laziness' or 'naughtiness' are adduced and this increases the child's guilt.

Many psychological symptoms, as we have seen earlier, are defensive manoeuvres against expressions of impulses which are associated with anxiety: the first step in helping a child to give up his symptoms is to reduce his level of anxiety and his guilt. Unless psychological rather than organic explorations are made, the reverse effect results and there is no increased understanding of the child's symptoms.

For hospital staff and indeed parents to be capable of attending to children's emotional reactions and to carry through an active prophylactic programme when a child is ill in hospital, they themselves need opportunities to express their anxieties and fears. Parents must be able to approach nurses and doctors freely with their questions and nurses must be helped to feel more comfortable in their roles and to communicate more easily and frankly with senior staff. There is much evidence to support the view that the traditional hierarchical staff structure in hospitals is an obstacle to such free communication.

Well-adjusted children of well-adjusted parents are likely in the long run to cope adequately with physical illness and with their relationships to doctors and nurses. Hospital staff in turn will be less anxious in their handling of such children and their parents than when confronted by disturbed children and hostile, complaining or even absent parents. It is essential to provide the staff of paediatric hospitals with psychological skills over and above their paediatric skills. This is necessary not only so that they can discriminate between symptoms caused by physical illness and those due to underlying emotional conflict, and can actively help sick children deal with their anxieties in relation to their illness and stay in hospital. It is also necessary in order to enable the medical and nursing

73

staff to become aware of those parents and children who are emotionally disturbed, either as a consequence of the illness itself or for other reasons. It is only when such families can be identified and their difficulties understood that one can hope to help them.

5. Bereavement

Death is on the whole a fortuitous event. Except for suicide and fatalities where accident-proneness plays a part, we do not ourselves determine whether we live or die. The loss of a parent through death is as likely to occur in a family that has previously functioned well as in one that has not. In contrast, when a child loses a parent by divorce, separation or desertion, complex personality disturbances in the parents have usually preceded the event by many years and it is then often difficult to distinguish between the impact of losing a parent, and the effect of being raised by people who were incapable of sustaining their relationship with each other. When a parent dies, however, the effects on the child are more likely to be due to the event itself and to its consequences.

There is evidence that the harmful effects of bereavement are more often due to its long-term social consequences and to the emotional reactions of the surviving parent than to the impact of the death itself upon the child.

THE CHILD'S VIEW OF DEATH

Sylvia Anthony, whose early study of children's ideas about death at different ages is the most comprehensive,[5] found that death as such holds no particular terrors for most children. She used *three experimental approaches:*

(1) In the first she aimed to discover how often and in what way children make spontaneous references to death. In this experiment nearly a hundred children were asked to complete stories whose beginnings they had been told. Death did not feature in these story openings. Despite this, however, almost half the children referred to death, funerals, killing or ghosts

75

and a few others mentioned death obliquely by saying, for example, 'he got run over', or 'she lost one of her children'. The theme of death appeared most frequently when the openings concerned people who were sad or frightened. For example a story about a sad mother evoked the ending that her child had died. A story about a child awake in bed at night might lead to the conclusion that he was afraid in case his mother died or in case he himself was killed. In these stories death was often a retaliation for misdeeds and was itself frequently followed by remorse and the revival of the dead persons. The one boy whose father had actually died did not mention death at all in response to any of the story openings.

Further investigations were done to define changes in the concept of death and in the reactions it evokes in children of different ages. (2) In the second experiment nearly a hundred children aged three to thirteen years were asked for the meaning of the word 'dead' among a number of other words which they had to define. Clear age differences were found: some *five-year-olds* did not respond at all. Some said they did not know what the word meant, some gave limited definitions such as ' 'adn't 'ad no dinner' or 'gone to sleep'. These young children often equated death with 'going to hospital' or being ill. Children *between seven and nine years* gave responses that showed they understood the meaning of the word and applied it to human beings. Their definitions were however neither logical nor biological. They said it meant 'when people's dead', or 'when you're in your coffin and you're laying in it'. *Ten-year-olds* would either give semi-logical explanations including some reference to biological facts, e.g. 'when a person doesn't live any more' or 'when you're dead, you can't come alive again'. Alternatively they produced logical definitions including the biological essentials, e.g. 'it means not living' or 'when you have no pulse and no temperature and can't breathe'. The changes with age in the nature of these definitions correspond to Piaget's stages of intellectual development: rational, logical explanations of death cannot be given by children under about eight years old.

(3) In the third experiment mothers were asked to keep notes of their children's contact with death and reactions to it. These descriptions also showed definite changes with age.

Very young, *pre-school children* ignored death. Later they re-acted by being puzzled, for example, by a dead fly on the windowsill. The earliest concepts of death were limited and erroneous. Bodily reactions were associated with the idea of death. Children would shrink from contact with dead things or alternatively they enjoyed killing small animals and watched with interest the consequences of their own attacks on them. It is common experience that small animals often serve as experimental victims for young children. Sometimes they are even eaten. A four-year-old boy known to the author removed the goldfish from the goldfish tank and swallowed it whole. Another mother reported that one day she found her two-year-old child in the garden eating a worm.

After the age of about five, the children studied by Anthony began to have some idea of what death is but misunderstand-ings of its implications and of how it comes about were still very common. Death now formed an integral part of the child's magical thinking. It had become invested with emo-tions: with aggressive feelings and with fears of punishment for wrong-doing. At this stage, between five and eight years children did not accept death realistically. They asserted that one can live for ever and that once dead, one can be reborn. Death was not recognized as an accidental, fortuitous event. When it happened it was always for a reason, usually as a retaliation for wrong-doing, often the result of the child's own bad wishes. A six-year-old was shown a picture of a tiger looking at a monkey in a tree and was asked to make up a story about the picture. This was his story:

Once upon a time there was a big tiger with sharp teeth and he says 'I'll eat you' and he caught him by the tail so that he couldn't get him. The tiger fell down . . . and the monkey went home and got some poison and gave it to the tiger and he was dead for ever. The monkey feels that he was ill too. No. He was ill in bed 'cos the tiger spitted out and the monkey had his mouth open and the poisonous came into his mouth.

Asked what happened then, he went on:

He was dead for ever too and I don't know anything else about him.*

* I am grateful to Miss Janet Hassan for allowing me to quote from one of her psychological reports.

This child distinguished between being 'dead', in which case all was not lost, and being 'dead for ever'. When children actually experience a death in the family during the animistic stage, they often become especially good and conscientious as if expecting that this will revive the dead person. Only *at about nine years of age* do children accept death realistically as a biological fact.

In summary, children react to death as our knowledge of their intellectual development would lead us to expect. Under the age of about four or five they ignore the phenomenon or else respond with puzzled and somewhat callous interest. Between five and eight they become intrigued with death, associate it with aggressive feelings and fears, regard it as a punishment for misdeeds but also as reversible. It is not until they are about nine years old that they acquire a rational comprehension of death. It is at this age also that sorrow begins to be expressed in response to the death of a loved person. Before then children often do not react emotionally at all or else they merely take a detached interest.

Sylvia Anthony studied children's ideas about the phenomenon of death; but what happens when a child meets death, not as an event befalling a loved but for him inessential being like a relative or a pet? What happens when the child loses a parent through death?

'MOURNING' IN INFANCY

Certainly even babies and toddlers react to parental loss. But because their capacity to anticipate the future is limited and their understanding of verbal explanations almost non-existent, a temporary separation evokes the same responses as a permanent loss. Death and absence have the same effect.

Bowlby equated early childhood reactions to separation from the mother with mourning following bereavement.[21] He described three phases in the young child's reaction when separated from his mother. These can be observed in children from six months to about two years of age. The most common situation in which these reactions occur is when a child is admitted to hospital. In the *stage of protest*, which follows immediately on the loss of the loved object, the child actively expresses his grief and his anger. He cries loudly and demands that the mother should return. He cannot be consoled by others and even if his mother returns during this stage he may continue to be angry with her for a little while before allowing her to comfort him. In the second *stage of despair*, the child stops his wailing and presents the appearance of apathy and inward grief. Whereas in the first stage he stood up in his cot, expectantly watching the door for his mother's reappearance, he is now no longer anticipating her return. He barely reacts to other people who try to play with and talk to him and he may spend his day rocking to and fro on his mattress or sucking his thumb. If his mother reappears at this stage it can take some days before he accepts her as before. He may not welcome her at first; he may then express anger, and lastly he may become excessively clinging, crying whenever she leaves the room and attempting to follow her about everywhere even into the toilet. The third and final *stage of detachment* follows if, instead of the mother returning, separation is prolonged still further. The child now no longer appears to care. He becomes cheerful and responsive to others. He seems to have 'forgotten' his mother. If she returns now he does not recognize her and she may find that she has to build up a new relationship with him as if with a stranger. It is at this stage that a substitute mother can start to make a relationship with an infant who has permanently lost his own mother.

Bowlby considers that once this third stage is reached, as it inevitably is after a permanent loss such as a bereavement, the child remains vulnerable: he is likely to react abnormally to any future disappointment or loss of a loved person.

LONG-TERM CONSEQUENCES OF BEREAVEMENT

What is the evidence that a prolonged separation from or permanent loss of the mother indeed has such serious consequences in later life? Many groups of psychiatric patients have been compared with non-patients to see if there is a greater incidence of parent loss in childhood among patients. Often the difficulty has been that no strictly comparable control group of non-patients has been found for whom data about parent loss in childhood was available. The other great difficulty is that loss of a parent results from many causes. Loss other than that due to bereavement is usually associated with other features of family disorganization. One cannot therefore attribute later psychiatric illness to parent loss as such. There is evidence that patients with personality disorders,[41] patients who have attempted suicide,[66] and delinquents[67] more often have a background of family disruption than controls. What part childhood bereavement alone, in an otherwise well functioning family, contributes to the causation of mental illness in later life is not known. It does not appear to predispose an individual to develop a depressive illness, as Bowlby has suggested.[116] It may, however, contribute to abnormal personality development. Even then the adverse factor is probably not the experience of the loss itself but the impairment of family life that results as a consequence.

There are few factual studies of the social and emotional sequelae of parental death. It is known that the death of a mother generally leads to greater disruption of the family than the death of a father. Few men undertake the double roles of breadwinner and home-maker. Society does not expect it of them. They cannot stay off work to mind the baby. Indeed it is often regarded as unfitting for men to cook and clean and launder for their children after work, without at least the help of a teenage daughter. Widowers with young children are generally forced to accept help from relatives or local authority children's departments. All too often such help takes the form of splitting up the family and providing care for one or two children together in the house of a grandmother, an aunt, or else in foster homes or children's homes. Meanwhile the widower has lost not only his wife but his family. Whatever personal decisions he makes for his children or himself are made while he is still in a state of grief and mourning, unlikely to bring to these issues a realistic appreciation of the future. Because there is usually an urgent need for the children to be physically cared for by somebody, hurried decisions are sometimes made, which in retrospect appear unnecessary and could have been avoided had there been a period of time during which the home was kept going without any major changes. A good home-help service is the ideal solution. But, and this is particularly so in working class areas, women do not like going regularly into the homes of widowers because their position in such families may appear to be ambiguous. Middle class widowers suffer a different kind of hardship. Here the ordinary social welfare services often decide that help is not necessary merely because the man earns a higher salary. Such fathers may not get the opportunity to work out the correct solutions to their many problems in discussions with a professional outsider. Moreover, they may not be offered the sort of material help that is made available to working class men. It is often not realized that to engage a resident housekeeper is beyond the means of most middle class families and that to find a really suitable woman for such a post on a permanent basis is often extremely difficult particularly in less populous areas.

Fortunately the mortality rates for young adults have fallen steadily and are now quite low. Accidents are a major cause of death. More men than women die in early adult life so that the problems of widows are numerically greater than those of widowers. It is perhaps for this reason that a recent investigation into the effects of bereavement concentrated on widows.[112]

Seventy-two London widows whose husbands died in youth or middle age were interviewed about two years after their bereavement. Three aspects of their subsequent lives are described by Marris in his book *Widows and Their Families*: their emotional reactions to the death, the help they got from friends and relatives and their financial position.

Although none were widowed for less than eleven months at the time of the interview, only fourteen appeared to have recovered completely from their loss. In a half, physical health was impaired following the bereavement, a finding substantiated by Parkes.[122] Medical consultation rates of widows both for psychological and physical complaints rise considerably after the death of their husband compared with their consulting rates prior to the bereavement. Marris describes too most vividly the intolerable distress suffered by young widows. They are characteristically apathetic, not caring whether they live or die; they are often resentful and hostile even towards those who try to be helpful; they withdraw socially from other people. If no one bothers about them they feel deserted; if people offer company and support they feel

intruded upon in their grief. Yet in the midst of all her emotional distress the widow has to take on more work and responsibility than she ever had before and with grossly inadequate
financial aid. In addition she has to cope with her children's
reactions to the bereavement. Marris describes how some of
the mothers managed this and how some of the children responded to the event.

Most mothers thought it was best to shield their children
from the rituals surrounding death. No child under sixteen
wore mourning and only about one in ten attended the
funeral. Many had never seen their father's grave. Some
mothers even avoided telling the children that their father had
died. A three-year-old persistently asked 'Where's my Daddy?
When's he coming out of hospital?' and his mother silenced
these questions. An eight-year-old was told her father 'had
gone into another hospital'. She found out the facts at school
and the shock was all the greater: she became silent and withdrawn. The reactions of the children varied with age. The
youngest of them did not seem to react at all. Some between
five and nine years were quoted as commenting on the event
in an apparently callous way such as 'My daddy's gone to
heaven, hasn't he?', despite the fact that they were also tearful
and anxious. Older children reacted in diverse ways: some
were depressed and weepy; one had angry outbursts whenever his father was mentioned; some became withdrawn and
solitary; and a number of older children inhibited their own
feelings so as not to upset their mothers towards whom they
became especially solicitous and protective.

On the whole, it was the widows who were most deeply
affected by grief, not their children. Only in a few cases in
which the marriages had been unhappy before the death were
the children found to be more seriously disturbed.

These two findings, that when a parent dies the grief of the
surviving parent rather than the sorrow of the children
dominates the household and that children are more likely to
be badly affected by a bereavement when the previous marital
relationship between the parents had been unhappy, were
confirmed by an American study.[74] Here a group of mental
hospital patients who had lost one or both parents in childhood were compared with a random sample of people in the

general population who had also been bereaved in childhood but who had not been admitted to a mental hospital. One of the questions studied was what memories these people retained of their grief and mourning. When the bereavement occured *under the age of nine* none recalled any feelings of grief they themselves had had. Girls recalled their widowed mother's reactions vividly; boys were more impressed by the circumstances of the death and by the funeral. *Over the age of eleven* personal feelings of grief were usually recalled and memories of mothers' reactions and of the funeral were less prominent.

Of particular interest in this investigation is the comparison between groups of well-adjusted and poorly adjusted adults both of whom had suffered parental death in childhood. Among the well-adjusted the relationship between their parents prior to the bereavement had been a happy one.

It is a well-known fact that to mourn a beloved person is painful but does not evoke those haunting feelings of guilt and self-loathing that afflict the survivor of a close but hostile partnership. To the extent that children invariably share in the hostility and guilt of their parents towards each other, they too appear to suffer more when such a strained union is forcibly ended.

Another feature distinguished the group of well-adjusted adults bereaved in childhood. Their homes were kept intact by widowed mothers who were independent, hard-working and energetic, rather than warm and affectionate and who took on their additional, more masculine, working role with little conflict.

Among the hospital patients bereaved in childhood were many whose widowed mothers lacked this capacity to manage independently. They clung to their children for support, especially to their sons, getting them literally to take their father's place. This tended to impede the children's maturation. Sons of widows were especially handicapped during adolescence in establishing independent relationships with others. Although their working lives were successful, they frequently failed in their sexual adjustment and either remained single, tied to their mothers in the parental home, or else made unsuccessful marriages dominated by their concern for their widowed mothers.

Many studies of the later effects of bereavement in childhood are of necessity retrospective. They depend on the recall by adults of events that happened many years ago. To this extent they are not likely to be reliable. Moreover, a host of other factors have intervened between the bereavement in childhood and the observed outcome in adult life.

DOES BEREAVEMENT CAUSE PSYCHOLOGICAL DISTURBANCES IN CHILDREN?

Dr Michael Rutter was the first to examine systematically the relationship between bereavement and psychiatric disturbance in children themselves.[138] He compared children referred to the Maudsley Hospital Child Psychiatry Department with control groups of children attending paediatric and dental clinics, matched for age, sex and occupational class of fathers. He found that more than twice as many children attending the psychiatric clinic had lost a parent by death than had children attending a paediatric department. Nearly six times as many psychiatrically disturbed children had been bereaved than had children attending dental clinics. The proportion of psychiatrically disturbed children who had lost a parent by death was, however, small. Less than one in twelve had been bereaved. Rutter compared disturbed and control groups of children for bereavement rates at different ages. He found the differences between disturbed and control children to be most marked when the death had occurred during the child's third or fourth year of life. He suggests that loss of a parent at three or four years is especially damaging because this is the time at which parents are most needed as models for identification. To test this theory he examined the relationship between the sex of the child and the sex of the dead parent. If lack of an identification figure is the important factor then death of the same sex parent should be most closely associated with later psychiatric disturbance. This relationship was indeed found in the case of girls: maternal death and psychiatric disturbance are especially related. The relationship did not hold for boys, but the numbers were very small.

Rutter compared the bereaved children among the psychiatrically disturbed group with the rest of this group. He thought that doctors might more readily refer children who had lost a parent, being alerted to possible emotional disturbances by the death. Bereaved children, however, had not been referred earlier or for milder disorders. They tended rather to be older than other referred children. The onset of their psychiatric illness only rarely followed close on the bereavement. In nearly a third there was a gap of five years or more between the death and the onset of symptoms in the child. Bereavement at three or four years of age most commonly led to referral at puberty. The only group of children whose illness began within six months of their bereavement was a group consisting mainly of adolescent boys. They presented either with depressive illnesses, resembling adult grief reactions, or with antisocial behaviour. Except at adolescence, the long-term consequences of parental loss are more important than the experience of the death itself. Even these long-term consequences most frequently come to the surface in late childhood and adolescence.

THE EFFECTS OF HAVING ONLY ONE PARENT

When a parent dies the family generally becomes impoverished. Marris showed that even the financially better-off widows, those who work full-time, have to raise their families on a much-reduced income.[112] Widowers have to pay housekeepers and home helps for essential services and get no income tax relief as they did when they were maintaining a wife. Bereaved children become poor children. Their clothes are not as new and their toys not as numerous as those of their schoolfellows. Often they depend on hand-me-downs. Like their surviving parents they react to the pity their position evokes from others by experiencing a loss of self-esteem.

When one parent dies, the other is forced to withdraw from the child also. Widows often withdraw emotionally from their children because they are preoccupied with their own feelings of grief. But there is in addition an actual decrease of parent–child contact. When she takes on the role of breadwinner for her family, while at the same time maintaining her home, the widow has very little time left for her children. She is not free to take them out for pleasure, to read them stories at night, to supervise homework, to play games with them. The children have lost their father but they have lost a part of their mother too. Moreover, their mother has changed. It is not only grief that has altered her but her state of widowhood. To make a success of this new role she must mobilize parts of her personality that were previously hidden: masculine attitudes of energy and independence are called for. Feminine needs and the wish to provide maternal care and affection can no longer be fully indulged and have to be repressed. The children must now assume some of the responsibilities for running the home, looking after themselves and minding their younger brothers and sisters. Four-year-olds are sometimes entered for school before they are ready for it to free their mothers for work. Younger children attend day nurseries and see little of family life. When a mother dies, as we have seen, the family often breaks up altogether.

No child likes to feel different from his peers. Yet neither poverty nor restriction of shared family activities appears to affect children adversely provided the relationship between them and the surviving parent is good and the home remains intact. What does seem to matter is the gap in their intimate experiences of how mothers and fathers behave towards each other and their children within the family circle.

We have seen earlier that during the genital stage of development children model themselves on the parent of the same sex. When they imagine their own future, boys and girls see themselves as becoming like their fathers and mothers. The core of our personality, the part we think of as permanent throughout our lives, is largely built around these early childhood identifications. When a parent is absent during these critical years, personality development is impaired and the task of identity formation at adolescence is likely to be difficult. Rutter showed that for girls the loss of a mother between two and four years of age is especially damaging. Hilgard showed that of children who lost their fathers boys are more liable than girls to have difficulties in their own sexual and marital adjustments in later life.[74]

Often when a parent has been lost, other people, e.g. uncles and school teachers, serve as models for identification for the bereaved children. Such people are never known as intimately as one's own father and mother, and to this extent they are less satisfactory.

Before discussing this further, it must be stressed that although among psychiatrically disturbed children more have been bereaved than among non-disturbed children, we do not know what proportion of bereaved children are in fact disturbed. It may be quite small. We cannot know what the psychological hazards of parental death are for children unless a special study of bereaved children in the community is undertaken.

GRIEF REACTIONS IN CHILDREN

Babies between six months and two years, as we have seen, react to the loss of their mother with a well defined sequence of emotional responses. Between two and five children may surprise their elders by not reacting with manifest grief at all so long as they are assured their remaining parent will look after them, and their everyday lives are not radically changed. The fear of being abandoned altogether is uppermost in their minds rather than sadness and grief.

Between about five and eight years of age children are aware of death as such. They ask questions about it unless discouraged, and they give themselves magical explanations for the event. If parental death, or indeed the death of any close family member, occurs in the setting of other strains and difficulties, behaviour disorders are likely to arise, which to adults often appear to make no sense.

Allan, a five-year-old boy, had been deserted by his father in infancy. His mother had then married a farmer and there was now a step-brother aged two. Allan adored his step-father, and one day he was running to join him in the lambing shed. The younger brother followed. Allan shouted back at him to stay behind, as he himself climbed over a low wall to reach the shed. The brother, however, toddled after him over the wall, fell into a well and was drowned. Allan's behaviour now changed completely. He became a very aggressive child, frequently in fights with other children at school and unable to concentrate on his lessons. He climbed dangerously and sustained several bad falls so that his mother was constantly afraid he would seriously injure himself. To the psychiatrist who spoke with him then and later he revealed the recollections of his brother's death. He was able to remember the event in great detail when he was ten years old and the steady conviction that he had been responsible for the baby's death never left him. This feeling of guilt which he carried about with him for many years he was not able to discuss with his parents. He felt he must not upset his mother by 'reminding' her of the baby. She never talked of him and Allan felt he could not do so either. He wanted her to 'forget' the child and its death although he could not. His guilt makes sense in terms of his repressed jealousy feelings towards his brother, his rival for his step-father's affection, of which he was not absolutely sure. 'He's not my real father, but he loves me just the same.' The baby died and Allan felt his own wish to prevent the brother from joining him and the step-father in the lambing shed were responsible for the child's death. The only way in which Allan could get relief from his guilt was by inviting punishments and hurts from outside. He became naughty in school and was constantly in trouble. He became accident prone.

Above the age of nine years grief reactions of the adult type begin to occur. Children now participate in mourning, have fits of crying, become withdrawn and apathetic and often hostile. It is this last kind of reaction that grown-ups often resent and find baffling although it is a prominent feature of mourning at all ages. One of the widows described by Marris actually attacked her doctor physically and many accused doctors and nurses of not doing enough for their dead husbands. Most widows found themselves irritable with neighbours and relatives, angry because other people had so much in life whilst they had nothing left to live for.

Children also often react to bereavement with aggressive and even antisocial behaviour.

Mary was thirteen years old when her parents were involved in a road accident. The mother, who was driving the car, was killed instantly. The father was admitted to hospital with minor injuries. Mary was informed of the accident by her headmaster at school. She accepted the news calmly and became distressed only when she visited the father in hospital. An aunt came to look after her and Mary remained pleasant and cheerful at home. When she saw her mother's coffin arrive at the house she ran out of the house to a neighbour. The father and aunt decided she would be too upset by the funeral and arranged for her to stay at home. Following the bereavement Mary's behaviour at home did not change. At school, however, she became a different person. She was now truculent and stubborn and on one occasion when her art master remonstrated with her, she tore his glasses from his face and had to be restrained from attacking him.

Mary was an only child. Her father had been off work for long periods because of illness. The mother, a somewhat mannish woman, drove a delivery van. Mary was rather closer to her father than to her mother, who was stricter. When younger, Mary suffered from epileptic fits and at school she always did badly. This had been a source of much friction between herself and her mother. One month after the event, Mary could not remember how she felt when she heard of her mother's death. She said, 'It was in the newspapers. I just glanced at the name. That's all. And that's all I saw. It was in the *Express*. I just saw the name.' When asked to describe her mother she said, 'She had black hair, and she had a kind of . . . I can't remember anything. She had a white handbag. . . . When I see other cars I start getting worried . . . I'm afraid something's going to happen.' When pressed to talk about her feelings further, she suddenly became dazed, put her coat on and began to leave the room. Later when asked to recall her interaction with the art master she again became dazed and could remember nothing.

One month after losing her mother with whom the relationship had been strained this girl was still defending herself against the impact of the event: emotionally she denied that it had occurred and at home she behaved as if nothing had happened. Instead she felt anxious whenever she saw strange cars. At school, where her poor performance had earned her disapproval from her mother and where she had first learned of her mother's death, she puzzled her teachers by her unaccustomed hostility.

Janet, aged fourteen and the youngest of a large family, reacted to a double bereavement in a much more normal way. Yet her sullen behaviour made life almost impossible for an aunt with whom she now lived. She often sat as if in a dream, did not answer when spoken to, refused to wash or to help in the house and became very angry if anyone complained about her behaviour. In her interview with the psychiatrist she said, 'It all started when my mother and father died. It was on a Friday night. My mum told me to wake up Dad for his pills. He wouldn't and I told my Mum and she came through and found he was dead and told me to tell my brother, Billy. And then she told me to go to a neighbour and I went for her and she and her son came and my Dad was dead and we phoned for the doctor and on Saturday I told my sister that he'd died and my aunt came with me. My sister said she'd come on the Monday and on Monday my mother passed away at half past one. And the doctor said it would be better to tell my sister and we went and she was out and we waited for her and when she did come in, we told her and she came over with her husband. . . . I cried and the doctor gave us pills on the Monday. . . . My mum and dad got taken away on Tuesday and cremated at half past ten. My mum died of cancer and shock, my auntie said. My auntie promised to come on the Saturday and I was alone in the house with my brothers and she never came and we were waiting for her and she had an accident. The letter came from her husband but it was all lies. I went to Auntie Anne. She was supposed to be a friend. Then my brothers broke up the house when I left. The house got sold. All the furniture. I went every day at quarter to four to make the beds and give them their teas and wash up. They weren't fair to give up the house. I told them I'd have helped them but they gave up the house. They said, 'You couldn't do much good.' Billy went away and I never see them. [They both joined the Army.] Our neighbours were pests. There were rumours that my brother was having a carry-on at home and he wasn't. When my mother died I went to the lady next door to sleep and all of a sudden they broke away from us . . . they wouldn't come near. I felt it was they didn't like me. I felt everyone was drawing away. The people my mother didn't like. I got put with Auntie Anne and I didn't like it because I was put with her young children and I had to look after them and I never got out to play and I didn't get on with her daughter [aged 18] and her son [14]. I didn't get on with him and not with Auntie Anne and she got angry with me. She took her spite out on me. As if everything was through me.' Here the psychiatrist asked her if she blamed herself for her parents' death and she said, 'Sometimes, I think if they were there in pain. My father was very ill and got oxygen cylinders. My mum was ill too. She had haemorrhages. . . . Everyone expected it with my dad. He lived six years instead of six months. But it was a shock with my mother. . . . When my mother lived, she helped me on. I was the youngest. With my Auntie Anne, I get on her nerves. I do things I'm not supposed to do. I don't wash the dishes. I make her feel angry at me. My mind goes back to something else. I feel it's hard. I feel they're [parents] still alive. I'm scared to go through the room they [parents] lay in. . . . My mum really loved me. My dad and my mum thought nobody was like me. I had a funny feeling she'd pass away. I told a lie, I said to Auntie Anne that a girl friend's father was dead and it wasn't true.'

HOW DO ADULTS EXPLAIN DEATH TO CHILDREN?

The belief that children are 'too young to understand' is often used to explain two common but contradictory approaches to life-and-death matters affecting children. Children are either regarded as insensitive, unable to take in anything of what happens, and therefore allowed to witness adult emotions and interactions without being given appropriate explanations. Alternatively they are endowed with exquisite sensitivity and vulnerability so that the facts of life must be carefully hidden from them.

When a mother fails to inform her three-year-old son that his own father is dead and that the man she has been courting for months and is now about to marry will be his second daddy, she may tell herself the child is 'too young to understand'. When a man whose wife is dying in hospital guards this as a secret from his young children and goes alone to visit their mother so that they should not see the ravages of her illness, he may give himself a similar explanation. In either case the behaviour of the parents is dictated by their own inner needs rather than by a realistic appreciation of their children's feelings. The mother may have a lingering sense of guilt towards her first husband for not remaining loyal to his memory and this may make it difficult for her to tell her child the facts. The father may only half face his wife's imminent death. With a part of himself he feels he can avert the tragedy magically: if he acts as if it will not happen, if he does not talk about it, then surely it will not take place. To prepare the children may seem like inviting death itself.

Only when parents are helped to master their own often conflicting feelings in the face of death, will they be able to adopt realistic and helpful attitudes towards their children.

HOW CAN OUTSIDERS BE MOST HELPFUL?

The occurrence of a death in a family is usually not a matter for shame and yet there is a tendency to withdraw from the bereaved. People shy away from mentioning the dead for fear of upsetting his survivors. Yet the expression of grief after a bereavement is essential if the survivor is to adjust adequately to his or her changed life situation. How can a widowed mother help her child with his feelings about the loss of his father if she has not been able to deal adequately with her own?

Some people hold the view that the decrease of ritual in modern life, the absence of funereal pomp and of public mourning, deprives the bereaved of the opportunity to express their feelings and come to terms with their changed life situation. Increasingly mourning, like other deep human emotions, has become a private, solitary matter. Yet Marris made it clear that the public display of mourning meant little to the widows he studied; that funeral ceremonies gave scant comfort. Nevertheless, other people can give considerable support to the bereaved. Freud stressed what he called 'the work of mourning':[56] when a person is bereaved he has to work through his feelings of grief, of loss, of guilt. It is as if a part of himself had gone and he has to make good this deficiency in order to be able to carry on. It may take the survivor some time even to acknowledge the death as a fact. Then he dwells on his memories, identifies with the dead partner, imagines his presence in the house, treasures the objects that belonged to him. Feelings of hatred at the cruelty of fate have to be mastered; impulses to run away, to make a new and different start in order 'to forget the past' have to be controlled. Gradually, over months and years, feelings attached to the dead partner diminish so that the bereaved is able to enter once more into new experiences and new relationships. During this process of readjustment other people can help by providing opportunity for the bereaved to talk about their feelings anc to face their innermost thoughts. Abnormally prolonged or severe grief reactions and impulsive life decisions which are later regretted (for example the sudden rush into a new marriage) occur most often when the individual has not permitted himself free expression of the emotions aroused in him by the death.

In our day it seems that standard mourning rituals can no longer be relied upon to provide relief. Individual reactions to grief often do not fit the conventional and expected patterns. We can be most helpful to bereaved parents if we are prepared to allow them to voice the very thoughts and feelings (such as hatred of the dead) which do not fit in with the common stereotype of grief. It is feelings such as these that prolong the state of mourning and result in guilt and a sense of unworthiness. Once parents can accept their own negative feelings towards the dead they will be able to tolerate such feelings in their children. When they begin to form new relationships without blaming themselves for disloyalty towards their dead spouse they will be able to accept such behaviour in their children also. When a parent has not resolved his own inner conflicts, for example between love for his new wife and loyalty towards the dead mother of his children, he may induce his children to participate in this conflict, to the detriment of the whole family. He may tacitly encourage their antagonism towards the stepmother, because it diminishes his guilt towards his first wife. At the same time he declares their behaviour to be intolerable and proclaims his support for his new wife.

The difficulties of children caught up in such parental conflicts are the subject of Chapter 7.

6. Illegitimacy and Family Disruption

Society on the whole treats bereaved families kindly. Material help, although limited, is forthcoming as of right; sympathy is offered even if the bereaved cannot always respond to it and the public burial ceremony legitimizes the loss. Divorce on the other hand or illegitimate birth forces those affected to shield themselves from the public gaze and to cope unaided with their more complex feelings. Even material help is less readily available to unmarried mothers and to deserted or divorced wives than it is to widows. The widow's pension is small, but it is hers by right. Divorced and separated women must either press their claims for financial support from their former husbands before the courts or rely on social security. Both processes can be painful and shaming, and many women prefer to give up their right to financial support altogether.

Families incomplete because of illegitimacy and those broken by divorce or separation are different from families disrupted by death in that the remaining parents tend to be censured by their own families and by society in general. This increases their feelings of resentment, guilt and failure. They resemble the widowed in being more dependent materially and emotionally on their families and on public services. Unlike the widowed, however, the help they receive is tinged with disapproval. Yet people who become single parents as a result of their own failures in intimate relationships are likely to have personalities that are much less well-equipped to cope with the resulting problems, both practical and psychological, than people deprived of their marriage partners by the accidental event of death.

That the children of unmarried parents or of parents whose marriages have failed are at risk emotionally is not disputed. Estimates of the numerical size of the problem are, however, hard to come by.

THE SIZE OF THE PROBLEM

National statistics in the form of census reports do not yield the kind of information that helps us to determine the proportion of disrupted families in the community. We know that about 8% of children are born illegitimately but not every one of these children lives to grow up in an anomalous family. A five-year follow-up study done in Leicester some years ago showed that of every 100 mothers who had had an illegitimate child, thirty subsequently married and forty were co-habiting, most of them living with the father of the child.[108] Almost all these mothers had kept their children. Of the thirty mothers in a hundred who were neither married nor co-habiting five years after the birth of their illegitimate baby, a half had parted with the child, usually by adoption, and a half had kept their children. Two thirds of these mothers were single at the time of the baby's birth and five years later most of them were living with their parents. Thus at the age of five years four out of every five illegitimate children were still living with their mothers. Of the rest, about half had been adopted, a quarter lived with relatives and a quarter with foster parents.

Census reports tell us about the marital status of all adults, but they do not relate this information to the numbers and ages of their children. Special surveys are necessary to arrive at estimates of the numbers of children exposed to different types of family disruption.

In a recent survey of primary school children in England, at least 8% lacked one or both natural parents.[33] Another survey was undertaken some years ago in Minnesota.[67] A state-wide 30% sample of school-children were given questionnaires to fill in during their ninth grade at school. From the figures published it can be calculated that by the age of fifteen years 5% of Minnesota school children had lost their father through death, 1.7% had lost their mother through death,

0.16% had lost both parents in this way and 6% had parents who were either separated or divorced. More than one in eight children, therefore, had a disrupted family background; the common causes were death of the father and separation or divorce. The incidence of paternal loss increased down the social scale. Only 1.8% of sons of professional parents had lost their father by death while 5.7% of sons of labourers had been bereaved in this way. Rates for divorce and separation were twice as high among labouring families as among professional classes. Boys who came from the large farming population of Minnesota were anomalous in having the lowest rate of parental separation or divorce. During their ninth grade nearly 8% of children were living with their mothers only, 1.5% with their fathers only, 2% with neither parent (presumably with relatives, foster parents or in children's homes) and 2.3% with step-parents.

One can only speculate how other Western communities compare with Minnesota. Certainly the large farming population with its very low rates of separation and divorce would tend to keep the overall figures for family disruption low. It is very likely that in our big industrial cities the proportion of fifteen-year-olds who come from disrupted homes is considerably higher than one in eight.

CHILDREN FROM BROKEN HOMES

There is much evidence to suggest that children from disrupted families have more behaviour disturbances than children whose homes are intact. Bereavement is somewhat less important in this respect than family break-up due to failure of the marriage.

Most of the evidence comes from investigations in which groups of psychiatrically disturbed children are compared for the incidence of broken homes with control groups of normal children. An early study along these lines was done in Cambridge during the war.[12, 13] Here one out of every eight children referred to a child guidance clinic was found to have lost a parent by death and one out of every four came from a home broken for other reasons. Among the control group of children attending similar schools, only one in eighteen had been bereaved, and one in twelve had lost a parent because their parents' marriage had failed.

In a more recent Edinburgh study in which a hundred primary school children referred for psychiatric treatment were compared with a hundred controls attending the same school classes, 28 of the psychiatric clinic attenders came from broken homes compared with only 6 among the controls.[179]

When other indices of emotional disturbance are used the same high incidence of family disruption is found. Among children in residential maladjusted schools, for example, it has been shown that 19% had parents who were divorced, 9% had been bereaved, 17% had a step-parent, 15% were illegitimate and 8% had been adopted.[87]

The drawback of studies such as these is that they tell us more about psychiatrically disturbed children than about children from broken homes. We know how many disturbed children have lost parents, but we do not know how many children from disrupted families are in fact disturbed. To find this out we need to survey a random sample of children from broken homes and to compare the incidence of psychiatric disturbances in these children with that in children from united families.

The Minnesota survey already referred to provides us with this kind of information.[67] In this survey of ninth grade school children, the incidence of one type of behaviour disorder, delinquency, occurring during the subsequent three years, was examined for children from different kinds of homes.

The incidence was highest in children who had lost parents through separation or divorce. Boys whose fathers had died and girls whose mothers had died showed the second highest delinquency rates.

When the family composition of the children was examined, the highest delinquency rates were found in boys living with their mothers only or with neither parent. For girls, the highest rates occurred in those living with fathers only, with neither parent or with step-parents. These relationships held for each social class separately. They support the idea that an important cause of delinquency is loss of the parent of the same sex, and the consequent lack of an identification model.

The 'broken home' as a cause of emotional disorder in childhood has become as much of a cliché as 'maternal deprivation'. Both notions have been overworked mainly because the facts concerning family composition are easy to establish, when other, perhaps psychologically more relevant, aspects of family life often elude satisfactory classification and measurement.

Nevertheless, as the Minnesota study shows, even crude factual data lend themselves to establishing more precise relationships once one gets away from global concepts. In Minnesota, *a specific type of disturbance*, delinquency, was related to *particular types of family background*, and an attempt was made to explore *the process* whereby the anomalous family composition led to the child's difficulties. Moreover, it is the fact of family disruption that attracts public attention and, potentially, help for children exposed to this particular stress, and not the more subtle aspects of family attitudes and relationships which from the psychological point of view may be more important.

WHAT PSYCHIATRIC DISORDERS CHARACTERIZE CHILDREN FROM BROKEN HOMES?

This question has again been looked at most often from the point of view of children who have come forward for psychiatric care. Both the Cambridge study[12, 13] and a later investigation in South-East London[168] showed that aggressive and delinquent children very often come from disrupted homes, while children with neurotic disorders generally have structurally united families. In Chapter 2 we related aggressive and antisocial disorders to defective socialization and neurotic symptoms to experiences of excessive anxiety. While many children from broken homes have been exposed to highly traumatic experiences, and may of course suffer from neurotic conditions too, more of them have been harmed by parental deprivation, inconsistent methods of child-rearing and failure of adequate socialization. These factors in the long run outweigh the effects of anxiety and stress and increase the child's difficulties in the outside world, especially since society is not as tolerant of delinquent as of neurotic children (see Chapter 3).

THE BROKEN HOME AS AN INDEX OF PARENTAL
AND SOCIAL DEPRIVATION

It is more meaningful to think of family disruption as an index of other adverse circumstances in the lives of children than to regard it as significant in itself. One of the common consequences of illegitimacy and family disruption is not only parental deprivation, but general social deprivation as well. Illegitimate children and children from broken homes more often find their way, temporarily or permanently, into institutions. If this happens in early childhood, their chances of developing the personality deficits associated with institutional care are high (see Chapter 1).

Even when social stimulation is adequate and the child's intellectual development and his capacity to form emotional relationships with others are unimpaired, the absence of a parent can have profound psychological effects. These are greatest when the loss occurs in the child's third or fourth year of life and when the absent parent is of the same sex as the child.[135]

Family disruption leads to a variety of quite different circumstances in later life, each of them likely to influence the future social and emotional development of the affected child profoundly and in different ways. When parents split up, most children remain with a single parent, usually the mother. More rarely they acquire a step-parent or, if they are illegitimate, they may be adopted. They may be looked after by relatives or foster parents. Finally, they may spend the remaining years of their childhood in an institution.

THE BROKEN HOME AS AN INDEX OF PARENTAL
PERSONALITY DISORDER

A greater or lesser degree of parental deprivation is an inevitable consequence of family disruption. But marriage breakdown is also an index of personality difficulties in the parents. These certainly preceded the disruption of the home and are often not cured by it, but continue. Children of unmarried, divorced or separated parents are children who are being brought up by a parent or parents who have either made an unrealistic marital choice or who re-enact within their marriage their own neurotic conflicts (see Chapter 7). Each parent denigrates the other in the children's eyes and when, as often happens, the mother dominates, the father is presented to his children in a poor light. After the break, children from such failed marriages, are left not only without a parent, but with an image of a 'bad' parent, and this endangers the normal personality development of the child of the same sex who identifies with this same despised parent and *is* often identified with the parent by others. We all have our parents inside us. In part we are our parents. Our self-esteem and our confidence are dependent on our being able to think well of our parents in childhood.

The image of a loved parent who has died is kept alive by his surviving partner and is presented to the children with pride and with the affectionate feelings that existed before his death. When a parent **disappears** because the marriage has failed the situation is entirely different.

Brian was almost eleven. He said he had come to have his stealing cured. He steals when he is unhappy or gets 'mad' and it all started during his stay in a children's home when he was five. He also said he did not have a dad; his dad was a bad man who used to fight with his mum. Brian's mother had been reared by her grandmother, 'and even to my family yet I'm sort of disowned'. Throughout her childhood she felt unwanted and jealous of her brothers and sisters. These feelings she carried over into her adult life. She married a man who was promiscuous from the start and who repeatedly cast her into the role of the jealous wife. She left him many times but always returned, until he finally told her to go.

Brian witnessed repeated, violent quarrels between the parents, yet whenever the mother prepared to leave home with him and his sister, she said 'we're going for a wee holiday.' After the final break-up of the marriage both children stayed in a children's home. When discussing Brian's stealing the mother said, 'He was never like this before they went into the home. There was too much freedom there. He wasn't upset. He was too young to understand. I tried to explain but I couldn't get through to him, he was only five. While he was there he got into trouble with another boy, stealing toys from Woolworth's. I then decided to take him out, to have him beside me,' and Brian was never thereafter allowed to play outside alone. He left the house only with his mother. He began to steal from his teacher at school and from a neighbour. The mother said, 'I blame myself. He hasn't got a father and I feel as if I've failed.' She also blamed the teacher for allowing the thefts to take place and now, in the boy's presence, she blamed him: 'He's like his father', she said, '*he* used to steal.'

Brian was handicapped by having a masochistic mother who once her early childhood had felt deprived and unwanted; by having no father but merely an image of an unstable man who exploited his mother and is regarded by the whole family as bad and dangerous; and, finally, by his mother's expectations that he will turn out to be like this father.

Emotionally disturbed children commonly come from broken homes. Marriage breakdown is known to be associated with personality disorders of the parents. Indeed, when these relationships are looked at from a slightly different angle and parents of disturbed children are compared with parents of normal controls personality disorder among parents, especially mothers, of children with behaviour disorders is found to be excessive. Just over one half of disturbed children have mothers with serious difficulties in their relationships with other people. The fathers of the children too are more often disturbed than fathers of normal children but the difference is less than for mothers and is confined to fathers with grossly deviant, antisocial personalities manifesting for example in alcoholism, promiscuity, violent behaviour and crime.

While mothers with serious and with moderate personality disorders contribute both to marital disharmony[127] and to the development of behaviour disorders in their children,[179] the father's personality disorder must be quite gross to have similar effects.[179]

THE LATER EFFECTS OF BEING REARED IN
A BROKEN HOME

Children become grown-ups and their childhood experiences help to determine their adult life patterns. Many investigations have related parent loss in childhood to various kinds of psychiatric and social disturbances in later life.

Personality disorder,[41] neurosis,[58] delinquency[60] and attempted suicide[66] in adult life are all statistically related to having experienced a disrupted family life during childhood.

Once again however, although we know how many adult patients with such disorders had been exposed to family disruption in childhood, we do not know how many children from broken homes in fact develop these difficulties in later life and how many escape unharmed. Nor do we know what are the characteristics of those children who grow up normally despite adverse circumstances of upbringing, nor what qualities of temperament or of their later environment protected them against the emotional hazards to which they had been exposed.

FAMILY PATTERNS TRANSMITTED FROM
ONE GENERATION TO THE NEXT

Mrs Brown, driven to distraction by her son's asthma and by his nocturnal cough, reported to the psychiatrist that she herself together with an older brother had been reared from infancy by her maternal grandparents. During the war her father was in the Navy and her mother joined the Land Army. The parents never lived together again. 'I never knew the real story, but no, they didn't get on. I don't think my father liked children. I don't know anything about it really.'

The grandmother was senile and 'It was more me looking after granny than the other way about.' When Mrs Brown was nine she and the grandparents came to live with her mother. 'She was too soft. I never knew my mother to have a temper and I would have liked her to. I always feel that now, if I don't get what I want, I go in a huff and go in a tantrum. If she had battered me . . . [Yet] I didn't want to stay with her. I went for a week once when I was eight and I ran away. She had an 'uncle' with her who didn't like me. It was his house and he looked after us when she was on night shift.' When Mrs Brown was ten, she woke up in bed one day to find her granny, whose bed she shared, dead beside her.

At school 'I never liked it. The teacher used to say to my mother "She has a brain, but a lazy brain" and then in the town school the teacher was more for the bright ones and I didn't do anything because all the others had brains and not me.' During her adolescence 'I was restricted by my brother and my mother . . . but I'm not sorry in a sense. All the time I felt I wanted to get away. I wanted to be a hairdresser, but my father died and there was no money.' She took a factory job. 'I didn't like working. I got restless. I can't stick to anything, I never was able to in my life. I hate to be confined.' She had a series of jobs.

At eighteen she married to get away from home. The husband she married came from a 'very broken background'. His parents too had separated and his mother with whom he lived was alcoholic. 'He had looks – he was nice-looking and that's all you thought about. He lacked something. Duncan [her asthmatic boy] reminds me of him. . . . He [the father] can't even write. He tried to be something he wasn't. He never worked when I knew him' and when Mrs Brown became pregnant he began going about with other women. 'He was never able to face up to anything.'

After Duncan's birth, Mrs Brown's mother persuaded her to leave her husband and to come back home again. This she did. She went back to work while her mother looked after Duncan and then she got a divorce. Duncan called her 'Mummy' and his grandmother 'Mamma'. When he was two, Mrs Brown went to live with Mr Brown. She has been with him ever since and has two other children. Duncan remained with his grandmother until he was four and she too old to cope with him. It was at this stage, after he had rejoined his own mother, that his asthma started.

Mr and Mrs Brown are not married. 'It's not really a worry. We got on better than if we married because we had a lot of debt and three children and there's a respect for one another because if you're married you can pack up and go. I feel we take each other less for granted.' But she is not really happy. 'We're happy enough, but not happy enough for them [the children] to let them see. We have an awful lot of worry with Duncan being ill. He [Mr Brown] wants to send him to school when he's ill and I want to keep him home. He thinks he's dodging the queue, but he's not.' Sexually 'I'm that wee bit backward all my life' and, now weeping, she accused herself of doing nothing right, ever. 'It's me, it's what's wrong with me. I can't do nothing right. I never did things right as a child. If I went a message and got the wrong thing, I'd hide it so I wouldn't get battered. My granny once promised my mother she wouldn't hit me and when my mother left she did. And yet I loved that woman more than my own mother.'

Mrs Brown attributed Duncan's asthma to his 'bad upbringing'. Instead of being allowed to play with other children as a toddler, she felt he was restricted by his elderly grandmother and 'great uncle'. 'At the time I didn't mind. I probably was relieved she would take him in a sense. There was a sort of mixed up feeling between he and I. My mum did wrong. She took him off my hands and gave me my freedom. If someone takes someone away from you, it's like putting you in a puzzle.'

In fact Mrs Brown's failed marriage and her inability to claim

her first child firmly as her own must at least in part be as-
cribed to her own ambivalent relationship with her mother
and to the fact that she herself never felt really wanted and
secure.

It is very likely that to take Duncan helped Mrs Brown's
mother to feel less guilty about rejecting her own daughter as
a child. Mrs Brown, alone at eighteen, was not equipped to
make a stand against her mother. The result is two generations
of children confused about their place in the world and divided
in their loyalties towards parent figures.

That this sequence of events is not rare, at least among
children referred for psychiatric care, has been shown by
Wardle in a study already quoted. He found not only that
such children commonly came from broken homes but that
their parents too had had this experience in childhood very
often. Only one quarter of the children he investigated 'could
boast two generations of unbroken homes'.[168]

The case of Duncan Brown and his mother illustrates too
how the stresses and confusions of childhood can become incorporated into adult personality structure and can lead to a
re-creation of the anomalous situation. The child, now parent,
holds in her hands the fate of her own offspring. Mrs Brown,
rejected by her parents as a child, felt she could do nothing
right. Her misfortunes she attributed to her own shortcomings.
Her poor view of herself was reinforced at school. Wherever
she was, she felt she should be somewhere else. She could not
settle. She married a boy from a similarly disrupted home and
the marriage was a failure. She allowed her mother to take
charge of her child and when finally she got him back, her
guilt towards him made it impossible for her to tolerate any
expressions of discomfort from him. A night-time cough following whooping cough turned into a wheeze and as she became ever more solicitous and also more exasperated with
Duncan, so the asthma assumed increasing proportions until
it dominated the life of the whole family.

At what stage of this cycle is intervention most likely to be
effective? Help was not sought until Duncan became asthmatic. Could help have been more effective if it had been
offered at the time of Mrs Brown's pregnancy or even during
her baby's early months? Her marriage was breaking up then

and she was under medical and nursing care. Could she have used help at that stage if it had been made available to her?

ILLEGITIMACY AND ADOPTION

Illegitimate children are no longer hidden from public view, but they continue to be shut away psychologically. Barriers often exist between them and their parents that are not found in ordinary families. Shame motivates this behaviour as it did in the case of children hidden in attics in Victorian days. A hundred years ago mothers could not bear to look at their unwanted offspring. Now they find it hard to face their feelings towards them. This barrier of shame between parents and children can be found in any anomalous family situation. Mrs Brown for example had never explained to Duncan that Mr Brown was not his real but his second father. Yet she felt a strain between herself and Mr Brown because Duncan, who was causing so much upset, was not even his child.

Another mother living with her parents, who was forced by pregnancy to marry at eighteen and whose marriage broke up a year later, had never explained the situation to her son, then eight. When the little boy asked where his daddy was, the mother mentioned the town the father now worked in. One day the child reported that a boy at school had asked him about his daddy and he had said he was away 'at sea'. Again the mother did not provide real knowledge but allowed the child to persist in his face-saving explanation.

Illegitimacy, even more than other causes of anomalous family situations, results in barriers of silence if not of actual falsification of facts. Children reared by grandmothers are still sometimes taught to look on their mothers as older sisters. They grow up with feelings of uncertainty and doubt. A pact of secrecy prevents them from voicing their suspicions. They feel guilty because of them and they are permanently deprived of a really frank relationship with the adults who care for them.

A man of thirty reported that he was adopted at a year. Once when he was five a lady spoke to him in the street. She said, 'I know you, Michael Jones, I know your mother,' and she offered to buy him a cup of tea. 'But I was too shy and I told my mother and she got Mr

Jones to kick up a row with her to keep away and later I knew that she was my mother. I took her to be just a big girl at the time, fifteen or sixteen. Even to this day my mother wouldn't talk about my own mother and all she says is detrimental, which is true apparently, because I have a sister and a brother all illegitimate. . . . I knew I was adopted since I was thirteen, although I wasn't told till I was twenty-one. It was just suspicion over the years. . . . Knowing and suspecting all these years from when I was thirteen to twenty-one I think had a bad effect on me. There was an aunt and my father kept telling me how fond of me my Aunt Mary was and I suspected *she* was my mother. But I was quite wrong as it turned out.'

Illegitimate pregnancy is by no means confined to the young or to the unmarried. In the Leicester study mentioned earlier, only one sixth of the mothers were under twenty years old and only just over a half were single at the time of conception. Such single mothers are faced with a major decision about their child: whether to give him up for adoption or whether to take on the inevitably hard struggle of bringing up a child without a father.

In such a situation the mother must come to the decision most appropriate for herself and her child. Ideally too she should learn from her experience so that in future she will manage her love relationships better and will be able to provide stability for the family she may have. For both processes skilled psychiatric or social work help is needed. At present this is generally offered to moherst of illegitimate children to help them in their decision making. It is less readily available for the second, and more protracted, task that faces such mothers: that of improving their own personality adjustment.

A recent study in Gloucestershire found that the decision of whether to keep the child or offer him for adoption was often made firmly well before the child's birth.[182] Out of one hundred and sixty unmarried, pregnant girls two thirds had made up their minds before the child was born and over one half had had a constant intention throughout the pregnancy either to keep or to relinquish the baby. Only one third were still undecided at the time of confinement and only 17 changed their minds once the child was born, mainly in favour of keeping the baby. By the time the children were a year old, 88 mothers had chosen to keep them and 72 had decided on adoption.

Three factors were associated with the choice of adoption: the presence of other children, legitimate or illegitimate, a married putative father and a negative attitude on the part of the mother's parents towards having the child in the family. Other factors such as social class and age of the mother, strained family relationships and a broken home, were not related to the decision. Most of the mothers who elected to keep their babies although they had other children, although the putative father was married and their own parents unwilling to help with the child, were psychologically grossly unstable.

Relatively little research has been done into the later results of illegitimacy as such or into the outcome of adoption. This is because until recently it was thought that the people in volved would want to guard jealously their right to secrecy. In the case of adoption this is certainly not so. Adoptive parents, and even adoptive children when grown-up, are quite ready to discuss their experiences in order to provide information that will help other people in similar situations in the future. Several long-term follow-up studies of adopted children are now under way, and one retrospective account of adults who had been adopted in childhood has been published.[110] This showed that of 58 people adopted as children only 21 were well or fairly well adjusted. Unfortunately the sample studied was by no means representative either of a general population or of a population of adopted children, consisting merely of subjects known to their family doctors to have been adopted and willing to participate in the survey. Family doctors inevitably know more about patients who consult them often, and people with excessive emotional needs are more likely to reveal to their doctor the details of their past lives than patients who are well-adjusted.

Short-term follow-up studies of adopted children have shown a much less gloomy picture.[107] At least two thirds of adoptions seem satisfactory to professional outsiders and in the eyes of the adoptive parents themselves only between one in seven and one in ten are unsuccessful.[89]

One of the main factors shown by most studies to be associated with outcome is the age of the child at the time of adoption. Intellectually adopted children tend to resemble their adoptive parents; even children of supposedly dull mothers do quite well educationally when reared in a culturally stimulating adoptive home. Early placement is therefore more important than protracted diagnostic examinations and tests designed to make quite sure the baby is physically fit and intellectually compatible with his future parents. The fact remains that we know very little as yet about the long-term results of adoption and that we know more about its failures than its successes.

Child guidance clinic figures show that adopted children make up between 5% and 13% of their referrals while the prevalence of adoption in the community is between 1% and 2%. Referral rates may be high because adoptive parents tend to belong to middle class families and such families make greater use of clinic services. It has been suggested also that familiarity with social workers, an inevitable accompaniment of the process of adopting a child, makes such parents less reluctant to take up a psychiatric referral.[18]

We do not yet know whether adopted children in general have more psychological disturbances than others nor to what extent such children are predisposed to emotional disorders in later life. But we do know something about the special problems facing illegitimate children and adoptive and other substitute parents. Such parents have to cope with many extra responsibilities which they have voluntarily undertaken and the child himself must face his own anomalous life situation. How can he do this without impairment to his developing personality? Clinical experience indicates that the crucial factor is his parents' capacity to face honestly their own feelings so that they can relate to the child with frankness and with unambivalent affection.

When parents decide to adopt a child, they are forced to make a deliberate choice, not demanded of natural parents. Much more than other parents, they see themselves as the active manipulators of their children's fate. They have behind them in addition the experience of disappointment and sometimes the sense of failure that comes from not having children of their own. Unless parents can honestly face these feelings they may find themselves becoming very anxious indeed when they have to deal with the minor difficulties that crop up with all children. When their children are not completely happy or do not behave perfectly, they irrationally feel themselves to blame. One mother felt her adoptive son to be so handicapped by his adoptive status, and by what she perceived as his extreme sensitivity, that she could not treat him naturally. The fear of harming him in some way was always with her. Towards her own son, conceived shortly after the adoption, she felt quite different.

Overwhelming and irrational guilt sometimes finds distorted expression through denial, projection and rationalization. Consciously the parents allow themselves to be aware only of the good they have done the child by taking him into their home. They cannot bear the thought that they have sometimes made him unhappy or that they may have something to do with his temporary misbehaviour. Instead they blame the child. But there is another ready-made scapegoat. The badness in the child comes from his true parents who, unknown as they usually are, are perceived in fantasy as immoral and highly sexed. The notion that these qualities are latent in the children they have adopted is not rare among adoptive parents. Although it stems as we have seen from their own feelings of insecurity, its effect can be devastating for the child. Minor misbehaviour on his part is responded to as if it were but the forerunner of major delinquency.

Mrs Cunningham was very worried indeed about her adoptive daughter's repeated stealing. She had adopted Jean after some years of marriage. 'I thought it might happen after Jean, but it didn't. I'd read about people adopting a child and then getting one of their own.' She followed the advice of the adoption society and when the child was five, she told her she was 'chosen' because her parents could not have a baby of their own. Mrs Cunningham never again referred to the subject fearing that if the child really knew she had had another mother, she would want to join her. One day after starting school, Jean told some neighbours her parents were 'only my step-parents'. This upset Mrs Cunningham very much but she did not take the opportunity to enlighten her daughter. She dreads the possibility that Jean, now 12, might want to raise the topic again. Mrs Cunningham was told that the child's real mother was 'very attractive to men, not a good mother type. She left her baby.' What worries Mrs Cunningham most of all is

Jean's 'untruthfulness and the stealing. Well, I don't know what's causing it. Because she gets plenty of pocket money and she has a happy home life. Sometimes I feel there's something there, that if only she'd *tell* me, truthfully. She's different to what I am in so many ways. I sometimes think there's a sort of ruthlessness about her. All my husband's and my relations, to me these children are very much like their own parents: dull, ordinary people, who wouldn't steal and lie and when I took Jean I was under the impression that a child absorbs her environment. What worries me is my husband. He just adores that child and he gets let down by her so often. She was such an attractive child. What worries me is in case she does something really bad in the future, the uncertainty.'

Mrs Cunningham felt Jean was hiding her true feelings from her. She did not realize that her own lack of frankness about the adoption contributed to the barrier between them. This example illustrates a very common cause of difficulty between adoptive parents and their children. The parents are afraid that their children harbour a secret longing to rejoin their own family. The children in turn fear that because they were once rejected, their adoptive parents too may one day let them go. Certainly adopted children commonly think about their own unknown parents and, because they in fact have two sets of parents, they may in fantasy split them into the good parents and the bad parents. In the process of coming to terms with their family situation, their feelings towards their adoptive parents fluctuate wildly. This is one of the extra tasks that adoptive parents have to face: to provide unconditional acceptance and security, while their children's feelings towards them, especially at adolescence, alternate between affection and hostility. If the security of the parents depends on their children's positive feelings towards them, if the child senses that his place in the family is conditional on his own behaviour, tensions may rise to an unbearable pitch. The child becomes more and more difficult in order to test out his parents' tolerance; they in turn become increasingly disapproving and rejecting. In such a situation the first helpful intervention is often to let the parents see that what the child wants above all else is to have them as parents always, and to let the child see that what his parents really dread is his rejection of them. Only such recognition of mutual dependence

will make it possible for child and parents to begin to communicate more fully with each other and to understand each
other better.

CHILDREN AND STEP-PARENTS

An adoption is a public transaction which always involves a
legal decision and, increasingly, the participation of some
kind of social work agency. When a parent marries for a
second time, this is a much more private matter. Not surprisingly even less is known about the special problems facing
step-parents and step-children than about those involved in
adoption.

There are obvious differences between the two situations.
Most children are adopted at birth. They have two sets of
parents but they know only one. The other exists merely in
fantasy. Step-children on the other hand have had to part
from a known parent and accept a new one. They have never
had to face total rejection, because one parent remained with
them, but they have had to master conflicts of loyalty towards
their old and their new parent and also feelings of jealousy
against this new parent who now takes first place in the affection of the surviving parent.

The step-parents' problems too are very different from those
of adopters. A step-mother, for example, has a new child and
a new husband all at once. She must not only prove herself a
good mother to someone else's child, she must also be a good
wife. The way she succeeds in one role may determine her
success or failure in the other. If she is not absolutely sure of
her husband's love, if she feels him watching her critically, she
may be quite unable to tolerate the negative feelings her step-
children will inevitably show her at times. The children then
become very powerful in the marital relationship and carry a
corresponding load of guilt and blame for any discord between the parents.

Adoptive parents and step-parents have one important problem in common. Both are ready to offer substitute care to a
child who for one reason or another has been deprived. In
this sense, they give more than parents are usually called upon
to give. What many find hard to understand is that the children

they benefit do not respond only with love and gratitude. Very often they are ambivalent, especially at adolescence. They both love and hate their new parents. Their past experiences of having been rejected or of having lost a parent make it harder for them to accept a new relationship. They need to test it out. They feel themselves in part to blame for their past experiences and to that extent they feel bad. They need to show this badness to their new parents in order to make sure they will be accepted as they really are.

CRISIS INTERVENTION

All situations just described involve an active choice on the part of one or both parents. Almost all are public in the sense that doctors, social workers or the courts know about the changes in family structure as they occur. The nautre of the parents' decision has far-reaching consequences for their children. Sometimes it is made hastily, under conditions of excessive practical and emotional stress, and sometimes it is regretted later on.

A group of Boston psychiatrists have instituted special psychiatric services for people in such situations of crisis, believing that crisis intervention can be a very potent technique in preventing mental ill health (see p. 182).[91]

7. The Neurotic Family

A marriage in which the unresolved childhood conflicts of both partners are repeatedly enacted is the basis of a neurotic family. Children inevitably are involved in this drama and the roles allotted to them have a profound effect on their personality development. Such a family may appear perfectly stable and united. Respectability, high standards of home management and impeccable social behaviour outside the family is the rule. Yet the relationship between the parents and between parents and children is characterized by frustration and discontent. Maladaptive behaviour on the part of one parent finds a counterpart in the other, and their union endures despite repeated violent quarrels and even temporary separations; despite constant belittling of one by the other; despite the genesis of psychoneurotic symptoms or antisocial acting-out behaviour. Such families may attract medical attention because of the symptoms of a parent, a travel phobia for example in the wife, or alcoholism or promiscuity in the husband. Very often however such families express their problems more indirectly, through emotional disturbances in one of their children.

NEUROSIS AS A MARITAL BOND

When Tolstoy wrote 'All happy families are alike but an unhappy family is unhappy after its own fashion'[164] he was expressing the view that the sources of human misery in intimate social relationships are individual and idiosyncratic. The particular mood attached to certain unhappy childhood years, the individual traumatic events that happened, the peculiarities of negative parental attitudes and behaviour become built into the developing personality and may colour all subsequent relationships. When a married couple is unhappy the precise quality of their unhappiness is found to have its origins in those early traumatic life experiences that were of unique importance to each individual. Happy experiences do not have this permanent and idiosyncratic effect.

Michael Barnett was nine when he was referred to a child guidance clinic because of a stammer, recurrent nightmares and timidity. Although at the top of his form he disliked school. He was a shy, nervous boy, lacking in self-confidence and he avoided outdoor play with other children. He was preoccupied with scenes of violence on television: he wanted to be sure that 'it was just a story' and not 'real'. The mother felt he had his father's temperament while she saw the two younger children as being more robust like herself. She resented having to be careful about what she said to Michael in case his feelings got hurt, just as she resented her husband's vulnerability. Gradually she revealed that the marriage had been punctuated by repeated violent quarrels almost from the start and that their sexual relationship was very unsatisfactory. In an interview together with her husband she said to him: 'Why can't you be like my brothers-in-law, who, when my sisters attack them in public, just shrug it off because it's not meant seriously?' He replied, 'They don't really shrug it off, it goes home.' Later in the interview she turned on him, saying, 'Why can't you be a man? *I* always have to see to everything. I have to make all the decisions.' She wanted him to take over and yet unless she had the final say she did not feel things would turn out right. He accused her of refusing to have intercourse with him. She said, 'How can one have intercourse when one's just quarrelled? He's lucky, he forgets. But I can't, I feel wounded.' He said, 'I feel if only I could convince her that I have real feeling for her and that it's not just a physical urge then she would react differently.' He seemed to accept her accusation that he was inadequate. His wife however went on to reveal her own deep fears of intercourse. 'It sickens me, the thought of it. It makes me feel like vomiting.' The quarrels which had the power of 'wounding' her so were often pretexts to avoid intercourse.

As a child she had been a tomboy and had had repeated accidents. Her husband reminded her of a previous love affair in which the unadventurous and timid boy who was then her fiancé had on one occasion terrified her by his unexpected sexual advances. After the marriage she told her husband he would have to be patient with her because of this experience which, she indicated, had given her a horror of intercourse. The next question to be explained was why she had been so terrified at the time. Again the husband helped her to recollect an experience she had had still earlier, at the age of seven. 'There was a woman in the street, who sold toffee apples and she had a cock, a wild animal, who loved toffee. The ritual was that as each child came away with his apple, he gave the cock a bite of toffee. The cock was so fierce, it was due to be killed. One day I went to buy a toffee apple and as I left with the apple I thought "no, I'm not going to give him his bite". I went off, past the cock who stood quite still. Then on an impulse I put out my tongue at him and suddenly he flew at me. He bit my tongue and he wouldn't let go and I ran home home with the cock still clinging on to my tongue and then, as always, my mother put the blame on me.' She has a big scar on her tongue and feels ashamed of it. 'And then the cock was killed.'

This terrifying assault had become symbolic of the sexual act for her. In future she chose men who appeared timid and were themselves vulnerable. She had the upper hand. She adopted the attitude 'I'm not going to give it to him.' Yet she also longed for the men to be aggressive. She was contemptuous of her husband's inability to assert himself with her as a man and yet she made it quite impossible for him to do so. She said she might feel better if he went out and got drunk. It was his being such a 'goody-goody' that got her down.

When Michael, her first son, was born she worried about his tongue. She thought he might be tongue-tied and not learn to speak properly. When at two-and-a-half, like many children at that age, he stammered slightly, she became exceedingly anxious. Her brother had stammered as a child and she had never ceased to feel guilty for teasing him about his disability. Her feelings towards Michael were a mixture of guilt and exasperation. He also was 'too good' in her eyes. She was afraid he might become 'womanly' like her husband.

The father's personality pattern was the counterpart of his wife's. He had indeed been very shy as a young man, self-conscious and subject to blushing. When they first married Mrs Barnett felt 'My childhood was wild and rowdy, and he was kept down. I felt sorry for him and protected him, but now I want him to be like my sister's family and do it on his own.' His father was a cripple who spent most of his time out of the house, nagged as he was by the mother who slaved away for the family. 'She drove him out of the house and into the pubs.' Mr Barnett resented his mother's nagging as he now resented his wife's. In fact he found himself responding to his wife's nagging and incessant complaints by evading his family responsibilities just as his father had done a generation before. When his wife's nagging stung him to retaliate, he got the sort of satisfaction that he had longed for as a child when he saw his mother dominating his father and wished he could take action.

He was impatient of his son's frailties for which he blamed himself, especially since his wife was forever telling him that, although he ought to play a more active part as a parent, he was 'too hard on the children'. On one occasion she said she liked it when he went fishing with the boys and he countered with, 'There you are again. You say you want me to go fishing and I immediately feel that you're organizing me again and that it's really not me that's doing it.'

The neurotic distortions of personality resulting from this mother's childhood experiences dovetailed with those of the father. Although both were unhappy and the mother had even considered leaving her husband, an equilibrium had been reached. For years they had lived a life of repeated quarrels and mutual frustration. Michael, their older son, who resembled his father in temperament and who had a predisposition to stammer, finally drew medical attention to his parents' plight by his own neurotic behaviour disorders.

Psychiatric treatment in this case achieved an improvement in all the child's symptoms, except the stammer, and a dramatic change for the better in the marital relationship. This last change however was achieved at a price. Although much happier with her husband and able to enjoy intercourse, Mrs Barnett now had two symptoms: she complained of abdominal pain, which she felt might be caused by a stomach ulcer, and the thought that she might have cancer occurred to her repeatedly. Her childhood fear that she had been badly wounded, that there was something seriously wrong with her, had not left her. But whereas previously she had seen this bad thing, which was both vulnerable and wounding, in her child and in her husband, she now felt it was within herself.

Manifest marital strife existed in this family. The mother's fear of having been damaged through a sexual assault deter-

mined her choice of a man she could think of as non-threaten-
ing sexually. She taunted him and fought with him. Her
aggressiveness aroused guilt in her which was intolerable and
she projected this on to her husband: it was his fault; he was
not manly enough. He in turn had identified with a father
whose position in his childhood family had been inferior. He
felt unsure of himself as a man. This made his wife even more
guilty because it confirmed her view of herself as not only
damaged but damaging. When she nagged at him she gave
him the opportunity to re-experience the same feelings of
righteous indignation that his mother had induced in him as
a boy.

Because of his mild stammer both parents saw their son as
damaged. The mother reacted as if once again she had been
the cause: *she* had damaged her child. She had caused her own
tongue to be hurt and now his was hurt. The guilt was more
than she could bear and she projected it onto her husband. He
in turn was only too ready to accept the blame. Did not his
son resemble himself in his sensitivity and vulnerability? Because of their own neurotic difficulties neither parent could
tolerate the child's handicap. They reacted by pulling him up
whenever he stammered, making him 'speak slowly' or repeat
phrases. The result was that he became self-conscious and
stammered even more.

MARITAL CHOICE OR NEUROSIS BY CONTAGION?

That marriage partners resemble each other is an established
fact. Husbands and wives are more alike in intelligence, in
stature, in social background, attitudes and interests than can
be accounted for by chance. Many of these characteristics such
as intelligence, height and social background are clearly attributes of each partner that were present before the marriage
and are not influenced by the association itself. The similarity
between the couple for such attributes must be due to a combination of two factors: opportunity for encountering each
other and marital choice. Opportunity for meeting depends
not only on the geographical area of residence. Social class,
religious affiliation, school, occupation and cultural interests
also determine the social circles within which an individual

moves and are responsible for the fact that the kinds of people a person is likely to encounter resemble to some degree himself. Quite apart from the opportunities for contact with like people that exist within geographical areas and within social groupings, there is evidence that individuals actively choose their marriage partners in their own image. This biased choice is called *assortative mating*.

Intimate knowledge of families leads us to suspect that neurotic distortion of personality is yet another, and an extremely important, point of resemblance between spouses. What is the evidence that this is in fact so, and if it is so, how can we be sure that the couple chose each other for these qualities of neurosis? How can we know that they did not grow to resemble each other in the course of their marriage? An early investigation of this problem was done by Slater and Woodside.[153] In the 1940s they interviewed 200 hospitalized soldiers and their wives. Half the soldiers were in hospital because of a nervous illness, half were physically ill. Slater and Woodside found that in both groups husbands and wives resembled each other with respect to age at marriage, height, number of brothers and sisters, intelligence, education and premarital sexual experience. There was no resemblance with respect to 'good looks'. All husbands and wives were rated for neurotic disposition and considerable similarity between marriage partners was found.

A recent study by Kreitman based on a series of personality questionnaires filled in by husbands and wives showed that the degree of similarity of marriage partners varies with the duration of the marriage.[89] Two groups of married couples were investigated: in the first one partner had attended the local psychiatric clinic; the second group was composed of couples living on the same housing estate who had not been to a psychiatrist and who were comparable to the first group in age, social class and duration of marriage. Tests for neuroticism and for nervous illness showed that in both groups the marriage partners tended to resemble each other. But, whereas in the non-patient group the resemblance in neuroticism and mental health between partners was high in the early years of their marriage and decreased as time went on, the reverse trend was found in psychiatric patients and their spouses.

They grew to resemble each other more and more with increasing duration of marriage. From these findings we can conclude that in the general population marriage partners resemble each other at the time of marriage on a number of indices for neurosis. Usually this initial similarity gets less with time. It is an outcome of assortative mating. Some couples do not resemble each other in this way initially; one partner being more neurotic than the other to start with. People who become psychiatric patients often have spouses who, although previously un-neurotic, have become neurotic also by the time of the psychiatric referral. Kreitman suggests that lack of social involvement outside the family, a common characteristic of psychiatric patients, may account for this change. Lack of outside social contact increases the tensions within the family and may in this way contribute to the development of neurosis in the marriage partner.

THE CHILD'S ROLE IN A NEUROTIC MARRIAGE

Mrs Rogers described her five-year-old daughter Linda as follows: 'You can't discipline Linda. She's very insecure, just a bundle of nerves. She talks all the time, she drives you mad and she fidgets. She never played with other children when she was small and now she wants to but she isn't accepted. She ruins their game. She always needs to be top dog and she complains "No-one will play with me." I'm afraid how she'll grow up if no one wants her. She makes friends with adults but resents other children. I get exasperated with her. She's easily bored, nothing pleases her for long. She got a pram and a doll for Christmas and she just covers the doll and that's it. She's in and out, in and out and she never plays. She talks all the time and at school her work's erratic.' Linda began to wet her knickers again when she was two and she was still often wet. At meal-times she fussed and dawdled so much that after months of battling with her the mother finally decided to let her go without food altogether whenever there was a fuss.

Mrs Rogers had found herself getting irritated with Linda since the child was a year old. It was her 'getting into everything' that then used to anger the mother. Whenever she was cross she felt guilty and her husband added to this guilt by saying she was too impatient with the child. It was a relief to her when finally at the age of five, other people too found Linda difficult and even the father had to admit that something was wrong with her. Now both parents were united in their criticism of the child.

Mrs Rogers remembered little about her own childhood except that it was unhappy. She was an aggressive, rather destructive child who wet her bed until the age of fourteen. She had a poor relationship with her vigorous, dominating and obsessionally houseproud mother whose constant ailments dominated the family. 'I love her because she's my mother, but I don't like her as a person.' Her father was 'a saint' but a distant one. He left the running of the home entirely to her mother. Mrs Rogers used to envy other children who were given more freedom than she was and one of the things that later appealed to her about her husband was that he came from what seemed to her a large, affectionate, free and easy family. After leaving school she took up teaching. This satisfied her mother's ambitions and her own needs for independence. She managed perfectly her professional role of taking charge of others. It was not until she had her own child to look after that she began to have self-doubts. Repeatedly she found herself reacting to Linda's early strivings for independence exactly as her own mother had reacted to her. She hated herself for it and became even more rejecting of the child who evoked these feelings of self-criticism in her.

Mr Rogers had married his wife 'for her nice ways, her principles. I try to improve my rough ways to fit in with her.' When he was a child, 'It was terrible. My mother was a cripple and my father died young. I want my children to have a better education. Once we had a school play at the end of term and the teacher said to go home and dress, and I had no clean shirt and had to borrow one of my sister's blouses. I felt shabby and inadequate. I couldn't go into company. I was a scruffy kid.' Yet about Linda he said, 'I'm more for letting her be wild, a tomboy,' while his wife, he thought, wanted her to be 'prim and proper, a little girl'.

In this family both parents were in conflict about their social standards. As a result the child was given contradictory cues so that whatever she did was wrong. The mother had been restricted and inhibited in childhood. She married a man who represented freedom to her, yet she found herself repeatedly being over-strict with her own daughter. He in turn had suffered the humiliation of social inferiority as a child, had married his wife for her higher standards and then found himself constantly encouraging his daughter to rebel against these standards. It can be no coincidence that in seven years of marriage this couple had not yet managed to set up a satisfactory home together. At first they lived with the maternal grandmother while the father worked in another town. Then they were in a cramped flat which they had to share with relatives. They finally moved into a house of their own in the father's home town, but no sooner had they settled there than he again found himself a job elsewhere and came home only at weekends. The outcome of their failure to resolve their own long-standing conflicts was that their daughter, criticized by both parents, and feeling unloved and unlovable, became attention-seeking, restless and quarrelsome. Linda's recurrent complaint was that 'they don't like me', 'they' being in turn her cousins, other children, her parents and her teachers. Neither of her parents was aware of any discomfort other than the irritation induced in them by their child. The mother did not complain of her husband's frequent absences from home. The father was not made tense by his wife's insistence on maintaining the proprieties of a middle class home. They rarely quarrelled. Linda was the one sore point and they viewed her future with gloom and foreboding. She had become a *scapegoat*.

In this home there was no overt marital disharmony. The unconscious dissatisfactions of each partner with the other were expressed solely through the child. The mother had received little affection in childhood. Her husband from a free and easy family seemed warm and loving. Yet she got little affection from him now since he was always away. Her anger when the child did not entirely conform to her high standards was in part an expression of her frustrations in the marriage. The father admired her for her social and intellectual standards. She appeared to be able to stand on her own feet and to need little protection from him. Although he disapproved of them he had identified with the low standards that prevailed in his own childhood family and unconsciously he was undermining his wife's authority in the home by encouraging the child to be rebellious and a tomboy.

The child in this family was used to express the marital tensions which neither parent had faced.

CORRUPTING PARENTS AND IMPERFECT CONSCIENCE FORMATION IN CHILDREN

When children habitually steal, run away from home or engage in unacceptable sexual behaviour, although in all other respects conforming to ordinary social standards, their acting-out, delinquent behaviour can often be shown to have its counterpart in the personality of one or both parents. Some years ago the notion was developed by Johnson and Szurek that a parent's neurotic conflict commonly finds expression in the child's acting-out behaviour.[82] The parent, often the mother, is ambivalent; she gets vicarious gratification from her child's behaviour, subtly condoning and fostering it unbeknown to herself, while outwardly reacting with reproach and disapproval towards the child. The parent's unconscious permissiveness and inconsistency of discipline lead to imperfect conscience development in the child, to the formation of what Johnson and Szurek have called 'superego lacunae'.

Parents may induce antisocial behaviour by suggesting it as a possibility. Many mothers who are still guilty about their own premarital sexual exploits will repeatedly warn their adolescent daughters against 'getting into trouble'. Their warnings and constant checks on their daughters' behaviour suggest to the children that their mother's image of them is one of promiscuous sexuality. They begin to accept this image of themselves and behave accordingly. Mothers who are forever telling their small children not to 'go with strangers' similarly plant ideas in the children's minds that were not there before. They foster the very behaviour which they regard with such dread and fascination. Some mothers condone delinquent behaviour for years before finally and unexpectedly clamping down on the child, often only when the behaviour has drawn public attention to the family.

Mrs Cunningham, the adoptive mother described before, never liked to make too much of a fuss about Jean's petty pilfering from her handbag. She thought 'it would pass'. It was only when Jean stole a gold locket from a friend that the mother began to react. Her reaction then was to see a potential criminal in her daughter and to adduce hereditary causes for the difficulties. She gave a hint that there was something exciting for her in the child's stealing when she said, 'All my husband's and my relations, to me their children are very much like their own parents: dull, ordinary people, who wouldn't steal and lie.' Once Jean's stealing had been discovered outside the family circle Mrs Cunningham detached herself from the child emotionally. She now used the delinquency as a rationalization for her own long-standing feelings of anger at the child and for her disappointment and frustration at not being able to conceive a baby of her own, not even after the adoption, as she had hoped.

Delinquency in children may be an outcome not of a parent's inner neurotic conflicts but of tensions between the parents. Children are not uncommonly the battleground for such parents in conflict with each other and often the battle is waged far more openly than in the example of the Rogers family cited above. Some parents are so completely at the mercy of their neurotic impulses that they can offer their children little protection against their own conflicting attitudes and behaviour.

One pattern of such abnormal family interaction is for the mother to choose a husband of whom she disapproves while, without being aware of this, getting considerable satisfactions from his behaviour. Daughters of alcoholic fathers, for example, often marry heavy drinkers themselves. They seek to reform them, fail and, when their husbands become addicted to alcohol, resist all outside offers of treatment for the condition. Boys in such families encounter in their mothers the same ambivalent attitudes of seduction combined with disapproval. Their fathers present them with an equally ambivalent situation: a model for identification which must not be copied. This family pattern is particularly hazardous for boys and is found very often in delinquent and in sexually deviant children.

Mrs Black's son, aged 22, had just been imprisoned for assault and her youngest child, Anne, a girl of 12, was very nervous and had started sleep-walking. But Mrs Black's main source of unhappiness was her marriage. 'It's a worry with my husband fighting all the time and coming in drunk. It's been a problem for years. Some nights it's worse than others. We're not getting on at all. I don't talk to him now. [They sleep and eat apart.] . . . We had a fight the other day and it upset the children. Anne got a bag of nerves. She runs outside the house when he starts, at night. She'll shout at her dad "Don't fight, dad, don't fight" or she'll go away. He needs a drink to give him courage and he uses bad language to me in front of the children, a thing I don't do myself.'

Mrs Black's father used to drink. 'He used to want to fight like, with my mother. I seemed to be the only one who could quieten him and get him to bed. I was closer to him than to my mother.' As a child Mrs Black was delicate. One of her happiest memories was being in a convalescent home at eight. 'It was summer-time and we were all out in bathing costumes.' As a teenager she was shy. 'I never liked dancing. I could go and watch but not get up myself.'

Mr Black was born with a mild cerebral palsy. He limped and his arm was stiff. His mother died in childbirth when he was six. 'His step-mother wasn't very good to him and he stayed with his auntie and then he was put in a home. We've often heard him saying being put here and put there, staying with this one and the next one, he's always had to fend for himself.' About his physical handicap 'he didn't seem to let it bother him, unless he felt it inwardly himself'. In their courting days 'I felt a bit put out about it and *now* he says I don't want to have anything to do with him *because* of his bad leg. He's casting that up to me and I've never cast it up to him.'

The real troubles between this couple began over the children. Their first son was premature and often ill. The mother devoted much anxious care to his upbringing. The second boy, now in prison, had been in trouble with the police since he was twelve. 'They could never tell my husband they were in trouble. They'd always come to me, because he would cast it up to me, that it's *my* fault.' Mrs Black was over-indulgent; Mr Black was punitive. She sheltered the children from him and he reacted by withdrawing and indicating they were her responsibility and not his. When the second boy was in trouble 'he threatened to turn the boys out of the house. But I said if they go, I'm going too. He was jealous of them when the oldest was 18, because when he came in late after work he'd find them just sitting about.'

Mrs Black clearly condoned behaviour in her sons that she knew would agitate the father. Her reaction was to shelter the sons from his wrath. Unconsciously she derived satisfaction from their delinquent conduct and from his aggressive responses. Although all the family knew of the prison sentence, Mrs Black made them keep it a secret from the father.

Her ambivalence and the satisfactions she derived from her sufferings were revealed in much of her behaviour. In the early years of the marriage the father was only a social drinker but the mother prohibited alcohol. 'You know, the thought of drink, you feel everyone would go the same way, because when we got married I wouldn't allow a bottle of beer in the house.' Now that he had become an alcoholic, Mrs Black indicated with some pride that there was always sherry in the cabinet.

In latter years she suffered from poor eyesight but refused to wear spectacles. She was often very depressed but 'didn't want to bother the doctor'. Instead she elicited sympathetic concern from her children. She often consulted the doctor about her marital problem, however, but was unable to follow through any advice given to her. She agreed with the doctor that the best thing for her to do was to leave her husband, but she stayed. When the doctor suggested Mr Black should have treatment for his alcoholism, she felt it would do no good.

She was stuck in a pattern of behaviour whereby she, apparently a passive sufferer, in fact constantly provoked her husband to attack her. She was re-creating in her adult life a childhood situation that had been of immense importance to her. She had married her husband because he was like her father, and like her father, he disappointed her: he did not stop drinking. Her husband in turn was an outcast in his own family, just as he had been in his childhood family after his mother's death. He dealt with his suffering wife's accusations, with her disapproval and her determined efforts to have the children on her side by taking refuge in drink.

One son became delinquent. Whether the youngest girl, now reacting with anxiety and sleepwalking to the same experiences that her mother had had at her age, will continue to follow her mother's masochistic life pattern is an open question.

NEUROTIC REACTIONS TO PARENTHOOD

Children's symptoms as we have seen are often an expression of the parents' disturbed relationship with each other. Parental difficulties may arise however not in response to their marital relationship but as a reaction to their children's demands on them to act as mothers and fathers. Latent neurotic difficulties, inconspicuous up to now, may be aroused by the responsibilities of parenthood.

A woman whose childhood and adolescence had been made intolerable by an over-dramatic, controlling, attention-seeking, robust, but in her own mind always ailing, mother found herself full of resentment against her older daughter. This child then aged three had become clinging and demanding after the birth of a baby sister. Whenever her mother nursed the baby she wanted to be cuddled too. She refused to play with other children and demanded constant amusement. 'She's at me all the time. She's not a peaceful companion. I get irritable. I wish she'd go and jump in the lake.' The mother reacted to the child's behaviour as if it was an unfair, personal attack upon herself. Instead of seeing it as a childish claim for reassurance and responding to it as such she began to battle with her three-year-old. The little girl pulled her doctor upstairs on one occasion and said 'That's what I do with my Mummy because I like her to go where I go. Some little boys are very naughty. They quarrel with their mummies.' The more the mother held out against her child's demands the more difficult and bad-tempered the child became. This struggle came to an end only when the mother recognized that the feeling of being exploited that her daughter now evoked in her was exactly similar to the feeling she had had towards her mother as a child. 'She's like my mother, always wanting to talk and to relate to people. She can drive me up the wall.'

Of her relationship with her mother she spoke as follows: 'I was not affectionate. I stayed as far away from my mother as possible because I didn't want to be involved. I get furious with myself. I tell her what I want from life and hope about things and she knocks me back and then I think to myself "you silly fool". My brother was affectionate and she strangled him. She was making demands on him that should have been made on my father. He coped by being out of the house. When I wanted to move into a flat she felt rejected by me and had a nervous fit which frightened me. But if you took my mother seriously you'd find *you* were worrying and *she* wasn't. These sort of people are a bit of a menace.'

This mother's past reactions to her own mother were understandable; her present response to her child, who had aroused these same feelings in her once more, was irrational. At the end of the treatment the mother said, 'Things have sorted themselves out. I couldn't see how it happened. It was murder. But now she's really wonderful. Of course, she *can* be difficult. The other day she said "I'll throw you in the lake and have Daddy for my mother." ' The child was now able to express her occasional hostile feelings to her mother more openly. She no longer needed to pretend that only 'little boys' quarrel with their mummies.

Parenthood often evokes the long-forgotten feelings of childhood. Whether one approved of one's parents and resolved to adopt their methods of child-rearing or whether one decided they were wrong and that whatever happens one's own children must have a different start in life may be crucial. Many parents vow never to be to their children as their mothers or fathers were to them, but often they find themselves quite unable to keep to this resolve. One father, cowed into submission by a sadistic grandfather, was gentle and understanding with his own two children. But repeatedly he found himself reacting with sudden and frightening severity to minor misdemeanours of his little boy. He said, 'It's my father in me' that took over on these occasions and he disliked himself for it and felt ashamed. He had identified with a father whom he feared and hated. A part of himself, usually well disguised, was this father and his son had the power to bring him to life. The father was extremely concerned about his little boy's multiple fears for which he blamed himself. His response to the child's symptoms was neurotic: it served only to make the symptoms worse. The more anxious the child was, the more angry the father became.

'FAMILY PSYCHIATRY'

Because children's behaviour disturbances are so inextricably linked up with their parents' own neurotic life difficulties, it is often legitimate to regard them as symptoms of a more general family problem. Illness in the child may be a manifestation of neurotic relationships involving not only the patient who has been brought for treatment, but the whole of his family.

Child psychiatry as a separate discipline was born some fifty years ago. From the start treatment focused not on the child alone but on his parents too. Only if they could modify their attitudes and behaviour, it was held, could one hope for any permanent improvement in the child as a result of psychiatric treatment. At first it was thought that all that was needed was for parents to be given correct advice or 'guidance'. This optimistic belief was soon shattered.

Psychoanalysis has contributed greatly to our understanding that poor parental functioning is usually irrational, often neurotic and not under voluntary control. It is not due to bad intentions. Most parents mean to be good parents. They discover with dismay that what they actually do does not correspond to their ideal image of themselves. It is not what they want to do. This realization of the unconscious motivation of behaviour led to the recognition that parents of psychologically disturbed children require attention in their own right and that the techniques needed to help them to modify their attitudes and behaviour are not didactic but psychotherapeutic. Psychiatric social workers who help parents in this way have been essential members of the psychiatric team since the first child guidance clinics were established.

The last ten years have seen a further change in emphasis: the development of the concept of 'family psychiatry'. The main proponent of this concept in America is Nathan Ackerman.[1] According to his views all psychological problems of children must be seen within the context of family interaction. He aims at 'understanding health through the emotional "give and take" of family relationships'. Treatment must focus not on the child and on the parents' problems separately but on the total interaction between the child and his family. In family treatment, the ill child is seen by the psychiatrist together with his parents, his brothers and sisters, sometimes with the grandparents. Treatment aims to clarify the interactions between members of the whole family, to allow family members to communicate more freely with each other and, as a result, to understand each other and themselves better. In this country the aims and practices of family psychiatry have been described by Howells.[76]

Most people would agree that family treatment, that is psychotherapy involving parents and child together, can be extremely useful in certain circumstances, especially with older children. But there is considerable scepticism of family psychiatry as a blanket approach to all psychological problems of childhood. Such scepticism is based on three main arguments:

(1) Exponents of family psychiatry often pay scant regard to diagnosis, viewing all disturbances in childhood as reactions to neurotic family relationships.

(2) The technical procedure of family group treatment is not suitable for all cases even of neurotic family relationships.

(3) The processes of family group interaction are even more complex than those of the interaction between two people and the accurate description and evaluation of what goes on in treatment becomes even less feasible than it already is in more orthodox individual or group psychotherapy.

The first two points require expansion here.

Not all deviant behaviour in childhood is neurotically determined. We shall see in the following chapters that cultural and constitutional factors may be of over-riding importance in a proportion of cases. To ignore this is to burden parents unnecessarily and fruitlessly. Many mothers have spent hours of painful self-exploration to discover how they have failed as parents, when a proper examination and detailed psychological investigation of their children would have revealed minor but so far unrecognized, constitutional handicaps. Guilty parents are not better parents. The reverse.

The notion that all ills stem from 'the family' reached its climax in the hypothesis of the '*double-bind*' as a cause of schizophrenia.[15] The loss of contact with reality, the thought disorder and the delusional experiences of psychotic patients were causally attributed to their mother's child-rearing practices. Investigations of mothers of schizophrenic patients showed that these women would give one cue manifestly while at the same time subtly and covertly giving the opposite one. Such a mother might scold her child smilingly or tell her teenager to go out and enjoy himself while at the same time making it clear by expression and gesture that when he goes she will feel desolate and that he ought really to stay with his mother. Many mothers no doubt behave like this to their children and the children in turn may develop signs of emotional disorders, but that such behaviour causes a serious type of insanity has not been established. Several studies purporting to show such a connexion have not also examined parents of non-schizophrenics. They have failed to show that such double-bind responses precede the illness and are not reactions on the mother's part to having an ill child. They have failed also to explain how non-schizophrenic brothers and sisters of the patient escaped becoming ill. Moreover, the diagnosis of schizophrenia in the patients studied has often not been convincingly established. Other more scientifically acceptable investigations, which demonstrated that parents of schizophrenics do in fact relate and communicate differently from parents of normal offspring have not yet answered the question of whether these parents are constitutionally different because of genetic similarities with their children, or whether the parents' abnormalities have actually *caused* their children's illness.[25]

A recent investigation in Boston has gone some way to disprove the theory of the double-bind as a cause of schizophrenia. Fifty patients were found who had been admitted to a mental hospital with schizophrenia and who had also attended the Judge Baker Child Guidance Clinic in youth. They were matched for age, sex and social class with fifty other children who had attended the clinic at the same time. An analysis was made of the descriptions of the mothers recorded in the case notes of both groups of children. It was found that there were proportionally more psychotic or borderline psychotic mothers in the group of children who later became schizophrenic. On the other hand, neurotic mothers who displayed double-bind behaviour were in fact more common in the group of disturbed children who did not in later life develop schizophrenia.[169] We shall return to these questions again when we come to consider childhood psychosis.

Even when children's deviant behaviour is clearly neurotic and determined by disturbed family relationships, family group psychotherapy may not be the best treatment approach. Young children express themselves differently from adults. We shall see that the treatment techniques required by them are different also. Children are not a match for their parents in a treatment setting depending mainly on talking. They are not a match for them anyway, because they are dependent beings, while their parents are autonomous. Inevitably too in such a group children are outnumbered. The energy invested by the therapist in helping the child keep his end up in this setting restricts the parents' freedom of communication. Often too the crucial areas that must be explored by parents if treatment is to be effective are precisely those topics from which children are by custom excluded. Parents cannot for example discuss their sexual difficulties in their child's presence. Even to hear them express their feelings towards each other or towards the grandparents may be an unnecessary burden for a small child preoccupied with his own anxieties.

The concept of 'family psychiatry' has been very useful in emphasizing the intimate relationships between children's disturbed behaviour and their parents' neurotic problems. On the other hand, the practice of family psychiatry as a universal treatment technique cannot be recommended.

8. Culturally Deprived Children

Every child must learn to live with its family. In the last two chapters we saw how disruption of family structure and the conflicting demands of neurotic parents can increase a child's difficulties in adapting to family life. But there is a second series of requirements the child must meet: those of the outside world. When he leaves his own house to play in the street or in some other child's garden, when he goes to shop for his mother, when he rides in a bus or queues outside the cinema on a Saturday morning his appearance and behaviour come under public scrutiny. More important still are the demands made on him to conform to quite definite standards of achievement and of social behaviour at school. In all these public situations the child has reflected back to him the views that others have of him. Failure in the outer world, for whatever reason, is accompanied by loss of self-esteem and has profound effects on personality development.

Behaviour disorders induced by adverse family interactions can handicap a child in fulfilling his public roles. His level of anxiety may be such that it is quite impossible for him to concentrate in class and his school performance drops precipitously. He may feel unloved at home, assume he is not likeable and become a demanding and quarrelsome child. But failure in the outside world has many causes other than neurosis. Among the most important, because they affect large sections of the childhood population, are causes attributable to social and cultural differences between the sub-groups of our society.

CHILDREN FROM MINORITY GROUPS

All children from minority groups have extra problems to face irrespective of whether they are members of a particular religious sect or come from a foreign country. Let us consider first of all children from small social groups which are merely different from the larger group within which they live but which do not carry any particular stigma of inferior social status. There are a number of small religious sects whose children must conform to certain patterns of social behaviour, food habits and religious worship that are vastly different from those of almost everyone else. From the beginning the child grows up with the idea that 'we are different from other people'. During the primary school years children in general prize conformity. They want to be like everyone else. How do children from religious minority groups deal with this wish which is in direct conflict with parental instruction? Usually they do so by means of reaction formation: they become excessively devout adherents of the particular beliefs and practices of their group and they proclaim their pride to be members of it. With these attitudes they counter the curiosity and disbelief of other children and the headshaking of adults. Yet they cannot altogether identify with the beliefs and traditions of their own sub-group that deprive them of so many opportunities in the wider world. At the same time they are not allowed to identify completely with the standards of 'the others'. The result is a latent division within the personality which often does not become manifest until adolescence. Adolescence in children from such minority groups is often a particularly troubled period in which hidden conflicts surface for the first time. Sometimes such children will break away from their previous traditions at this point. But such a break involves a real rift between the generations that cannot be repaired. The more common alternative seems to be that the child apprehends fully the consequences of minority group membership and chooses to accept them for life.

Allan Robb was nearly thirteen when he was referred to a psychiatrist. His symptoms were obsessional rituals which seriously interfered with his everyday life, and violent temper outbursts at home, particularly against his mother. The family belonged to a small religious sect and lived in a country district. There were no other

children of their faith nearby. Both parents described the restraints imposed on them as children but they were brought up in
a city where the social life for youngsters within their own religious community was active.

Allan's difficulties began after the birth of his sister when he was
four. He was very jealous of her from the start, threatening on one
occasion to throw her in the fire. Because of their religious beliefs
the parents regarded Allan's expressions of anger as sinful and he
became excessively guilty. His school progress was slow and the
requirements of his religion restricted social contact with other
children outside school hours. The satisfactions in his life were
therefore few. His sister was cleverer and more equable in temperament. The more the parents disapproved of him, the more difficult
it became for him to master his jealousy and to subdue his rage.
Finally when he was ten his grandfather, the only person with
whom he had an unclouded relationship, died. It was at this stage
that his obsessional symptoms started. He found himself having to
straighten the objects in his room repeatedly, and reacting with
tantrums when some trivial article was shifted by his mother's
home help as she dusted the room. Dressing in the morning was
drawn out interminably since he had to tie and re-tie his shoe laces
and, as a consequence, he was often late for school. Once there he
was symptom-free, but as soon as he returned to his garden gate in
the afternoon he was again held up by obsessional activity and
ruminations so that he would often stand there for as long as a
half hour unable to move into the house. His mother interpreted
his symptoms correctly as an attack upon herself but she wrongly
assumed it was deliberate and within the boy's control. Both
parents were horrified when the symptoms took the form of compulsive swearing and uttering of obscene words.

Here is what Allan said:

'Sometimes I keep thinking I'm not like other children. My
sister is always down in time. She is quick, not like me. I'm more
careful. I'm too careful and too slow. I like to be tidy with clothes.
I used to spend a long time . . . I wish I was a normal boy. I'm not
saying that I liked my father better than my mother, it would be
wrong. They say they love me as well as my sister. Sometimes I've
said that I like my father better, that I hate my mother, but I
haven't meant it. I've said it in a temper and then I feel sorry. My
mother says thoughts are as bad as words. If I say "sorry" my
mother says my sorries don't mean anything and if I say sorry for
long enough she says "show that you're sorry". . . . I'm not blaming her for it . . . She's right . . .'
and later:

'I'm still as worried as I was about my mother being upset about me. I'll have to stop sooner or later. I'd have it on my conscience. If you do something bad, you have it on your conscience and then you tell your parents . . . [for example] that someone had smoked under age. It's disobeying the law. I'm positive there's a law. It can give you lung cancer and if I did start I'd get in the habit and I wouldn't be able to stop.'

Asked about masturbation he said, 'I don't do that much. It's not very bad to do that unless you do it in a rude sense like making a joke.' This he thought was a sin. 'Well, I think it's because of our religion. It's not the same as most people's. I would rather have it than other people's . . . You do wonder sometimes, but I wouldn't leave it. I've often threatened to in a temper to my parents but I didn't mean it. Smoking cigarettes is going against my religion. We're not like the church. You shouldn't smoke nor drink. It's O.K. to a certain extent, like wine at table, but it's very wrong in a bar. Dirty jokes are not as bad as smoking.'

This boy's obsessional neurosis arose from profound conflicts between his inner impulses for aggressive and sexual behaviour and the dictates of his over-strict conscience. The parents aroused his anger repeatedly by their preference for their daughter and their belittling attitude towards Allan. At the same time, guided by their religious principles, they reinforced his own guilt. His undistinguished school career and the restrictions on his social activities imposed by his religion deprived him of many ordinary satisfactions and outlets. A major contribution to his improvement was the parents' recognition that his isolation from other children was harmful and their greater acceptance of his friendships.

Children born in a foreign country of foreign parents face quite different problems. Both they and their parents generally strive to adapt themselves to the ways and customs of their country of adoption. They want to belong. Such adaptation is easier for children than for parents. Children, if they are young enough, soon learn the new language. They are as sensitive to minor shades of accent as they are to slight variations of social attitude and custom. In this process of adaptation their parents are left far behind and this impairs their usefulness as parents. How can they set social standards in areas of behaviour about which they themselves feel uncertain? If in the new society the dating patterns of teenagers are entirely different from those existing in their country of origin, how can parents advise their children what to do? How can they know what limits to set? Their children are left to find out for themselves. Without firm parental support they may become excessively timid and inhibited or on the other hand they may throw restraint to the winds. While children from minority religious groups have to cope with two discrepant sets of social standards simultaneously, children reared in one culture who have migrated to another country have to switch from one set of standards and aspirations to another. For them the discontinuity is in time. When the change occurs late in childhood, the individual may forever feel that a part of himself has been left behind: that part which is inappropriate in his new environment, which does not fit in. He may forever have a sense that the core of his personality is incomplete and that many of the new ways he has learnt are a disguise and not part of his true self. (Some of the problems of present-day teenagers and their parents are similar and may be related to the greater cultural differences between the generations that exist in our present, rapidly changing world.)

Children from minority cultures have extra stresses to cope with but as a rule no serious impairment of functioning results unless there are also intra-familial neurotic tensions.

Serious stresses are associated with minority group membership only when this group has in addition an inferior social status within the larger society and its members are stigmatized.

COLOURED CHILDREN IN BRITAIN

Surprisingly, there has been no systematic study of coloured children in this country. In the schools a problem is felt when there is a heavy concentration in a particular locality of non-English-speaking immigrants. This, as was pointed out in a recent review of the subject, generally leads to some action being taken by education authorities.[70] But many coloured children speak good English, and second-generation children of immigrants do not have language problems. But they do have difficulties. It has been estimated that 1.9% of all London primary school children in 1961 did not speak English. On

135

the other hand as many as 9.3 % of the London school population were immigrants, most of them coloured. Other urban centres, such as Liverpool and Cardiff also have large populations of coloured children. While we know something about the social life, housing and working conditions of adult immigrants into this country and there have been studies on race prejudice in children,[134] there is so far only one published study on psychiatric disorders in coloured children.[64] This is a comparative study of West Indian immigrant children and of white children attending a child guidance clinic. Among the West Indian in contrast to the control children, girls were as frequently referred as boys and they were also more anti-social than control girls. The group of West Indian children had experienced many more and often traumatic early separations from parent figures.

Low-status immigrant sub-cultures share many of the problems of low-status social classes. The biggest minority group of children in our society are children from lower working class families. We shall see that these children are faced with multiple handicaps, genetic, medical, psychological and social, each of which decreases the chances of success at school and in the wider world. The educational and social failure of unskilled working class children in turn provides the trigger for much aggressive and delinquent behaviour. This occurs especially at adolescence when childhood, with its ostensibly limitless potentialities, ends and the individual is forced to recognize and accept his now forever restricted adult roles.

CHILDHOOD AND SOCIAL CLASS

The socio-economic status of a family is often defined in terms of the occupation of the head of the household, income, residential area, and the education of the parents. All these are indices to customs, attitudes and beliefs, in fact to a way of life which is shared by members of a social class and which distinguishes one class from another. The most common single index used is the occupation of the father and one of the most widely applied social class groupings is that of the Registrar General's classification.[59] In this occupations are divided into: class I professional, class II managerial, class III other non-manual, clerical and skilled manual, class IV semi-skilled and class V unskilled, labourers. In 1964 a national survey of parental attitudes and circumstances related to characteristics of schools and school children was undertaken at the request of the Central Advisory Council for Education. It was found that 4% of primary school children in England came from social class I, 14% from class II, 11% from class III non-manual, 48% from class III skilled manual, 16% from class IV and 6% from class V. One per cent could not be classified.[33]

Differences in health, intelligence, attitudes and behaviour are found in people from different social classes, the differences between manual and white-collar workers being as obvious as those between skilled and unskilled manual workers.

It may be true that prejudice between social classes is decreasing, particularly among youngsters, and the wish to have class barriers disappear is certainly widespread. There is however little evidence of a decline in the disparity of attitudes and behaviour between social classes and, as we shall see, profound psychological and social processes operate to preserve these distinctions.

1. Genetic Disadvantages. Intelligence, like height, is determined in part by our genes and in part by the environment in which we grow up. Limits are set to maximum potential intelligence by hereditary factors but whether this potential will be reached depends on the environment. Under optimal environmental conditions, e.g. when equally good opportunities for education are available to all members of a society, genetic factors make the greatest contribution to individual differences in intelligence. When conditions are such that only a small, wealthy section of the community has access to education, individual differences of adult intelligence depend much more on the social environment in which the individuals were reared.

In Western society it has been estimated that heredity accounts for about 80% of the variation in intelligence between people, environmental influences for 20%.[30] Children resemble their parents in intelligence but, as in the case of height, if the intelligence of parents differs from the average intelligence of a population, then the average intelligence of the children will be nearer the population average than that of their parents. Children from dull parents will, on average, be less dull and children from intellectually superior parents less bright than their parents. Educational, occupational and social selection is responsible for maintaining differences in intelligence between the social classes in our society, assisted by assortative mating (see p. 118), which ensures that parents tend to resemble each other in intelligence and social background.

Upper class children have a higher average intelligence than lower class children and, while heredity contributes greatly to this difference, environmental factors, as we shall see, also play a major part.

There is no evidence as yet that psychological attributes other than intelligence are determined in quite the same way and social class differences in attitudes and behaviour can be accounted for most satisfactorily in environmental rather than genetic terms.

2. *Increased Birth Hazards.* Complications of pregnancy and of birth occur more commonly among mothers of low social class status. This was shown some thirty years ago by Sir Dugald Baird in Aberdeen.[8] He observed that the stillbirth rate of women who had their babies in voluntary hospitals was twice as high and the infant mortality rate three times as high as those of women delivered privately in nursing homes. The major cause of infant death was prematurity. Private patients were healthier and taller and Baird found a direct relationship between maternal height and stillbirth and infant mortality rates. The shorter the mother, the greater her chance of losing the baby. Lower class mothers are more often stunted compared with middle and upper class mothers and this is due both to poor genetic endowment and to inadequate nutrition during the mothers' childhood years.

Prematurity and birth injury can end not only in the death of the baby but in a variety of physical and mental handicaps, ranging from cerebral palsy (the condition giving rise to the 'spastic' child) and mental deficiency, to more minor disabilities such as epilepsy and specific behaviour difficulties known as the syndromes of 'minimal brain damage' (see pp. 157–9). Indeed a group of American research workers have postulated a 'continuum of reproductive casualty'.[123]

It must be remembered however that although obstetric

complications are class-linked, being more common in lower social class mothers, the absolute numbers of children with demonstrable physical or psychological defects caused by such complications are very small. Children who come to a psychiatrist with behaviour disorders have had no more difficulties at birth than children in the community.[178] Obstetric damage cannot as has been suggested explain the restless, aggressive and often antisocial behaviour that children from socially deprived homes so commonly display. Nor can it account for the intellectual deficits which also characterize this section of our childhood population.

An attempt to tease out the part played by birth injury and other physical impairments on the one hand, and by a poor social environment on the other, in causing low intelligence was made some years ago by the Aberdeen workers.[49] Their conclusion was that only in seriously defective children with a definite history of birth trauma can one be sure that mental defect is due primarily to the birth injury. Such clearly brain damaged children are found in families of all social classes. More common are children with less severe degrees of mental handicap. They come from dull, culturally deprived families and they may or may not in addition have suffered some degree of birth trauma.

C. M. Drillien in Edinburgh investigated the occurrence of both intellectual impairment and behaviour disorders in the later life of premature children.[40] She found that large premature babies (weighing $4\frac{1}{2}$ lb. or more) were not grossly handicapped compared with full-term controls matched for social background. Small prematures, however, (weighing under $4\frac{1}{2}$ lb.) were in later life significantly more backward and more disturbed than full-term babies from the same social class. The lower the birth weight, the greater the proportion of handicapped children. Of course, the number of such very premature babies who survive is small and neither prematurity nor other birth injury account for the bulk of children who in later life present with mental retardation or with behaviour problems. In Drillien's study the later behaviour disturbances of prematures were determined not only by their birth weight. The emotional and the social environment in which the children grew up played a highly significant part.

3. Impaired Physical Health. Malnutrition and severe chronic diseases, such as tuberculosis, have given way to accidents and acute infections as the most common illnesses in childhood. Accidents in general occur more often in children from over-crowded homes, and road accidents are more common in lower class children who play in the street for lack of adequate playing space.[7] Respiratory disease, especially pneumonia, and burns are known to have the highest incidence among the children of unskilled manual workers.[155]

Although the common accidents and the common infectious illnesses of childhood now respond very readily to medical treatment and usually resolve without permanent complications, each such event in the life of the child is associated with anxiety, with restriction of activities, often with pain and often too with admission to hospital. Children from the lowest socio-economic groups are more likely to be admitted to hospital for illnesses which, in another child, are treated at home. Diarrhoea, measles and whooping cough, for example, are conditions that often bring children from large, poorly housed families into a fever hospital. The illness must be very severe indeed before a middle class child is parted from his family on this account. Lower class children too, especially as toddlers, are still at times sent to 'convalesce' because their home environment is thought to hinder rapid physical recovery. This course of action is rarely recommended for the middle class child and middle class parents would protest vigorously at such a suggestion unless their child was very gravely ill. Lower class children are thus exposed to more experiences of deprivation and to more emotional stresses as a result of illness than middle class children.

4. Child Rearing and Personality in Different Sub-cultures. Child rearing practices differ in families from different social classes and these differences are reflected in the behaviour of the children who in turn develop the personality characteristics of their parents. A tradition of attitudes and behaviour is thus transmitted from one generation to the next. The link is adult personality structure, moulded and consolidated in childhood and in turn exerting its influences on the next generation.

One of the most important studies in this field is an American survey of the child-rearing methods of almost 400 mothers and of the nursery school behaviour of their five-year-old children.[150]

Working class mothers were generally found to be more indulgent during infancy, offering bottle and dummy more freely than middle class parents. By the time their children were five years old, however, these working class mothers were less openly demonstrative of affection, more often overtly rejecting and stricter about sexual behaviour, table manners and orderliness than middle class mothers. Their children were observed to be more dependent on adults than middle class children. While working class mothers tolerated aggression in their offspring, they also tended to use physical punishment readily. Working class mothers in fact used concrete rewards and punishments; middle class parents used withdrawal of love as a training method. Working class children were the more aggressive; middle class children developed a 'confession' type of reaction to naughty behaviour. An English study of mothers and their infants confirmed some of these findings.[118, 119]

Even in their first year of life infants of unskilled working class mothers experience more physical punishment than middle class babies, and even in their first year these infants themselves are more aggressive: they have more temper tantrums.

Some of the patterns of child-rearing are clearly determined by the material conditions under which families have to live. When one baby is born after another in rapid succession, the toddler is forced to be independent and socially competent earlier than if he remained the youngest child in the home for longer. When space is limited parents have to remind their children to 'sit still'. When families are crowded, bathroom facilities inadequate and there is little individual privacy by day or night, modesty and inhibition of sexual display must be insisted upon. But much parental behaviour is not situationally determined nor is it adopted by choice. It is an expression of permanent personality attributes formed by the constraints imposed on the developing personality in early childhood.

The outcome of a typical pattern of child rearing in a lower working class home is a child who tends to be dependent on others, who is physically aggressive in identification with his parents, who needs to have immediate tangible rewards, who responds to punishment but is not particularly plagued by the pangs of conscience and who tends not to plan ahead. It is not, I think, too fanciful to suggest that such personality characteristics ideally equip people to tolerate in later life the working conditions imposed on large sections of manual workers in our society: lack of privacy, complete dependence on employers and the state, short-term payment and little long-term security.

British sociologists like Young and Willmott[183] and Peter Townsend[165] have demonstrated another aspect of the persistence of dependency into adult life. In working class families the dominant figure throughout a daughter's life is her mother. Middle class families in contrast move away more readily from their parents, their most important adult ties being with their marriage partners and their friends.

Enough has been said, I think, to indicate that children from different social sub-cultures show differences not only in dress and accent, but also in behaviour, and that some of the obstacles both to communication and to free movement between social classes consist in personality characteristics determined by child-rearing practices. To establish oneself as an adult in a new social group requires not only a break with the past but the shedding of an integral part of one's personality. 5. *Lack of Cultural Stimulation.* Failure at school for whatever reason is one of the major stresses in childhood which can set the stage for lifelong feelings of inferiority (see Chapter 1). The experience of school failure is particularly damaging for the developing child because it often lasts throughout the whole of his school career. The psychological defences he must use to cope with the chronic anxieties aroused by this situation only add to his difficulties. Most commonly the child who fails appears not to care at all about his shortcomings. His teachers find him poorly motivated, disinterested in his work, restless and distractible, and some children become aggressive and delinquent. His coping mechanisms serve only to make his position in the classroom even more untenable.

In children from lower working class homes the dice are loaded against their making a success of their school careers.

One of the major factors responsible for this is the cultural environment of the home and the neighbourhood, which begins to have its effect long before the child starts school.

We saw in an earlier chapter (pp. 17–18) that full development of one fundamental aspect of intelligence, language, depends on adequate stimulation in early childhood. Language development is retarded in lower working class children and the poverty of language of such children is a major cause of poor achievement at school. Without a rich vocabulary, concept formation is impaired and the tools necessary for reasoning are lacking. Bernstein has demonstrated clear differences in the traditional use of language between people belonging to different social classes.[16] This is not really surprising.

In culturally impoverished homes there is little space, there is little by way of play material and there are few books. Parents are too preoccupied with their own troubles to interest themselves in their children's achievements. The children play out of doors most of the time and parental concern focuses on their health and usually on their happiness but rarely on their development and abilities. Parents and children do less together and they communicate less often and less proficiently with each other verbally. Fathers tend to leave educational matters to their wives and often play no part even in the choice of the child's school. When children from such homes arrive at school they often prove 'disappointing' to their teachers and consequently to themselves and their performance over the years declines. Research done for the Plowden Committee on primary school education showed that a child's performance at school is even more closely related to his parents' attitudes to education than to the material circumstances of his home.[33]

But attitudes and circumstances are closely linked and Douglas's survey of child health and development provides much concrete evidence for the relationship between poor social background and school failure.[38] He found, for example, that children of unemployed fathers performed less well academically both at eight and eleven years of age than children from similar, unskilled working class homes whose fathers had regular work. At the time of the study prolonged unemployment was rare and when it occurred, it was generally due to illness and not to low intelligence. Children of unemployed fathers were therefore unlikely to be genetically predisposed to poor intelligence. What did distinguish these children was that they lived in the most unsuitable and overcrowded homes and had little contact with their mothers who worked long hours. Douglas had found earlier that within each social class, poor housing and overcrowding were associated with low test performance. Children of unemployed fathers were often described as 'lazy' and inattentive by their teachers, who also thought that their mothers took little interest in their school progress. We shall see later that negative evaluation of the child by the teacher makes its own contribution to school failure.

Culturally deprived children experience actual family disruption more commonly than others. When such children are burdened with the anxieties of separation from parents and have to live in the often not only culturally but socially depriving environment of a children's home, their chances of success at school are even more remote. (It was shown in a recent study that three quarters of the children in a large children's home came from families belonging to social classes IV and V, which together constituted only just over one quarter of the general population.[57]) While such children have often achieved high levels of self-care and of practical and social competence (they have had to look after themselves from an early age and, compared with non-deprived children, they are better at dressing themselves, at knowing how to undertake household tasks, at shopping and at caring for themselves physically), their verbal skills are much worse.[88] Such children do not respond eagerly to classroom instruction as do less anxious children from culturally superior backgrounds. Their teacher's disappointment, reflected back to the children, in turn robs them of whatever motivation for schoolwork they may have had, and constitutes a further obstacle to learning and yet another blow to their self-esteem.

6. Educational and Social Processes Discriminate Against the Culturally Deprived Child. Educational and social processes favour the development of socially privileged children but operate against the child already handicapped. Douglas[38] found that primary schools with the best records of grammar school awards tend to attract middle class children whose parents are interested in their schooling. These children improve in performance as they get older. At such primary schools even children from disinterested families improve on their performance. Good teaching can, he suggested, compensate for lack of parental interest. In primary schools with poor records for grammar school awards, children do not improve in their performance in this way. The Plowden Report[32] makes it clear that schools in socially deprived areas are inferior in a number of ways to schools in the country as a whole. Their buildings are old and badly designed, they do not attract and cannot keep good teaching staff; and their pupil turnover is also high, the more intelligent children tending to move out of the district.

The very children for whom, in the view of the Plowden Committee, the school should provide a 'compensatory' environment are at present accommodated in inferior schools. Quite apart from the actual quality of the schools, social processes also discriminate against children from unskilled working class homes. Such children already function less well academically but in addition they are given poorer educational opportunities. Douglas found that the chances of lower manual working class children being offered a place in a grammar school were less than those of middle class children, when the level of measured ability at the time of the selection examination was held constant. Not only measured ability, but social class factors determine the selection of children for grammar school places. Teachers evaluate middle class children more positively than working class children and this encourages achievement in the socially more privileged child. The bias of teachers against manual working class children has effects similar to those resulting from the bias of women teachers against boys (see p. 37). Motivation for learning and attitudes to school work decline. One common reason may be the teacher's difficulty to understand and identify with the child's attitudes and behaviour if these are different from her own.

In his most recent book[39] Douglas shows that the social class differences in educational opportunity had increased by the time the children had reached the secondary school stage and then extended even to pupils of high levels of ability. For example, nearly half the lower manual working class pupils of high ability had left school before the age of sixteen and a half years, compared with only 10% of upper middle class pupils. Many manual working class children with the ability to benefit from education beyond the statutory school leaving age are failing to do so.

Communication between parents and teachers decreases down the social scale. It is not surprising that a manual working class mother, ruefully remembering her own school failures, needs more courage to approach her child's teacher than an academically successful wife of a professional man. Besides teacher and mother share much less common ground in the first case: their personality characteristics, their attitudes and their expectations are different. Yet the child has a better chance of educational success when his parents pay regular visits to the school and understand and identify with its aims and methods.

Emotional disturbance is frequently caused by academic failure. On the other hand it may itself contribute to a child's lack of success at school. Maladjusted children as a group perform less well academically than children who are symptom-free, and disturbed classroom behaviour, especially restlessness, distractibility, resistance to discipline and anti-social conduct, occur more often in children who are failing educationally. Such behaviour tends to evoke negative responses from teachers so that the motivation of disturbed children is likely to drop even further and the chances of academic success become ever more remote.

In summary we can say that children from socially deprived homes are handicapped in a number of ways. Genetic factors determine that their potential intelligence is on an average somewhat less than that of socially more privileged children. The disparity between the children's attitudes towards education and differences in the extent to which they avail themselves of educational opportunities increase as they grow older, as a result of cultural differences in home background and biased evaluation from teachers at school. Communication between middle class teachers and manual working class mothers is poor, one of the obstacles being class differences in personality resulting from differing experiences of child-rearing. The personality characteristics of children reared by the more punitive lower working class parents are such that they tend to react to the frustrations of educational failure with aggressive, antisocial behaviour and this in turn earns them further disapproval from their teachers. School life for such children is frustrating and engenders feelings of apathy in relation to work and achievement. Family disruption, parental death, illnesses and accidents befalling the child himself, and (more rarely) specific intellectual and behavioural impairments due to birth injury and prematurity, contribute to the stresses and handicaps of socially deprived children. It is from this pool of socially and educationally limited and discouraged children that our delinquent teenagers mainly come.

What part the technological revolution has played in sharpening the effects of the processes outlined it is impossible to say. Certainly today status is more than ever before related to intellectual ability and to acquired skills. Those who lack such capacities suffer in self-esteem. They cannot identify with an adult culture from which they see themselves excluded. Instead they create their own adolescent world. Moreover, the patterns of social behaviour appear to be changing more rapidly now than ever before and continuity between the generations is correspondingly reduced. The restraints on adolescent behaviour that arise from identification with adult standards are weakened because these standards are no longer seen as adequate in our changing world.

In this dilemma we look, perhaps over-optimistically, to our educational system in the hope that changes in school organization and teaching techniques can halt the process by which increasing numbers of our children are excluded from the mainstream of society.

9. *Constitutional Disorders and Mental Illness in Childhood*

The emphasis in this book so far has been on those common emotional disturbances in childhood that are brought about by adverse circumstances. It is a mistake, however, to think that *all* difficulties of children must be due to environmental defects or pressures. This view is still often expressed, disturbed family relationships in particular being blamed for all psychological disorders in childhood.

A withdrawn and eccentric thirteen-year-old had been a great problem to his parents for years because he was unhappy, awkward in his dealings with other people and had inexplicable outbursts of rage. His father felt the boy resembled him. The mother found it difficult to make him out at all. She was bewildered and guilty. The remark she heard that 'there are no disturbed children; there are only disturbed parents' caused her to re-examine her own attitudes and behaviour repeatedly. The more guilty she felt, the less she was able to tolerate her son's peculiarities and to make allowances for him. It was a great relief to her when his difficulties were diagnosed as a mild constitutional deviance of personality. Once she could view the child's problems as arising from within himself and not as the result of some hidden defect in her own capacity to be a good mother, she was able to accept and even to understand him better and as a consequence of her relief the pressures on him too were reduced.

Some constitutional psychological disorders affect children in the same sort of way as physical impairments. The child becomes aware of his failure in certain areas of functioning. He may be clumsy or distractible; he may be generally retarded or have a specific learning defect. More often than not, he does not know why he fails. He comes to feel different, inferior compared with other children and he responds to his sense of failure with disturbed behaviour. Such psychological handicaps, like physical handicaps, act as environmental stresses.

A second group of constitutional disorders affect behaviour not indirectly by adding to the child's stresses but directly through disorganization of brain function.

A psychiatric examination must discover any existing constitutional defect or organic illness and determine, if possible, precisely how this impairs the child's functioning and how it is related to his behaviour disorders. It is not enough to focus only on the symbolic meaning and psychological causes of symptoms.

CONSTITUTIONAL DISORDERS THAT ACT AS
ENVIRONMENTAL STRESSES

1. *Physical Handicap*

Jane was seven when she stole a pound note from her mother's bag and also money belonging to her teacher. With the money she bought sweets for the children in her class. Jane had been a premature baby, weighing just over two pounds at birth. It was not until the age of 4 months that her mother was allowed to take her home from the maternity hospital. Meanwhile, after ten years of marriage, the father left the family because of an extra-marital affair. A few weeks after coming home Jane developed pneumonia and was re-admitted to hospital. She did not finally return to her mother until she was six months old. Her development was generally slow. At the age of three, she was found to be mildly deaf, but with the help of a hearing aid and speech therapy she learnt to communicate quite well with others. On starting school at five, however, it became obvious that in addition to her deafness she was also intellectually backward. She herself now noticed that she was not as clever as other children and she began to be very self-conscious about her hearing aid: 'The doctor said I can wear my hair long. See, if I wear long hair . . . to let no one see what I got in my ear.' For the first time too she became painfully aware of her anomalous family situation. What finally precipitated her symptom was her sister Mary's remark that the father had really preferred her, the older child. Jane said, 'I haven't got a daddy. I had one in Birmingham. It was my daddy. He likes my Mary best. He doesn't like me.' The mother explained the older girl's remark in terms of her jealousy of Jane who, because she was handicapped, received more obvious affection and protection from the mother. The stealing did not recur. This child was fortunate in that the acceptance, understanding and affection she got from her mother and her teacher helped her to compensate for her multiple handicaps, physical, intellectual and social.

Once a handicap is recognized allowances are generally made for a child's failures. This happened in Jane's case. Unrecognized, *masked handicaps* are the greater psychological hazard. Deafness is one physical defect that may go undetected; mild cerebral palsy leading, for example, to clumsiness is another. Petit mal, an unspectacular form of epilepsy, manifesting solely as momentary lapses of consciousness, is a third.

Recognized defects may result in stresses for children when they arouse unconscious guilt feelings in the parents. Such parents see the handicap as an accusation against themselves and are unable to accept it. They may become over-protective or rejecting towards their handicapped child, whose emotional problems are then more a response to neurotic parental attitudes than to his own physical or intellectual impairment.

2. Intellectual Handicap

The following case-history illustrates that intellectual defect can be very stressful when parents have difficulty in recognizing and coming to terms with it. Parents of normal-looking children often have more difficulty in identifying their child's handicap and explaining it to others, than parents of manifestly defective children, such as mongols.

Elizabeth was nearly twelve when her parents asked for advice about schooling. She was a tall, good-looking girl, one of twins. Her twin sister and an older boy were both normal, healthy children. The parents first realized that Elizabeth might be backward when at the age of four she threw a ten shilling note on the fire, and did not apparently understand the significance of what she had done. At school she made poor progress and at the age of eight the parents were advised to send her to a special school for educationally sub-normal children. This they refused to do because of the stigma which they thought attached to mental handicap and because they feared that at the special school Elizabeth 'would not be mixing with such nice people'. They saw her losing the middle class standards they themselves cultivated so carefully and they envisaged for her a social decline and a future of delinquency. Both parents felt greatly threatened by their daughter and they reacted with rejection not only of her handicap, but of the child herself. The backwardness they said was of secondary importance; what really worried them was that Elizabeth was 'obdurate and inaccessible to reason'. They blinded themselves to her unhappiness, pointing out only the trouble she caused. At school and in the neighbourhood girls her own age refused to play with her once they realized that she could not follow their interests, and her only friends were five- and six-year-olds. The parents disapproved of these associations because they felt it was odd to see a handsome, well-developed twelve-year-old play with such small children. When they tried to keep Elizabeth indoors, however, her strident screams resounded in the neighbourhood.

She had spent seven years at the bottom of an ordinary primary school class, with some additional help in a remedial group. Although her reading and writing were at a nine-year-old level, her general intelligence was that only of a child of six. Often, especially when the class was about to have a test, she would run away from school and wander the streets. Often too she developed stomach-ache and missed school on this account.

Only when it was inescapably clear that Elizabeth would not manage the transition to an ordinary secondary school did the parents agree reluctantly to let her attend a school for educationally sub-normal children. At once the child became happier and made friends. For the first time in her life she found she could do some things better than other children. At home the mother found it no easier to tolerate her immaturity. When she lost her beret, allowed a four-year-old to break her watch or lost her season ticket on the bus, the mother could not contain her irritation. The tantrums at home continued and the parents finally suggested it would be better for Elizabeth to be away from home in some institution where she could be 'trained'. In view of her good progress at the special school the education authorities at first resisted such a plan. But after some months the stresses at home became too much for the child. She began to steal both from her family and from school: she was beginning to fulfil her parents' prophesy.

Many thousands of mentally subnormal children are helped by their parents to tolerate their handicap without too great a loss of social self-assurance. Special education in small classes of children with similar intellectual levels enables retarded children to develop their abilities and at the same time maintain their self-esteem. But we must face the fact that for some parents to have a backward child is so great a blow to their own feelings of self-worth that they find themselves unable to accept the help that is available. Special efforts are then needed to focus on the parents' problems and to understand their individual difficulties in relation to their child.

The earlier in the child's life that parents who need such special help in order to cope rationally with their handicapped child are identified, the more likely it is that they can be helped to change their attitudes. Once parents are middle-aged and the child an adolescent the task of modifying parental attitudes to the child and the child's own view of himself and his future becomes very difficult indeed.

3. Exceptionally High Intelligence – Not a Disorder but a Potential Stress

High intelligence is a source of delight to most parents. It also helps some children to weather a disrupted and deprived childhood which would have been catastrophic to a less well-endowed child. But exceptionally high intelligence also has its hazards and these are of two kinds. The first springs from discrepancies between the child's intellectual development and his physical and emotional maturity. Very bright children are highly observant. They learn to read early; their intelligence exposes them to a wealth of information from which other children are shielded; and they struggle early with questions of morality and matters of life and death. Often they are bewildered by the many concepts and ideas they have to master and, especially between the ages of three and seven, they frequently suffer from multiple anxieties. The danger is that adults may fail to recognize that these seemingly precocious children need at least as much protection and mothering as the average child of this age.

The second hazard springs from the fact that exceptional intelligence, by definition, is rare, so that the intellectually superior child is often a lonely child and an ordinary school or even an ordinary family may fail to cater for his special needs. Such children are generally precocious readers but their handwriting is no better than anyone else's. Their ideas come so fast that to set them down in their slow, childish script is tedious and frustrating. Teachers are sometimes unaware of having an exceptional child in their classroom because his written products are so poor. The repetitive exercises he is asked to do to improve his performance and the lack of recognition of his gifts add to his boredom and frustration in the classroom and the result is that motivation drops and work habits decline precipitously. It is a tragic paradox that some exceptionally gifted children arrive at psychiatric clinics because of educational failure and secondary emotional disturbances, often after years of misery and tedium at school.

Unless efforts are made to recognize exceptional children and to make special provisions for them at school, abilities may be lost, not only as we saw in the last chapter, among the duller and culturally impoverished children in our midst but also among the most able and promising.

In general, highly intelligent children also have intelligent parents who can to some extent make up for deficiencies at school by providing a stimulating and interesting environment for their child at home. The risk is greater for the exceptional child of average parents.

The authority on the later development and needs of gifted children is the Californian psychologist L. M. Terman.[160] His researches show that on balance it is preferable for the gifted child to be accelerated in his progress from class to class in an ordinary school than to be retained with his own age group, although he may be socially at a disadvantage with older and bigger children. An alternative and better solution for the exceptional child is to retain him in the class appropriate for his age but to provide him with an enriched curriculum. For part of the day he should engage in activities that really stretch his abilities and allow him to work at his own level, while avoiding the repetitive exercises necessary for his classmates. The third alternative, special schools for the exceptionally gifted, is feasible only in large urban communities and may not be the ideal solution.[23]

4. Specific Language Defects
Some children, although of normal general intelligence, suffer

from a developmental lag affecting a single function. Such selective impairment of development is found especially in the area of language. While considerable variations exist in the rates at which children learn to speak, some are conspicuously slow in acquiring clear speech. They continue to mispronounce consonants and retain babyish patterns of language when their motor skills and social behaviour are already quite mature. Often mispronunciation is accompanied by a general delay in talking. The child is late in acquiring his first words; he may be well over three before his speech is really fluent while he may not consistently be able to pronounce 'th', 's' and 'v' until he is seven or eight years old. Such *minor degrees of immaturity of speech* are common. The danger is that impatient parents will try to teach their children to 'speak properly', demanding conscious effort to acquire a skill that is normally learnt without any particular exertions. Children's eagerness to communicate usually outstrips their mastery of language and certainly provides enough incentive for learning to speak. When clever children are slow to acquire intelligible speech they experience frustration. If to this is added parental disapproval, learning is made still more difficult; the child may be driven to defensive manoeuvres to cope with his anxiety.

Serious developmental language defects are rare, but when they occur they require accurate diagnosis and treatment. Children often react to the frustrations imposed by such handicaps with behaviour disorders and these may obscure the clinical picture. Ingram provides evidence that mild as well as serious language lags together with certain difficulties in reading and writing all form part of the same clinical syndrome which is more common in boys than in girls and tends to be associated with ambidexterity, affected children failing to develop early a clear-cut preference for using the right or left hand and foot. In one third of Ingram's cases there was a family history of retarded language development.[78]

Despite the links between the developmental speech disorders, each manifests quite differently. We have already mentioned the minor disturbances consisting of mild delays in the onset of speech or of persisting defects of pronunciation.

Among the rarer serious defects the most worrying is *developmental dysphasia*. Here the onset of speech is grossly delayed and for the first three or four years of his life the child is mute. Yet he is not intellectually retarded; he learns to do everything appropriate for his age except speak; he is normally responsive emotionally; and he is not deaf. Very often only expressive speech is affected, the child understanding perfectly what is said to him. He learns to use gestures to communicate with his family and his frustrations usually begin only outside his home. There he finds that he cannot make himself understood by other children and that they react to him as if he were backward. Sometimes in addition to his inability to use the spoken word there are difficulties in comprehension so that the child responds to noise but is unable to understand the meaning of words. The name *word deafness* is sometimes given to this disability. A serious language defect is an obstacle to all human interaction and to all learning. Dysphasic children tend naturally to improve with age but it is important that they are diagnosed and treated early in the hope that their language development can be hastened sufficiently to allow them to start school at the normal time.

Gross speech defects are so obvious that they are rarely missed. Specific language impairments affecting not the spoken but the written word, however, often remain unrecognized.

Backwardness in reading and writing is very common indeed, even in children of normal intelligence. Most backward readers and writers are to be found among the culturally deprived children we discussed in the last chapter. Lack of stimulation and encouragement at home, poor teaching and high levels of anxiety from whatever cause make for inadequate scholastic performance in essentially normal children. But there are some children, probably not very many, in whom none of the above causes operate and who nevertheless make poor progress in reading and writing. *Dyslexia* (formerly 'word blindness') is the name given to a particular kind of reading disability. Affected children cannot easily remember written words, sometimes they can read aloud but not silently, sometimes they can recognize letters but are 'blind' for whole words and sometimes they cannot even recognize letters, tending to confuse one letter with its mirror image. They may also have difficulty in recognizing and reproducing shapes and patterns. *Dysgraphia* is the name given to a similar and often associated difficulty with writing. Here letters are poorly formed and the confusions between, for example, 'd' and 'b' or 'p' and 'q' that occur in all beginners persist for years.

Unless children with specific handicaps in reading and writing are identified, their teachers, their parents and they themselves may attribute their difficulties to 'laziness'. Children so labelled become discouraged and their motivation for learning drops. Reading and writing are basic for all later school subjects so that the child who has not mastered these skills in time is seriously handicapped. Children with specific dyslexia or dysgraphia need special help but, even more than this, they need to have their handicap recognized in order to preserve their self-esteem and their eagerness to learn. To describe a child as 'lazy' is usually quite inaccurate and always harmful. Teachers and parents resort to 'laziness' as an explanation for school failure when an unrewarding struggle to teach has become too much for them. They are in effect saying it is now up to the child and that they have given him up. Education has come to a stop. Most often the cause lies in a failure to make an accurate diagnosis of the child's difficulties.

Rather different from the developmental language defects just described is *stammering*. This abnormality of the rhythm of speech is not due to a developmental lag. Although common as a transient phenomenon in the pre-school years, established stammering (or stuttering as it is also called) increases in frequency up to the middle school years and then declines again.

A series of studies done in Newcastle[3] showed that about four per cent of children have an episode of stammering at some time in their lives. About a quarter of affected children have a transient, developmental stammer between the ages of two and four. Almost one half have a benign stammer lasting only about two years. Less than a quarter develop a stammer that persists for over five years. A hereditary tendency to stammer has been shown many times. Given this predisposition there are at least two types of stammerers. In one, the speech defect is associated with intellectual dullness, poor social circumstances and perhaps birth injury; in the other, with high intelligence, upward social mobility and a perfectionistic and over-anxious mother. Stammerers of this second type were the subjects of the best known controlled investigation of this problem.

Wendell Johnson[83] compared a group of stammering children, mainly of university parents anxious enough to ask for treatment of their child, with a control group of non-stammerers. He found that parents of both groups reported frequent hesitancies of speech when their children were three years old. Parents of stammerers however were less easily satisfied with their own and their children's achievements and they tended, more than other parents, to correct and comment on their children's speech hesitancies and to label these stammering. Johnson suggests that in his particular group of subjects the onset of stammering took place not in the child's mouth but in the parents' ear and that, like the centipede immobilized by being asked which foot comes after which, children made aware of speech hesitancies find it harder to maintain their verbal fluency.

Stammering is not in itself a symptom of psychiatric disorder and it occurs no more commonly in children referred to a psychiatrist than in non-referred children.[177] It is common in childhood but rare in later life and when it persists it can become the focus of considerable emotional disturbance which then requires treatment in its own right.

CONSTITUTIONAL DISORDERS THAT AFFECT
BEHAVIOUR DIRECTLY

1. *The Syndromes of Brain Damage*

Many diseases and injuries of the brain result in neurological impairments such as loss of sensation over a particular area of the body, weakness of a limb, blindness or loss of speech, without altering behaviour or personality in any way. Some lesions of the brain have an effect on both bodily functions and on behaviour. Yet other illness and injuries known to have damaged the brain leave behind no neurological impairments but are associated with marked changes in behaviour. The size of the lesion bears no relationship to the degree of behavioural change. Nor are there in children special areas of the brain where damage is more likely to result in behaviour difficulties. All we can say is that children known to have been exposed to an illness or injury affecting the brain sometimes show specific disturbances of behaviour and that children with such behaviour often have a history of brain damage, for example a difficult delivery or an attack of meningitis or encephalitis in early childhood. In some cases the only concrete evidence for malfunctioning of the brain is epilepsy, in others an electroencephalogram will show changes in the electrical recordings from the brain. In yet other cases behaviour typical of a 'brain damage' syndrome is found without any other evidence for an organic lesion.

In the most common syndrome of brain damage, known as '*hyperkinesis*', motor restlessness and distractibility outweigh all other symptoms.[77, 120] Affected children usually come forward for treatment at the age of three or four when their overactivity and failure to acquire impulse control can no longer be explained as due to their age alone. Hyperkinetic children characteristically are never still. They are on the move all the time and they cannot pursue a single aim for long. They are abnormally responsive to all incoming stimuli and unable to select and focus their attention on any particular one. Every object in the room calls for exploration but as soon as the child has picked up one thing, he is already diverted by the next. Learning is grossly impaired and this affects not only formal learning at school but the acquisition of social skills and standards.

Disturbances of attention and concentration can occur without marked over-activity. In such cases parents are usually most troubled by their child's failure of social learning. The change from impulsive anal stage behaviour to the control that goes with conscience formation is delayed and the child appears not to take in parental strictures and demands. He has no sense of danger, wandering out of the house for example and into the street with no thought for his own safety. He continues to climb dangerously despite repeated warnings and he remains inaccessible to reason and unaware of the consequences of his own actions. In school such a child too has great difficulties in learning and his school work is usually far below his capacity.

The behaviour disturbances of 'minimal brain dramage' can

occur with or without general mental retardation. Often, even in normally intelligent children they are associated with mild impairments of motor skills and of visual coordination, some children being noticeably clumsy. On intelligence tests such children do much better on verbal items than on tests requiring visual and motor skills. They often function better in a quiet environment so that, while disorganized in a big and noisy classroom, they may manage quite well when taught in a small group. They respond very well to drugs such as tranquillizers and often excitatory drugs such as amphetamines have a paradoxical, calming effect. Pheno-barbitone usually makes matters worse. In any case the tendency is towards improvement with age.

Some years ago Leon Eisenberg drew attention to the common but false assumption that behavioural changes associated with brain damage must be fixed and immutable while those reactive to environmental pressures are essentially modifiable.[44] It may in some cases be very difficult to induce changes in the environmental pressures on a child. On the other hand, children with a clinical syndrome of brain damage generally improve with age especially if the demands made on them are modified to fit in with their particular difficulties and they are given appropriate drug treatment.

Not all behaviour disorders of brain damaged children are directly caused by their organic lesion. Secondary, reactive disorders, for example stealing or soiling, often occur as a result of the child's social and educational failures for which, unless his condition is correctly diagnosed, he is given the blame. Among schoolchildren with organic brain dysfunction psychiatric disorders are five times as common as in the general child population.[65]

One aim of early diagnosis is to make parents, teachers and the child himself aware of the inherent difficulties he has; only then can parents offer the kind of support and patient social teaching the child requires and teachers structure the child's classroom activities to suit his particular needs. Undiagnosed, a brain damaged child not only suffers from his handicap. He suffers even more from his sense of hopelessness and loss of self-esteem which results from the irritation, exasperation and disapproval that his behaviour repeatedly evokes from others.

2. Schizoid Personality

Constitutional but normal variations of temperament, such as great drive and energy or on the other hand sensitivity and quiet thoughtfulness can make adjustment for some children hazardous if their parents, for reasons of their own, are unable to accept these qualities in their child. Thomas, Birch and Chess, and their co-workers, showed that behaviour disorders are most common in children who are intense in their responses, predominantly negative in mood, irregular in their biological patterns of sleep and elimination and slow to adapt to changing circumstances.[161, 140] All these characteristics of temperament are normal in the sense that they occur often and do not by any means always lead to trouble. Difficulties arise only when the child's qualities of temperament conflict with his parents' expectations of how he ought to be.

There is one constitutional variation of personality, however, that although not amounting to illness (in the sense of there being definite symptoms and a clear-cut onset and course to the difficulties) and not due to recognizable brain damage, is so stereotyped and so often associated with trouble that affected children must be regarded as deviant. This condition is often called schizoid personality disorder. Sometimes affected children are called '*borderline*',[170] meaning that without being mentally ill, they have some features in common with children suffering from a true mental illness or psychosis. Moreover the previous personality of adult patients with schizophrenia is often of this type.

Among over two hundred children referred to the psychiatric department of the Royal Hospital for Sick Children in Edinburgh about five per cent had this kind of personality disorder. Of the twelve children studied eleven were boys and almost all had been referred to hospital because of difficulties at school. Some were clever children who were failing in their school work and all had troubles in their relationships with other children and with teachers. In fact difficulty in making contact with other people was their main disability. All children were socially withdrawn and preoccupied with their own pursuits. Some were very shy and quiet (two refused altogether to talk in school) and some talked freely about their often idiosyncratic ideas. Several children showed an interest in and a knowledge of politics quite beyond their years, others were experts in electronics. The children themselves felt different from other people.

As one boy put it during his first interview: 'I'm an odd person, different from most people. I have different tastes. I like being by myself. It's my nature. I'm more fond of things than people. I see a lot of people with each other and I can't fit in. They have interests like fishing and pop records and I'm a square. I don't mind it; it's other people who object. They're nasty to me and I have to put up with it. I don't like fighting back much; I'm not a destructive type of person.' This boy had made a number of radio and television sets and kept lists of all suppliers of electronic equipment in Edinburgh. He corresponded with many of them. He also excelled in mathematics at school. In all other subjects he was at the bottom of his class. At the age of five he invented an island peopled by peculiar inhabitants. He found that his stories about the island entertained other children. At the age of thirteen he was still preoccupied with this 'dreamed-up island, square and on wheels, on the ocean bed' but found that he now had to keep these fantasies to himself because other boys, if they knew, laughed at him.

These children are often very rigid in some areas of behaviour, insisting on getting their way and refusing to conform to ordinary social demands. If they are thwarted they have temper outbursts. Such disruptive outbursts were the cause of psychiatric referral in some children, parents and teachers finding themselves quite unable to understand what had upset the child in the first place, or why a refusal of some apparently trivial wish had aroused so much feeling.

Those children who were not withdrawn but communicated easily used metaphor freely and rather concretely, making the kinds of associations between ideas that normally occur in dreams.

One boy when asked whether he felt that as a result of his interviews he was 'getting somewhere' said quite seriously 'I like travelling.'

Another, asked how he felt about being an only child said, 'I don't know any different.' He was drawing two dinosaurs at the time. To the comment that even a dinosaur had a mate, he replied, 'It's not a mate, but a sworn enemy. Would you like it if a certain animal wanted you for food?' This boy just before a move of house and school said, 'People tell you you have to make friends, and then when you do, you have to move and they want to get rid of you.'

Another said, 'I prefer animals to human beings, they don't pick fights with you unless you bother them.'

The parents of all the children had noticed personality difficulties since the pre-school years. Often they were puzzled by their children. They described them as remote, lacking in feeling, solitary. One mother said, 'He never lets his feelings go although he looks as if he'd like to'; another, 'He finds it difficult to show affection; questions only result in a closing up'; and a third, 'There's a strangeness about him.'

In almost all families a parent or a grandparent appeared to have the same kind of personality disturbance.

One father said of his son, 'He demonstrates a number of things which are personality characteristics of my own, I'm afraid' and he went on to describe how a minor professional disagreement with a colleague led him to give up a remunerative occupation in order to devote five years to a research project designed to prove his point. This he was able to achieve. Of his son he said, 'His approach has been to bang his head against a brick wall. I've a sympathy for him, but his mother says she can't understand him.'

One mother likened her son to her father whom she described as 'brilliant, but odd and impossible to live with. He couldn't make contact with other people and preferred to live alone.'

None of the nine parents diagnosed as being themselves schizoid had in fact been psychiatrically ill, except that one mother had had a brief delusional experience following childbirth. One father was often unemployed because he vaguely felt other people to be against him and his enthusiastic propaganda for the Communist Party of Great Britain in fact antagonized his work-mates. Judging by the fate of their parents, the chances of the children themselves becoming mentally ill in later life seem small. However, their difficulties during the school years are formidable, because this is the time in which the demands for gregariousness and social conformity are higher than they were in early childhood and higher than they are ever likely to be in later life. Once more the primary need is for children with a schizoid personality disorder to be recognized. When a child's difficulties are not understood they act as a threat and as a challenge to parents and teachers. Adults feel incompetent in the face of such children and they often react by increasing the pressures on the child. Once the diagnosis has been established parents and teachers find it easier to decrease their demands for conformity, to educate the child by building on his particular interest and aptitudes and to insist on the essential requirements of social behaviour with less hostility.

3. Childhood Psychosis: Autism

For practical purposes it is true to say that only one major mental illness or psychosis occurs in young children. This is the illness that used to be called childhood schizophrenia but is more correctly referred to as childhood autism after the label 'Early Infantile Autism' used by the child psychiatrist, Leo Kanner, who first described the condition in detail.

The illness begins in the first three years of life and one can do no better for a start than to quote Kanner's own description of its characteristics.[85] He mentions five. Firstly, and this is a universal feature of the condition, there is 'the children's inability to relate themselves in the ordinary way to people and to situations', a phenomenon he also calls 'an extreme autistic aloneness'. ('The word autism stands for 'self-incapsulation in an isolated world',[80] for 'being turned in on oneself and one's own fantasies with no regard for outer reality'.[81]) Secondly there is failure to use language for the purpose of communication, some children having no speech at all, others using language in an abnormal way. The main feature of the autistic child's utterances is parrot-like repetition of what has just been said or of stored up phrases. The third feature described by Kanner is 'an anxiously obsessive desire for the maintenance of sameness', limiting the variety of spontaneous activity and leading to attacks of rage or panic when external conditions conflict with the child's demands. Fourthly, Kanner mentions the child's fascination for objects and his high level of skill at fine motor movements and lastly he stresses that there are good cognitive potentialities at least in some areas of functioning which distinguish the condition from mental defect.

Subsequent studies of the behaviour of autistic children
have drawn attention to their repetitive motor behaviour,
flapping movements of arms and hands, especially when ex-
cited, and rapid fine finger movements often in front of the
child's eyes as well as jumping and repetitive manipulation of
small objects, string, pebbles, little threads, being characteristic.

In a study of fourteen autistic children attending a special
school in New York, Wolff and Chess[180] found that the severity
of the illness is very variable indeed. Some children were
mute, almost totally withdrawn and spent their day aimlessly
jumping and running about, often masturbating. Others,
although impaired in their social contact with other people
and in their language, did participate in some normal play
with other children, learnt to read and write and managed
many ordinary activities appropriate to their age. The most
reliable sign of autism was found to be the child's failure to
look other people in the eyes. He either avoids visual contact
with others altogether or else he stares at people, looking
through them rather than at them. The other universal
feature, and one that was thought to underlie many of the
behavioural abnormalities of autistic children, was the stereotyped repetition of patterns of behaviour that really belonged
to a much earlier stage of development (e.g. the repetitive
manipulation of and staring at small objects, which resemble
the repetitive explorations described by Piaget in the first two
years of life) or that had been appropriate in a previous social
context. Such remnants of previous activity appeared over and
over again in a child whose general behaviour often indicated
quite a high level of maturity and an accurate appreciation of
his present social setting. This repetition of past patterns
seriously interfered with current behaviour and seemed to be
the basis for obsessional insistence on certain environmental
conditions. One little boy refused all honey unless it came out
of a 'Gales' jar; many children insisted on predetermined
verbal responses from their mothers and had tantrums if the
expected reply was not exactly as they wanted it. One child, a
great encyclopaedia reader, asked his mother repeatedly 'El
Greco is a . . . ?' and became very upset indeed if, instead of
saying 'a painter', she pointed out that really he knew the

answer. The 'insistence on sameness' showed itself only in areas where such obsessional patterns had formed. The children often ignored other changes altogether or else made the necessary adjustments. Much of the child's language and also his non-verbal expression of wishes could be understood in terms of the exact repetition of past experiences without modifying them to fit in with new circumstances. One boy always asked for ice-cream by saying to his mother, 'You want some ice-cream, Thomas? Yes, you may.' Several children instead of asking for food or water would push their mothers to the stove or try to induce them to turn on the water by moving their hand towards the tap. One child when hungry would just sit at the kitchen table and wait.

How common is this condition? In a recent survey it was estimated that between four and five out of every 10,000 children are autistic.[104] Rutter has pointed out that this estimate makes autism more common than blindness and nearly as common as deafness in children.[125] Affected boys outnumber girls at a ratio of about 4 to 1.

What is the outlook for the future for the autistic child? There have now been several follow-up studies[35, 45, 139] and all indicate that only one in six children diagnosed as autistic managed to cope in an ordinary school environment. Several, although living a relatively independent existence, continue to display oddities of behaviour. Almost half the children required institutional care and the remainder were at home, perhaps attending special schools. Two pointers to the prognosis for the individual child exist. Firstly, children developing the illness imperceptibly during their first two or three years of life do rather better than children whose early development seemed normal and who have a setback (with loss of language and withdrawal from emotional contact with others) during their second or third year of life. Secondly, children who have useful speech at the age of five tend to do well while those who are not yet speaking then do badly. Language skills in these children correlate very well with their performance on intelligence tests and these are even better predictors of outcome.

It must be stressed that all these follow-up studies were of children in whom the diagnosis had been made at least ten, in the older studies as much as twenty, years ago. It is possible that in those days, when the diagnosis was not often made, only the more severe cases were diagnosed. Now that psychiatrists are better informed, milder cases may be recognized more often and the overall prognosis is likely to be somewhat less gloomy.

Certainly autism in childhood is a serious condition and for some affected children the outlook in our present state of knowledge is poor.

What causes autism in childhood? Some autistic children show evidence of brain damage; in others there is nothing in the history or on examination to suggest neurological impairment. The fact that a number of parents of autistic children, like the parents of schizoid children, are themselves emotionally withdrawn, obsessional, intellectual, often clumsy in their relationships with other people and at times over-sensitive and perhaps suspicious, has led in America to the idea of 'the schizophrenogenic mother'. This term is often used rather loosely to indicate that 'schizophrenia' is caused by adverse mothering. Although autism in childhood does not lead to schizophrenia in adult life, and adult schizophrenics never seem to have been autistic as children, the notion that mothers 'cause' schizophrenia in their offspring has been used to explain both the origins of the adult psychosis as well as autism in childhood. This explanation does not answer the question why only one child in a family is affected by his mother, nor does it solve the problem of how a personality deviation in a parent that is difficult to define and to detect can produce such early and gross disturbances in the child, when many infants and young toddlers, exposed to far more obviously abnormal parents, are not harmed in this particular way. Orphanage children, for example, do not become autistic.

There is little doubt that the often very careful studies of parents of autistic children and of adult schizophrenics are valid. Parents of both groups of patients probably display schizoid personality traits. Even Kanner, nearly fifteen years ago, suggested that many parents might have a milder form of their children's abnormality.[86] The most reasonable explanation is that both the parental abnormality of personality and the child's illness are dependent on hereditary factors.

Despite this, the fact remains that many parents of autistic children are perfectly normal, well-adjusted people.

In Britain most psychiatrists believe autism, when not associated with recognisable brain damage, to be due to an as yet undiscovered biochemical abnormality of the brain based on hereditary factors. In America many psychiatrists believe that it is caused by emotional factors. Even the belief in an organic basis does not imply that environmental factors are unimportant. How the autistic child is handled and what stresses he has to meet affect his condition profoundly. Moreover psychoanalysts like Margaret Mahler have contributed greatly to our understanding of the autistic child's world in terms of the nature of his relationships to the objects and people around him.[111]

What has treatment to offer? With psychiatric help the majority of parents of autistic children can manage to keep their child within the family and aid him towards improvement. Parents supported by the psychiatrist can do more for their child at home than an expert child therapist in weekly one-hour sessions. In addition almost all autistic children can benefit from education. Only in an educational setting can they learn to function in a group of other children and begin to acquire scholastic skills. The illness varies so much in severity that no single educational setting suits all autistic children. Some fit in quite well at ordinary nursery schools and schools; others benefit from attending schools for maladjusted or even physically handicapped children, depending on the numbers and the kinds of children in the class and the particular skills of the teacher. Many autistic children are currently accommodated in classes for backward children. In some cases this may work out well, in others the child is there only because no other special class is available. The danger for an autistic child in a backward class is that he may not get sufficient individual stimulation and that his latent skills remain unrecognized and unused.

An energetic parent association exists in this country; one of its aims is to provide and to promote centres for the treatment and education of autistic children. The clinical picture and current approaches to the illness have been well described in two recent books, one brief and one more comprehensive.[174, 175]

All the conditions mentioned in this chapter raise profound questions about the interaction between organic and psychological factors, between brain function and behaviour. These questions remain at present largely unanswered. But to those with experience in the field the clinical syndromes described are clear; their course and outcome are beginning to be defined and their response to different treatment approaches is being studied.

It will have become apparent that several of the conditions described superficially resemble those of the more common behaviour disorders that are due to environmental pressures. The child psychiatrist's particular contribution is to decide whether for an individual child's difficulties psychological explanations alone suffice or whether the field of explanation must be extended to include constitutional and organic factors.

Part III
TREATMENT APPROACHES

10. *The Social Environment*

This chapter is an examination of how society as a whole, its organizations and institutions, can contribute to the prevention and relief of psychiatric disorders in childhood.

Children cannot be viewed in isolation from parents. A continuous process of mutual influence exists between the generations. Contented parents who function adequately in society are likely to have well-adjusted children, and the chances are that children who cope satisfactorily with the stresses of childhood will become well-adjusted in their later lives. When adults are exposed to major crises, their children suffer indirectly and when children have to master inherent handicaps or calamitous life circumstances in their early years, their adult functioning is often impaired. Any therapeutic help given to adults has indirect beneficial effects on their children and, although this has not been substantiated because of the difficulty of long-term follow-up studies, the hope is that if we can make specific improvements in the environment of our children this will contribute also to their mental health as adults.

WHAT PSYCHIATRIC DISORDERS RESPOND TO ENVIRONMENTAL IMPROVEMENTS?

We should be clear at the outset about the kinds of psychiatric conditions in childhood and later life that environmental improvements can hope to prevent and cure. On the whole they consist of behaviour disorders and psychoneuroses in childhood and of psychoneuroses and personality disorders in later life. There is little evidence as yet that improvements in our medical, educational and social services can reduce the incidence of the constitutionally determined, major mental illnesses such as the psychoses. Improved medical care has, if anything, added to the numbers of our constitutionally handicapped children by making it possible for more such children to survive. For example, small premature babies now have a much better chance of reaching adult life, and we know that such babies are prone to have numerous physical, intellectual and emotional handicaps.

Preventive psychiatry, like preventive medicine, focuses not on the individual patient nor even on the individual family but on wider social groups. The behaviour disorders of childhood, the neurotic illnesses of later life, the neurotic and antisocial personality distortions that interfere with work, with intimate relationships such as marriage and parenthood and with orderly social conduct, all these are psychiatric disturbances which theoretically at least are preventable. They occur in people who are not on the whole constitutionally deviant: their basis is experiential.

In considering what society can do to prevent and ameliorate such psychiatric disorders it is worth once more viewing them broadly as caused by two sets of circumstances: experiences of overwhelming anxiety and experiences of inadequate socialization often associated with parental and cultural deprivation.

THE REALTIONSHIP BETWEEN SOCIO-CULTURAL INFLUENCES AND PSYCHIATRIC ILLNESS

The attempt to relate wider socio-cultural factors to psychiatric disorders has many pitfalls. In simple, less diversified, non-industrial societies it has been possible for example to relate broad patterns of child-rearing to personality development and adult behaviour.[172] In these societies one can to some extent identify the particular stresses which the culture imposes on its members. But such studies merely demonstrate relationships, they do not suggest ways in which the social life of a community can be 'improved' nor do they throw light on the relationship between culture and illness. One might think that a transcultural comparison of psychiatric illness rates could be related to differences in social organization existing in different communities. But illness rates of different cultures may be influenced by factors quite other than the social factors under investigation. For example, the recognition of illness and its manifestations can differ widely from one society to the next and this is especially so for those illnesses whose causes are environmental. Nor can we legitimately make comparisons between one generation and the next within the same culture. For example, in the late nineteenth century Western European society was characterized by its paternalistic family structure and by the low status of women. At the same time, although actual rates are not available, the incidence of gross female hysteria appeared to be high. From clinical experience we know that hysteria in the form in which it manifested in the late nineteenth century is now rare and that our most troublesome psychiatric disturbances in adult life are the personality disorders, in particular antisocial personality disorder or sociopathy. But there is no way of relating these apparent changes in psychiatric disorders to the general social changes known to have occurred, because on the one hand no relevant measurements of illness were made a hundred years ago and in any case too many unknown variables will have changed also.

It is not on the whole profitable to try to find relationships between global social factors and mental illness. A more rewarding exercise is to examine the interaction between quite specific social variables and particular aspects of psychological functioning occurring within a single culture and within the same period of time. There have been many studies, for example, relating the incidence of various mental illnesses to socio-economic class and area of residence. The pioneer work in this field established the fact that schizophrenia occurred most often in deteriorated urban areas where people lived alone in hotels or lodging houses.[50] The question then arose did social isolation cause schizophrenia or did schizophrenia lead to a social decline in the people affected so that they drifted into the poor slum areas of the city? Subsequent research supported the latter 'drift' hypothesis, indicating that the environmental factors examined were not a cause but an effect of the illness.[51]

An apparently similar conclusion was arrived at by Robins who found that antisocial children, in contrast to neurotic children, often had sociopathic fathers with poor work records and themselves often became sociopathic in later life.[133] In contrast to the neurotic group, such antisocial children more often came from the lowest socio-economic class and their social status in adult life too was low. Robins considers social class factors to be largely irrelevant in the causation of juvenile delinquency and adult sociopathy. But her work, which demonstrates the importance of childhood experiences within the family in causing this particular personality deviation, does not rule out the possibility that social intervention outside the family could interrupt the sequence of antisocial development from childhood into adult life.

Most research into the relationship between social factors and mental illness has aimed to uncover either the causes of psychiatric disorders or their long-term effects. Few investigations have been set up which could provide a scientific basis for administrative action. One such is the study by Hare of the prevalence of psychiatric ill-health among the inhabitants of an old part of Croydon compared with that among people from the same suburb who had been resettled in a new housing estate.[68] Hare showed that the fears often expressed previously, that neurosis increases in new housing estates, are not consistent with the facts: there was no difference in prevalence rates between the two areas studied. Douglas's work on primary schools is another example of a study that has direct relevance to administrative action.[38] It provided evidence that early streaming of children according to their apparent ability is detrimental to the educational progress and classroom adjustment of the lower class child and the less able child.

The field is still wide open for exploration. Housing policies, reforms in education, the administration of the National Health Service and changes in our legal system are all social processes likely to affect mental health. There is room for more experimental investigations of the effects of proposed policy changes before they are implemented on a nation-wide basis, and there is room also for testing out whether certain administrative changes can contribute to the prevention of specific psychiatric disorders.

It is an established fact, for example, that among children with behaviour problems, however identified, boys outnumber girls. It has often been suggested that this has to do with the different social expectations to which boys are exposed. A recent follow-up of young adults who were originally a part of a study of nursery school children showed that while women maintained into adult life their individual characteristics of passivity or initiative, and of dependence or independence which they had shown between the ages of three and six years, no such stability for these personality attributes was found in males.[84] This research established a clear difference in personality development between boys and girls, a difference moreover which is likely to be due to social factors. The social variables concerned were not however sufficiently explored to lead to any practical conclusions (see also Chapter 3).

Douglas, as we saw in Chapter 3, provided a further clue to factors prejudicial to the emotional adjustment of boys.[38] He suggested that the negative evaluation of boys by women teachers in primary schools contributed to a drop in their school performance relative to girls. Whether such negative attitudes on the part of female teachers also contribute to the excess of behaviour disorders in boys is an unexplored matter, but one that could relatively easily be tested and possibly remedied.

HOW CAN SOCIETY BEST USE ITS RESOURCES TO PROMOTE THE HEALTHY PSYCHOLOGICAL DEVELOPMENT OF CHILDREN?

We shall consider this question under three heads: (1) Prevention of avoidable stresses and avoidable deprivations; (2) Amelioration of unavoidable stresses and deprivations; (3) Identification and treatment of psychiatric disorders.

1. Prevention of Avoidable Stresses and Deprivations

Discussions of preventive mental health often focus on the early identification of illness. In particular, when the prevention of delinquency is at issue, the belief is voiced that identification and treatment of 'pre-delinquent' children will be helpful.

But to identify a child as a potential delinquent can be the final step in determining his downfall. Such predictions have a way of fulfilling themselves. Of far greater value and much less hazardous are society's attempts to improve the environment for all children so as to reduce those stresses and deprivations known to cause psychiatric disorders.

The Schools. Society takes responsibility for a considerable part of child rearing. All children go to school. The experiences that are provided for them there, in contrast to their experiences at home, are in large measure under public control. Through the training of teachers, and the organization of schools and classrooms, society has a chance to improve and modify a major part of the environment of its children.

The past ten years have seen great changes in the school curriculum and in teaching methods. Increasingly these take into account the importance of a child's motivation and of his intellectual capacities at each developmental stage. A recent brief report on Primary Education in Scotland,[147] for example, provides an excellent survey for teachers and parents of current ideas. Even this up-to-date report, however, which stresses the importance of emotional and social development, does not focus on actual teaching techniques. Methods of maintaining discipline in the classroom or of modifying group interactions between children are discussed only in the most general terms.

Teachers are aware that classroom experiences provide opportunities for children not only to acquire knowledge but also to mature socially. But it seems that techniques for conducting the class with these aims in view are not often specifically taught. Increasingly the expectations are that schools and nursery schools should not only compensate children for cultural deficiencies in their own homes but should in addition provide an environment in which generally acceptable social standards can be acquired, especially by children from disorganized families in which these standards are lacking.[32] But to transmit social standards requires techniques quite different from traditional teaching methods. When people set out to instruct children in social behaviour the effect is often the reverse of what was intended. For example, warning school children of the dangers of smoking does not deter them,[158] and punishment may actually increase their later consumption of cigarettes.[121]

Social behaviour can be modified only when the teacher sees herself as a role model for her pupils and, with expert knowledge about group processes, deliberately conducts the interactions in her classroom in such a way as to foster satisfaction rather than frustration, cooperation, efficiency, cohesion, trust and mutual identification. It may surprise us to learn that, despite the long history of research in this field, the *first* text to help teachers understand the factors influencing group behaviour in the classroom was published only in 1964.[14]

Lippitt and White studied the effects of different kinds of group leadership on children as long ago as 1943.[103] Their study took place in the setting of boys' clubs engaged in hobby activities. Three types of adult leadership were investigated: autocratic, democratic and *laissez faire*. In autocratic groups all policy was decided by the leaders; instructions were given one at a time so that future steps were always uncertain; task assignments and work companions were selected by the leader; praise and criticism were 'personal' and the leader did not himself participate in activities. In democratic groups policy and goals were determined by group decisions; children were free to work with whom they liked; leaders took part in activities and praise and criticism was 'objective'. When his advice was sought the leader would offer alternatives to choose from. In *laissez faire* groups there was complete freedom with minimal leader participation and no attempt to appraise or regulate the course of events.

It was found that groups of boys react either with submission or rebellion to an autocratic leader. The autocratic submissive groups were efficient but much aggressive behaviour occurred when the children were released from the group. Autocratic rebellious groups were less efficient and aggressive behaviour occurred most of the time. In both types of autocratic groups there was evidence of considerable dependence on the leader, of lack of initiative and individuality, and of hidden discontent. Scapegoating was common. The *laissez faire* groups were less efficient. The boys did little work, playing most of the time, and the situation was experienced as less satisfying by the children themselves. The democratic groups were efficient and task-oriented. The children were more friendly to each other than in either of the other two settings and they were less aggressive not only in the presence of their leader but outside the group too. This study demonstrates beautifully how techniques of social organization within a group can have profound effects on children. It is not so much what is said but the techniques used to convey information that affects the social behaviour of children in a class room. An authoritarian approach provokes counter-aggression and when this is not tolerated within the classroom setting it is expressed outside.

It seems to me that in our schools there are as yet quite untapped social forces which, if explored and skilfully used, can counteract the frustrations of our duller and socially deprived children and could even offset rather than, as at present, reinforce the effects of antisocial family influences.

Quite apart from their responsibility for the educational and social development of the group of children in their care, all teachers are at times faced with the problems of individual children with behaviour disorders or of children struggling with educational handicaps. A commonsense approach based on personal life experiences and traditional social customs is not generally rewarding when it comes to dealing with emotionally disturbed or even merely anxious people. When teachers are knowledgeable about the causes of disturbed behaviour in children, they will react by reducing the pressures on the child, thus enabling him to function better. For example, when a child engages in petty stealing from his teacher or from other children, the teacher will want to know what particular stress the child is currently facing. Perhaps he is trying to keep up with a class of children all cleverer than he. Perhaps his parents are in a marital crisis and he is suffering from relative neglect. In the first case the teacher is in a position to provide the remedy. But even in the second case her reactions to the child can have profound effects. If she disapproves of the stealing but conveys to the child and to the class as a whole that she knows there are reasons for the thefts, then the child will feel understood and may get satisfactions from his relationship with the teacher and the other children that will to some extent compensate him for his deprivations at home. If, on the other hand, the teacher too begins to reject the child, and the class, taking their cue from her, do so also, then a child already under stress will be in an even more difficult situation and further acts of delinquency are likely to occur.

Teachers who are informed about human behaviour will not expect parents to react completely rationally if their child is failing at school. They know, for example, that when faced with the fact that their child is backward, parents will need opportunities to voice their own, often irrational anxieties, their anger, their fears for the future and their guilt feelings, before they can participate in realistic decisions about the child's future education.

School teachers can contribute greatly to the prevention of emotional disturbances in children by shielding them from excessive pressures within the school setting. They can also contribute to their therapeutic management where difficulties spring from the home environment. Finally, they can help anxious parents towards a more realistic view of their children by focusing on the parents' own view of the problem. But in order to undertake these responsibilities teachers need to have special training in this field and they need in addition adequate supporting services from psychologists and psychiatrists.

The Medical Services. To cure a patient of a physical illness is no longer sufficient. The responsibility of doctors and nurses extends beyond the preservation of life. Treatment of the common infections of childhood rarely presents a problem in these days of antibiotic drugs and many formerly fatal or chronic diseases such as meningitis, tuberculosis and osteomyelitis can now usually be cured. Small prematures and babies with a variety of inborn abnormalities which would formerly have been fatal now survive. The advances of surgery, for example, have made the prospect of normal physical health possible for children with severe inborn abnormalities of the heart. Often the problem is less one of how to keep the patient alive than how to help him and his family adjust emotionally to his illness, its treatment and its possible residual effects.

Quite apart from the debatable issue of how harmful

hospital admissions are to later personality development, there is no doubt that they are often very distressing. The general policy of most children's hospitals is to avoid admission if at all possible and, in cases which must come in, to give mother and child ready access to each other. Many illnesses previously necessitating hospital admission can now be treated at home. Planned surgery is in some hospitals performed on children as day-patients and long-term stays in convalescent homes are rarely advocated for young children.

Children from socially deprived homes, however, still tend to be admitted to hospitals with illnesses, such as dysentery and measles, that rarely call for admission of children from better-off families, and they also continue to find their way into convalescent homes. A study of hospital admissions 'for social reasons', as they are often described, would be of great interest. Does the child really benefit in health from an admission for a relatively mild illness merely because his home is disorderly? Does his mother manage to visit him in hospital as often as a mother from a better organized and better-off family? What nursing, domestic or even material help could the mother be given to enable her to nurse her child at home? What are the merits of home management versus hospital admission as far as the child's emotional adjustment is concerned? We need to know much more about what actually happens before we can judge the common policy of more ready admission and longer stays in hospitals and convalescent homes for children from socially deprived families.

In Chapter 4 I mentioned that operations of doubtful value are still often done precisely at an age when their emotional ill effects are greatest. Much more attention can profitably be paid to the timing of necessary but non-urgent operations. If surgery can be put off until the age of seven or eight when the stage of infantile realism is over and children can understand explanations about their illnesses, the risk of emotional disturbances is reduced.

Doctors and nurses have it in their power to minimize the psychological stress of illness. If they are to do this effectively they need a basic training in child psychology and they also need ready opportunities to discuss with psychiatrists the day-to-day management of those children whose responses to illness are unusual or who suffer from severe or rare physical handicaps.

Just as medical staff need to care for more than the physical health of their patients, it is their business too to look beyond the patient himself at his family as a whole. Parents of chronically ill or physically handicapped children are in special need of attention since their explanations and attitudes to the child will determine his own adjustment to his handicap. Parents of a dying child will need to discuss their own feelings and also the responses of their surviving children. A much mourned first son, for example, can hang like a shadow over the life of a later child who, unless his parents are helped to overcome their grief, may feel that he can never match up to his dead brother.

When young adults become ill, the effect of their illness on the rest of the family needs to be considered. When a young mother for example develops poliomyelitis and, after months of treatment, is left with a paralysis of one leg so that she must wear a caliper and is no longer able to run after her young children, her reactions to this handicap require to be noted and she will need definite opportunities both to discuss her own feelings and fears and also the responses of her children. Parents often need help from professionals to know how to explain their illness to their children. Long-term illness in any member of a family has profound effects on all the others and the resulting anxieties and deprivations require to be understood and alleviated.

We have discussed the impact of death on a family at some length (see Chapter 5). Most deaths are witnessed by doctors or nurses. Without special training neither is able to give the professional help required to the surviving members of the family. All too often even doctors shy away from the bereaved, sharing perhaps their magical belief that they should have been able to prevent the death. The subject of children dying in hospital has recently been reviewed by Yudkin, who indicates that because nowadays older children rarely die in hospital, doctors are ill-prepared to help families, other patients in the ward, and perhaps the child himself to face the fatal outcome.[184]

Other Social and Public Services. Family disruption, if not due to death, generally follows on poor family functioning because of personality defects of one or both parents. The actual split could in many cases be prevented if public policy focused its resources to this end. Over half the children who come into the care of *local authority children's departments* do so because of confinement of the mother or short-term illness of a parent. A comparative study of children taken into public care during their mothers' next confinement showed conclusively that even the request for short-term care is a symptom of poor family functioning, and that the children involved are vulnerable children.[146] The authors question the wisdom of a social policy whereby doctors and social workers invariably complied with mothers' requests to have their young children taken into care. Alternative practical help is recommended: a more flexible home-help service and financial support for fathers or relatives acting as substitute mothers.

For children in need of long-term care planning is often inadequate. Too many foster home placements break down, and there is evidence of a gap between knowledge and practice in child care.[36, 37]

More effort is now rightly expended in attempts to prevent family disruption. It is generally recognized that to evict a family from their home because of rent arrears is neither economic nor a therapeutic proposition.

How far proposed reforms in *sentencing procedure of courts* will go towards preventing family break-up remains to be seen.

Crime often arises on the basis of long-term family conflicts. The imprisonment of the culpable member is prejudicial to the resolution of their difficulties. Sexual offences in married men, infanticide in women, property offences occurring in people with a blameless past history but currently under stress, all these are instances in which imprisonment adds yet further to the burden of people already in difficulties, without the least likelihood of being in any way remedial.

2. *Amelioration of Unavoidable Stresses and Deprivations*

Crisis Intervention. In situations of crisis individuals are generally more ready to make changes in their personality adaptation and therapeutic intervention is likely to be more effective than at any other time (see p. 112). At these times it is always necessary to look beyond the immediate crisis at the past and future of the afflicted person and at his or her family.

Death and physical illness or deformity can affect all families. Yet there will be some for whom the event is more traumatic, perhaps even pathogenic, because of previous personality disturbances.

If such families can be identified and given special help to cope with the event at the time it is likely that a real contribution to their future functioning will be made, while treatment later when the family presents with a clear-cut psychiatric illness may be far less successful.

For example, a not very happily married couple watched their thirteen-year-old son die slowly of cancer. When his illness was first discovered the affected leg was amputated. He was then sent home and his mother nursed him until he died. She talked to the doctors about the boy's diagnosis when it was made but she could not bring herself to discuss it with her husband and kept the fatal nature of the child's illness a secret from him. It made the son more wholly hers. When the boy died, his father became depressed and silent, refusing altogether to talk about the child. Communication between the couple was worse than ever. Two years later the mother became pregnant for the second time and during this pregnancy she developed asthma which has continued ever since. The second child, also a boy, grew up surrounded by pictures of his brother, and the dead boy's dog, a puppy when he died, grew up with him. An atmosphere of mourning persisted in the home, the mother was always ill and her feelings for her second child never matched those for her first. Increasingly the parents felt they had little in common. The death of an aunt finally precipitated a state of acute anxiety and depression in the little boy and his parents were unable to comfort him. It was at this point that psychiatric help was sought.

A joint interview with both parents at the time of their first son's illness would certainly have revealed the tensions between them. Then, or when the boy died, they could perhaps have been helped to come closer together and to support each other in their grief and this would have enabled them later to invest their affections anew in their second child.

Of course, in the case of a single family, it remains entirely speculative whether earlier intervention would have prevented illness later on. The effectiveness of prophylactic intervention of this kind however is open to investigation and a planned study needs to be made.

Other situations that come to public attention are themselves indices of previous psychiatric disturbance. There is considerable evidence, for example, that mothers of illegitimate children are more neurotic than other girls. Kidd showed that among unmarried women students who became pregnant at any stage of their university career nearly a half had consulted their doctor for a psychiatric disability during their first year at university. Among a control group of students the proportion was a sixth.[90]

A neurotic pattern of family interaction found fairly commonly in working class families was illustrated in the case reported in Chapter 6. Here the mother is often her own mother's first and premaritally conceived child. The grandmother's guilt, never worked through, is expressed as rejection of her daughter. The unloved daughter then fulfils her mother's predictions by herself becoming pregnant out of wedlock. In part this pregnancy is an attack on the grandmother, an act of revenge, and the guilt that accompanies it can only be made good by giving the child over to the grandmother. *She* looks after the baby, while the mother goes to work and when she finally marries and tries to settle down with her child, the conflicting triangular relationship between mother, grandmother and child, to which the step-father is a relative outsider, produces endless tensions in the family.

There are good arguments for providing skilled psychological help for unmarried mothers focused not only on the pressing problem of the unborn child's immediate future, but on the mother's own past life and future expectations. Only when she can resolve the inner conflicts that have led up to her pregnancy is she likely to be able to cope adequately with her future love relationships and with the children she will have.

Help for the Handicapped Child. Our school system provides special facilities for many types of handicapped children but only in very recent years have attempts been made to evaluate the special educational services and to compare the results of different educational approaches.[163]

While mentally retarded children left in regular school classes are on the whole superior academically to children placed in special classes, children in special classes are better adjusted socially and do not suffer the isolation and rejection from their peers to which dull children in normal classes are exposed. Tizard suggests that the conclusions from such studies are open to different interpretations because the quality of the teaching both in normal and special classes is a factor that has as yet been insufficiently explored. With better teaching methods and smaller classes less segregation of all kinds of handicapped children may be necessary than is thought at present.

Currently, children are often placed in special schools or classes because teachers in ordinary classes are so over-burdened that they cannot provide the sort of teaching they would like for the deviant child. When classes are too large conformity is insisted upon and the child who cannot easily conform is under considerable stress. When classes are smaller and teachers trained to understand the whole range of child-hood behaviour, and when they have ready access to medical, psychiatric and psychological services, then many children with a variety of handicaps, from partial deafness and intellectual retardation to emotional maladjustment, could be retained in normal classes. This would avoid the sense of isolation and of being different that special class children often have, and could contribute to the broadening of experience and the greater mutual understanding of all the children.

Cultural deprivation constitutes a handicap that has only recently been recognized. In the United States attempts have been made on a nationwide basis to prevent the loss of intellectual ability that cultural impoverishment in early life brings about. 'Project Head Start' sees to it that every child from a poor slum area has at least a brief nursery school experience. In Britain nursery school facilities have decreased since the end of the last war despite evidence that the intellectual development of children from culturally impoverished homes is demonstrably improved by nursery school attendance. If economic considerations such as teenage unemployment could be set aside, it is debatable whether instead of extending the minimum school leaving age to sixteen it would not be preferable to provide nursery education for at least a section of our population. Under present conditions it is the middle and upper working class child who is likely to go to a nursery school and not the child from a semi-skilled or unskilled working class home who really needs it. It is these lower class, culturally deprived children who as teenagers, disheartened by long years of school failure, resent their life at school and long for the increased self-esteem that comes with the wage packet. For such youngsters an additional year at school imposes stresses that often lead to apathy and delinquency.

Before committing ourselves to this course on a nationwide scale it might be well to conduct local experiments, extending the school age in some regions only, and observing the effect on different kinds of children.

Children from Broken Homes. It is the policy of local authority children's departments to give preference to foster home care. In the last chapter we shall discuss the kind of help that should be made available to foster parents and the child-care workers who supervise such placements.

Because as many children as possible are placed with foster families those who remain in children's homes are generally disturbed psychiatrically. More often than not they are children with grossly disrupted and deprived backgrounds whose behaviour disorders cannot be tolerated in an ordinary family not their own.

Such children require skilled care. Yet the people who are asked to look after them, the houseparents and assistants in children's homes, are generally underpaid and often untrained. Because of the pressure of work on trained children's officers and child-care workers, houseparents also lack intensive supervision and in-service training. One hears little about the children in children's homes. They do not as a rule swell the numbers attending child psychiatric clinics. When their behaviour becomes too disturbed they may find their way into approved schools. Yet on the whole their abnormalities are tolerated and contained.

Clinical experience shows that such children in later life are at risk. Impaired intellectual development, unstable marriages, inadequate capacities for bringing up their own children, suicide and crime: these appear to be the hazards of an institutional upbringing. But we lack real knowledge. Follow-up studies of children in various types of residential care are badly needed. And it is time that units providing model residential treatment for such children were set up so that their achievements can be studied and the effects of different kinds of care on children with differing needs can be known.

3. Identification and Treatment of Psychiatric Disorders

The search for early signs of emotional disturbance in childhood may do harm rather than good. A label of psychiatric illness may for example induce a teacher to give up the struggle of trying to understand and cope with a puzzling and difficult child. After all he has been told the child is ill. With some relief, often tinged with misgivings, he hands the child over to the doctors, telling himself that the experts should manage better than he. Parents may resort to the same inner detachment from their child's difficulties as they give him over to the psychiatrist. But when all children with emotional difficulties are identified there will not be enough psychiatrists to go round. And in any case, psychiatrists cannot be effective without teachers and parents who are prepared to continue their attempts to understand and care for their problem children. When it leads to abdication from effort by parents and teachers to understand the child, diagnosis is not helpful. When it leads to actual segregation of increasing numbers of children in hospitals, special residential schools and children's homes, away from the normalizing experiences of ordinary school, family and neighbourhood life, then we must pause to reconsider the whole position. Are we right to press our claims for more psychiatric treatment facilities for individual children and for ever more specialized educational facilities? Should we not rather exert ourselves to provide the training and support that would be necessary to enable teachers in ordinary schools, and indeed all professional workers concerned with the care of children, to give skilled help to those children whose behaviour is deviant?

The Treatment Needs of Deprived and Delinquent Children. It is not only in Britain that treatment facilities are least adequate for deprived and delinquent children. In the United States, where psychiatrists have taken more responsibility in the care and treatment of such children, many enter state mental hospitals, often as certified patients. Such hospitals are generally large and also poor and the best doctors do not choose to work in them. The result is that the care given to delinquent and deprived children although 'professional' is by no means preferable to our own far from ideal methods of coping.

Here, when children have no families and are too disturbed to cope in foster homes, or when they are unable to conform at school and in the wider community, when they truant for example and wander the countryside, when they steal, start fires or engage in promiscuous sexual activities, they find their way into children's homes and approved schools. The inadequacies of children's homes, which were not originally set up to cater for psychiatrically disturbed children will be described in Chapter 12. Although approved schools are staffed by teachers, their methods of control and training are not demonstrably effective in modifying personality development.

Kilbrandon and After. A landmark in current thinking about the needs of deprived and delinquent children was the report of the Kilbrandon committee set up in Scotland to consider all children who are currently dealt with by the courts.[149] An English White Paper, *The Child, the Family and the Young Offender*, incorporated a number of its ideas.[63]

The Kilbrandon committee made far-reaching recommendations for the reorganization both of legal procedures and treatment facilities for such children.

The plan outlined abolished many of the anomalies of our present legal apparatus for dealing with youthful offenders. 'The shortcomings inherent in the juvenile court system can . . . be traced essentially to the fact that they are required to combine the characteristics of a court of criminal law with those of a specialized agency for the treatment of children in need, whether in law juvenile offenders or children in need of "care or protection".' The report suggested a separation of the legal function of settling matters of fact from the therapeutic functions of caring for deprived and delinquent children. Treatment panels were suggested for this latter function (family courts were suggested in the English White Paper), which would have at their disposal specialists to help in assessing the children and a variety of treatment services. Treatment panels could follow up a child over a period of time and recommend changes in treatment as they seemed indicated. Delinquent children would no longer be extruded from society and cared for by a separate set of social workers and residential establishments. Their needs, overlapping as they do with the needs of other deprived or disturbed children, would be catered for by a unified group of social workers who would have access to every kind of residential establishment for children.

The Kilbrandon report was followed by a Scottish White Paper on social work and the community[148] and, in England, by the Seebohm report on Local Authority and Allied Personal Social Services.[129] Both describe plans for unifying and strengthening the social services. The Scottish White Paper, and the Social Work (Scotland) Act which followed it in 1968 came ostensibly as an answer to the Kilbrandon report. But they deal with only a part of the total problem. There is no provision for the perhaps most urgent task of improving and unifying the facilities for children who need special residential care or education. There are no plans for removing the distinction, widely recognised as false, between the procedures and treatment facilities for dealing with children who are identified as delinquent by the police and children recognized as disturbed by their teachers or parents. So long as delinquent children are segregated from the community in institutions which leave on them a mark of social ostracism and shame and which often serve only to reinforce antisocial conduct, we cannot begin to feel satisfied that we are making progress.

The Kilbrandon report suggested that the new social work services and all the diverse residential establishments for children should operate from within the education authority. It seems to me too, despite the controversy this recommendation has caused, that it is the school system that can most advantageously carry out these socializing functions, just as classroom teaching of normal children can with benefit concern itself more deliberately with social processes. The unification of all the social work agencies, provided for in the Social

Work (Scotland) Act and recommended by the Seebohm Committee, whereby the same authority is responsible for the care of the elderly as well as the care of children, seems to me to ignore the far greater need to integrate the social, educational and medical services for children.

The new Scottish legislation poses the practical problem of how to staff the unified social work agencies with adequately trained people and how to provide these with sufficient medical, psychological and psychiatric supporting services.

The changes necessary in the residential care for children involve more than practical difficulties. The whole question of the professional status of the teachers and house-parents who work in them requires consideration.

Although poorly socialized delinquent children may need a different kind of residential setting than neurotic children, or delinquent children with intellectual or other constitutional impairments, the knowledge and skills needed by the teachers who educate and care for these children are quite comparable. At present the career structure of teachers working in approved schools and teachers in schools for maladjusted children is separate and the two kinds of boarding schools are by tradition run on very different lines. Size, for example, distinguishes the schools. The average approved school for boys holds 92 children, while residential schools for the maladjusted tend to accommodate only about 25 children and an average children's home has room for 16 residents.[117] The size of an institution in part determines the kinds of rules needed to maintain its structure. Therapeutic community methods, known to be effective in the treatment of delinquents and known to work in relatively small communities, may lead to chaos if introduced into larger penal institutions. West has stressed that the sheer size of our institutions for young delinquents is an important factor militating against their therapeutic effectiveness.[171] To maintain discipline in such large schools, where staff and pupils do not know each other intimately, methods are sometimes used which even a psychologically unsophisticated public finds unacceptable.

A step towards improving our penal institutions for the young would be to incorporate them into our system of special residential schools, to break down their size into therapeutically effective small schools, to unify the career structure for all teachers working with disturbed children and to provide such teachers with special training. The size of the present approved school population should not be an obstacle to such a process of integration. The number of children in approved schools is about one third of the number of children living in children's homes and one half of children in other residential special schools.[117]

The residential care of children, whether delinquent or not, poses other problems too. Few professional workers are willing to commit themselves entirely to an institution and to share all their everyday activities with their charges. In any case the numbers of children who require to be looked after is far too great for this. Housemothers and housefathers, teachers in approved and maladjusted schools and wardens of hostels for children are still too often untrained in psychological skills. They tend to get their work satisfactions not from the professional exercise of a special skill and from discussing their activities with colleagues, but from their actual relationships with the children and other staff members. To the extent that they bring their own emotional needs into their job, their capacity to be therapeutically effective is impaired. To take a simple example, when a child's progress is poor, when he is unresponsive or persistently delinquent, the staff may feel profoundly disappointed and this disappointment, reflected back to the child, can in fact hinder his progress. Again, when a child expresses animosity to his housemother and the housemother reacts to this as a personal attack upon herself, and not as an expression of latent feelings aimed perhaps at the mother who had deserted the child in the past, when the housemother treats the child's expression of feelings not as a transference phenomenon but as reality, an opportunity for effective therapeutic intervention has been missed.

Two alternative solutions exist to this great problem of how to combine therapeutic skills with substitute parental care. Neither has as yet been exploited sufficiently to provide a standard of care and treatment for our deprived and delinquent children that is at all commensurate with present-day knowledge.

The first solution consists of institutions, whether maladjusted schools, reformatories or special children's homes, directed by an individual with exceptional gifts and a special and often highly individualistic philosophy of life which he is able to transmit to the rest of his staff. One such person, as we shall see, was August Aichhorn[2] who applied psychoanalytic theory to his work as director of a boys' reformatory. Over and above his skilled application of psychoanalytic principles, however, was his complete dedication to the treatment of delinquents and his capacity to transmit his enthusiasm to the people who worked with him. Several experts from educational, medical and social work fields have made contributions to the care of children by the exemplary running of their particular institutions and by combining dedicated care and love of children with high professional standards.[2, 17, 26] All these individuals combined a high level of psychological insight with administrative abilities, with educational skills and with complete identification with their own establishments.

The second solution, more practical because it depends less on the existence of exceptional people, is to provide an expert adviser for each residential institution for children. His task would be, by means of regular discussion groups with all staff members, to help them towards a measure of distance from their everyday tasks and, from the vantage point of this distance, to a greater understanding of the children and their own relationships with them (see Chapter 12).

Until houseparents in charge of children's homes have education, salaries and status comparable with teachers and nurses, they will not be able to undertake adequately the heavy professional responsibilities that their work demands. The time is past when the public care of children can be left to unmarried elderly women, untrained for their job. There will soon be no unmarried women left for this kind of work. The professionalization of child care may appear to conflict with the idea that children's homes should be small units run 'as a family'. But this is not necessarily so.

In the field of residential child care there is much room for experimentation with different methods carefully evaluated.

At the present time the greatest needs that society must meet are twofold. Firstly, to provide proper training and continued specialist services to the many professional persons whose job it is to look after children; and secondly to subject all treatment services, out-patient and residential, to careful and continued evaluation.

Although many questions remain unanswered, we do have growing areas of knowledge. Administrative decisions in the field of child care need no longer rest on opinions alone but can, and should, increasingly be made on the basis of established fact. Optimal administrative provisions must be worked for vigorously. Nevertheless, the actual care of children and their parents will always depend on the psychological awareness and skills of individual professional workers.

11. Psychological Treatment of Children

When a child's behaviour is persistently at variance with what is expected of him by his parents, his teachers or society at large and he is brought to a psychiatrist for help, the first important step is *diagnosis*. Certain basic questions must be answered before treatment can begin. Is there a constitutional handicap, however trivial, that contributes to the child's difficulties? What are his intellectual abilities? Is there a discrepancy between the social and cultural background of his home and the expectations he encounters at school? If the difficulties are primarily emotional, one must decide whether past or present stresses provide a sufficient explanation for the child's symptoms or whether he has behind him a period of serious emotional deprivation in early life which has limited his capacities for normal social responsiveness.

Most children who come to see a psychiatrist are not in fact constitutionally handicapped in any way, and children who have suffered gross early deprivations are also rare among clinic attenders. At least eighty per cent of children brought for psychiatric care are reacting with deviant behaviour to upsetting life experiences in the present or in the past. In such children the precise meaning and origins of symptoms can only be guessed at in the initial interview. As the child gradually reveals his inner life and the parents talk more freely about their own problems, the personality characteristics of the child and the causes of his difficulties become clear.

In this chapter the focus will be on psychological treatment methods rather than on other, more specifically medical, approaches. Only the doctor can prescribe drugs, but many other professionals and non-professionals who care for children can benefit from an understanding of psychotherapeutic techniques. While the child who is seriously disturbed emotionally must be assessed and treated by experts, many other children in temporary situations of stress or with minor psychological difficulties will be helped if the people who look after them are aware of techniques to relieve anxiety and to help children modify maladaptive behaviour.

Almost all psychological treatment approaches to children derive from the work of those early psychoanalysts who in the 1920s began to devote themselves to the study and treatment of children. It is no coincidence that even then the child analysts working in their consulting rooms mainly saw children with neurotic disorders who came from socially competent, middle class families, while seriously delinquent children with acting-out behaviour disorders were then as now treated in institutions.

Anna Freud[52] and Melanie Klein[92] laid the theoretical foundations for all subsequent psychotherapeutic approaches to neurotic children; August Aichhorn was the first to apply psychoanalytic principles to the treatment of delinquents and he did this in the setting of a reformatory.

THE PSYCHOLOGICAL TREATMENT OF NEUROTIC CHILDREN

1. Psychoanalysis

Four basic treatment principles derived from psychoanalysis apply to children and adults alike. These are:

(1) A completely *non-critical acceptance* of the patient and of all his actions and communications. When difficult behaviour such as a nervous tic or stealing or soiling has a neurotic basis, that is, when it is an outcome of excessive defences against anxiety, disapproval makes matters worse because it adds to the child's stress. Acceptance of difficult behaviour as a problem to be understood, rather than as something that must at all costs be stopped, helps to reduce the child's level of anxiety so that gradually he can give up his excessive defences and allow himself direct expression of feelings previously repressed.

(2) *Empathic understanding* of the patient's feelings. The

therapist endeavours to enter the child's world, to see things as they appear to him, to understand and to use his language, verbal or non-verbal. Only when the child feels that he is being understood on his own level will he be able to communicate with increasing freedom and frankness.

(3) When symptoms are an expression of repressed impulses in conflict with how the child feels he ought to be, then the task of treatment is to help him give up his defences, to allow the forbidden impulses to surface so that he can face them realistically, accept them as a part of himself and come to terms with them. Treatment is structured by the therapist *to help the patient express those parts of himself which his conscience and his ideal self have rejected.*

(4) *The use of communication* between the patient and the therapist *as the treatment tool.* Adult psychoanalysis depends on verbal communication between patient and analyst. Indeed there is little activity apart from talk. The patient relaxes on a couch, the analyst sits behind him, not even glances, only words are exchanged between them. Clearly this kind of interaction is not for young children. Their capacity to express themselves in words is limited and during the animistic stage of development they do not bother to make their thoughts clear because they believe the adults know what is going on in their minds anyway. Moreover they do not find inactivity relaxing. On the contrary it acts as a restraint. Children are doers rather than talkers.

The first psychoanalysis of a child was Freud's treatment of little Hans who had a phobia of horses.[55] Freud bypassed the problem of how to communicate with children by working almost entirely through the father. The father reported to Freud his son's symptoms and also the boy's thoughts as expressed in his conversations and drawings. Freud suggested to the father how these might be interpreted and the father acted as therapist. Nevertheless even in this first psychoanalysis of a child it was the one direct encounter between little Hans and the professor that proved crucial for the success of treatment.

During this encounter little Hans was able to tell Freud in his father's presence that the latter was not always the benign and controlled figure he presented to the outside world. This very morning he had smacked Hans, a fact the father had altogether repressed. This communication was salutary for the father. It also established the fact that the boy's fears were not entirely without foundation. He left the interview with his self-esteem increased and with the knowledge that the professor was on his side. His ego had been strengthened and as a result he was better able to master his anxieties.

Freud nevertheless believed at that time that children would reveal their innermost thoughts only to their parents and that parents alone would know how to make sense of what their children had to say.

It is in the area of communication with children that Melanie Klein, the inventor of *play therapy*, made her greatest contribution. She considered that even at two or three years of age psychological treatment was possible. At that age children are not very fluent verbally but they play. One of Klein's fundamental tenets was that all play has symbolic significance. Adult psychoanalysis consists of interpreting to the patient the hidden meanings of his verbal communications. In child analysis play is regarded as an equivalent form of communication and is treated in the same way. Everything the child says or does to the analyst directly or in play is used as material for analysis.

Melanie Klein equipped a playroom with small, simple, non-mechanical toys: small men, women and children, small animals, cars, trains and aeroplanes, small houses, trees and fences. In addition she provided drawing and cutting-out material, running water, bowls, basins and sand. Children, she found, express their feelings in play with little toys, in drawings and modelling and also in role-playing games, such as mothers and fathers or playing school, in which the child often involves the analyst. In all these activities the child lets the toys, or the objects he has created, or the roles he adopts in play, stand for the important people in his life and his activities and verbal comments demonstrate how he feels about them and how he thinks they feel towards him.

A big car for example may stand for the father, a little car for the child himself, a crash between the two represents a clash of opinions and the final outcome gives a lead to the hoped-for solution.

Treatment consists of facilitating these activities, participating in them when invited to do so but always leaving the initiative with the child.

The analyst's main task is to understand and to interpret the symbolic content of the child's play. Melanie Klein summed this up as follows: 'The assessment and interpretation of the patient's material by the analyst are based on a coherent framework of theory. It is the task of the analyst, however, to combine his theoretical knowledge with insight into the individual variations presented by each patient. At any given moment we are confronted with one dominant trend of anxieties, emotions, and object-relations, and the symbolic content of the patient's material has a precise and exact meaning in connexion with this dominant theme.'[93]

The 'work' of analysis consists of a long process during which the child is helped to act out in play or to go over verbally those feelings and thoughts about which he is most anxious.

The hidden meaning of his communications and the sources of his unrealistic anxieties are interpreted to him repeatedly until his activities within the treatment setting and his behaviour in general indicate that he has mastered his anxieties and is functioning better.

Melanie Klein saw the process of child analysis and the analyst's role as exactly comparable with adult analysis except that the personality structure of children and their modes of communication are different.

Anna Freud added to our understanding of the distinguishing characteristics of the relationship between child patient and analyst.[52] She stressed that in contrast to adults children do not seek treatment of their own accord. They are brought, sometimes against their will. Often they themselves are not suffering at all from their disturbances: it is their parents who complain. She sees the analyst's first task to be that of making a contract with the child himself by helping him to identify his trouble, indicating that the analyst is there to help him but that the process of getting better may at times be hard work.

With children who are not aware of suffering, who do not see the analyst as a helpful person they can trust and who are not prepared to come to a decision in favour of treatment, Anna Freud described what may be called a process of seduction. She would make herself as pleasant and helpful as possible to the child, taking his side at all times; she would show the child that she had all the qualities of people he admired and also that she was very clever and knew a lot of useful things; she would make toys and doll's clothes and gratify the child in every way. She would act as intermediary for him with the adults he feared until he became extremely dependent on her. Instead of a decision on the part of the child to enter treatment, a tie of dependency formed the basis for future analysis with such children. A positive tie of some kind between patient and therapist is essential for the patient to be able to face up to the often very painful revelations of repressed material.

Apart from pointing out the differences in the contract between patient and analyst that exist with children, Anna Freud also stressed that for the child the analyst is always another grown-up, a real person. When adult patients react to their analyst as if he were a very powerful figure, this reaction, known in technical language as a *transference reaction*, can be understood in terms of the patient's childhood feelings about his parents on whom he was then dependent. In reality patient and analyst are equal. The recognition of this reality provides a corrective experience for the patient. During treatment feelings that belong to the past or to some other external situation are 'transferred' to the present relationship between the patient and his therapist. The analysis of these 'transferred' feelings provides a therapeutic experience for the patient. In the treatment of children parents are not in the past; they exist in the present. Although the child can transfer to the analyst feelings he has towards his parents, the analyst is in reality in a much stronger position than the child and to that extent he in fact resembles the parents. Anna Freud sees the analyst's role not only as consisting of analysing the child's productions, not only as undoing his excessive repressions and other defence mechanisms. She sees it also as an educative one, as helping the child, with an as yet immature self and an incompletely developed ideal self and conscience, to accept the analyst as a model for identification. An over-strict conscience is replaced not as in grown-up patients by their own adult standards, nor by no conscience at all, but by standards the analyst considers reasonable. The analyst acts as an alternative parent figure.

Let us look a little more closely at the first principle of psychological treatment: *total acceptance of the patient* and of all his impulses. This too involves the role of the therapist as adult *vis-à-vis* the child.

Melanie Klein draws a distinction between acceptance of the child's feelings and impulses and passively tolerating every form of his behaviour.[94] It is important for children to express their feelings in treatment, to show their anger verbally and in play and to convert the playroom if necessary into a 'battle-field'. The importance lies not in the aggressive outbursts themselves but in the light they throw on the child's feelings in this particular situation and therefore on his feelings in other situations for which this one is a symbolic substitute. It is equally important that the child is not made too anxious by his own aggressive activities, that the burden of responsibility for preserving intact himself, the analyst and the physical structure of the treatment room is not, unrealistically, left to him. It is the adult's job to maintain safety. Without showing disapproval of the child, the therapist can indicate that he will not tolerate destruction and that he will assume control if the child cannot manage this himself. Often acceptance and interpretation of aggressive feelings will enable the child to moderate his behaviour. Sometimes the therapist must exert restraints, not by means of exhortation but by assuming physical control of a situation himself.

The second principle, *empathic understanding* of the child, is one that is sometimes hard to grasp for people such as teachers and nurses who are accustomed to an authoritative role in relation to children. It means that in a treatment setting the adult gives up the notion that he knows better than the child what the matter is and how it must be put right. It means that the analyst has an open mind, receptive to the novel ideas the child may introduce into the treatment hour. The child is listened to seriously and with respect and the analyst tries in partnership with the child to understand his wishes and ideas however childish and unrealistic they may appear to be on the surface.

The third principle of treatment, *helping the child to express repressed parts of himself*, assumes that what is wrong is that the child has had to repress and defend against wishes and impulses because they conflict with unrealistic demands from his conscience. His conscience, as we know, has been built up in the past from the incorporation of parental prohibitions, a process which began during the animistic stage when children commonly misperceive their environment. Very often however it is not only the child's animistic distortions that have resulted in an over-strict conscience, quite commonly parental demands are in fact excessive or conflicting and this not only in the child's past: they continue to be inappropriate in the present. It does not help a child to encourage him, for instance, to voice his sexual curiosity, which excessive guilt in this area had forced him to repress, when his parents cannot in fact tolerate such behaviour. If the analyst's standards are at variance with those of the parents the child can hardly benefit from the kind of treatment that has been outlined.

This led psychoanalysts in the early years of their work to restrict their practice to children of parents who were in sympathy with psychoanalysis, understood its principles and were able to cooperate fully in treatment although at times they had to put up with even more difficult behaviour on the part of their child.

2. Psychotherapy

Psychoanalysis concentrates on the child himself. It assumes that parents will with relatively little advice be able to maintain a helpful, interested but non-interfering attitude towards the treatment of their offspring. It is a method that intrudes greatly into the child's whole life since it involves daily sessions with the therapist. Psychoanalysts can undertake the treatment of only relatively few children and the cost of treatment, which is extremely high, is rarely borne by the National Health Service but by philanthropic foundations and by parents themselves. As a result the public financial resources available are in the main concentrated on the exploitation of psychoanalysis as a research tool and on providing this very specialized form of treatment for children with very unusual treatment needs.

A more practical approach to the large numbers of children who require psychological treatment is that of child guidance clinics and hospital psychiatric departments for children. Here help is provided by one or more members of a treatment team and involves not only the child but his parents too. Parents of emotionally disturbed children require help in their own right in order to adapt to the changes in their child which psychotherapy aims to bring about.

When a child is excessively shy, inhibited or fearful his behaviour is often but a reflection of an aspect of his mother's or father's personality, although they may ostensibly long for him to be different. Unless parents are helped to tolerate parts of themselves that have been repressed they may be quite unable to accept, for example, a temporary period of naughtiness and rebelliousness that treatment of the child, if successful, will bring about.

Often indeed a change in the parents alone and an increased understanding on their part of themselves and of their child is sufficient to allow the child to give up his excessive defences, to outgrow a temporary setback in emotional development and to function better. Very young children in particular and children whose symptoms have not yet become fixed reaction patterns can very often be treated indirectly through their parents.

When symptoms have become more fixed, when they derive largely from internalized conflicts and no longer respond merely to a reduction of environmental pressures, the child himself requires treatment.

Psychotherapy with children adopts the same treatment principles and basic assumptions as does psychoanalysis. The tool of treatment, communication between child and therapist, is the same and its adaptation to children of different ages involves exactly the kind of playroom equipment and play techniques that were devised by the child analysts. Treatment is however more circumscribed not only in time but in its objectives. Children are usually seen once or at most twice a week and treatment rarely lasts for more than six to nine months. Indeed quite brief psychotherapeutic interventions extending over only a few interviews with the child are often extremely helpful. In psychotherapy with children a decision is com-

monly made to focus only on that particular area which diagnostic explorations have shown to be the most crucial one for
the child's difficulties.

This approach was systematically used by David Levy for a
special group of children to help them release repressed feelings about particular past life experiences. He described
release therapy almost thirty years ago.[99] Levy viewed this procedure as treating the child by exploiting his own methods
of treating himself in play. He found it useful in those cases
where a definite upsetting event in the past had precipitated
symptoms in the child and where anxiety persisted despite the
fact that the current environment was no longer stressful. His
series of successful cases consisted in the main of young
children who had developed night terrors, specific fears, tics,
temper tantrums or negativism following such upsetting experiences as a hospital admission, an operation or the birth of
a new baby in the family. His technique was to confront the
child with a reconstruction of the traumatic situation. For
example, for the child who suffered from repressed feelings
of sibling rivalry he provided a mother doll, a baby doll and
an older child doll, all constructed in such a way that they
could be dismembered limb from limb and as quickly put
together again. Very young children were allowed to mess
aggressively with sand and water in order to express repressed
feelings of anger and frustration that were, for example,
aroused by a past experience of passivity and helplessness
during an operation. Interpretation was kept to a minimum,
the child getting relief merely from the opportunity of releas-
ing in play feelings which excessive anxiety had previously
caused him to repress. For older children this non-interpre-
tative method was less successful, and children who were reacting to more complex stresses persisting into the present
were not helped by it.

For such children, and they form the bulk of clinic attenders,
a combined approach of interpretative play therapy for the
child and psychological help for the parents is indicated.

3. The Treatment of a Soiler

In Chapter 2 I described the case of a six-year-old boy, Graham
Smith, who repeatedly soiled his trousers. Both parents were

with him on the occasion of his first visit to the hospital. When the psychiatrist greeted him in the waiting room he became flushed, hung his head and silently refused to leave his mother and father. The parents remonstrated with him and finally the father picked him up, prepared to deposit him bodily in the psychiatrists' room. The psychiatrist thereupon asked the father to put Graham down saying that she thought he would manage to come along on his own. This he did, allowing the parents to accompany the psychiatric social worker.

In the playroom Graham was entirely inactive and silently hung his head. The psychiatrist stood with him by the side of the bath. She indicated that she knew what his trouble was, mentioned it by name and said she would try to help him. She then offered him various play materials, but every offer elicited merely a shake of his head. She began to run water into the bath and he watched with some interest. She plopped a little boat into the water and handed him a second one. He took it, threw it in and gradually began to move the boats about in the water. During the next few interviews he began on his own to approach the bath, to run the water and, with growing spontaneity, to produce ever more violent 'storms' and shipwrecks. As he became less inhibited in his play he moved on to other play materials: sand and water, plasticine and paint. It was at this stage that he revealed his castration fears (see Chapter 2). He became increasingly more messy and his play involved the psychiatrist as a person more and more. The main interaction between the two now consisted of him trying to see how much mess, attack and what he thought of as naughtiness, the psychiatrist would tolerate without getting angry with him. This was interpreted to him repeatedly. On one occasion, he hung out of the window with a little toy knife poised over the sill. After repeated taunting glances at the psychiatrist behind him, he finally dropped the knife into the garden. Both went out to retrieve it and then it was time for him to go home.

During the following week he had a series of nightmares and at first he refused to come for his next interview. His anxiety about the knife was interpreted to him when he did appear.

His behaviour in the playroom now became not only messy but destructive. He proposed tearing up all the other children's pictures on the walls and he hurled wet sand about everywhere. The psychiatrist said she did not mind mess; that could be cleaned up, but that she would not allow him to destroy other children's paintings just as she would preserve his own. At one point she actually held on to him to stop him daubing paint all over a picture on the wall. When she let go he astonished her by climbing up a water pipe in the room, roaring with laughter.

The following week he appeared looking very pleased with himself and his mother reported he had been entirely clean since the previous visit. In the same week she too had been able to take a big step forward: she had told her relatives that to help in her father's shop was too much for her. Graham's behaviour in treatment now underwent a second change. From being concerned only with messing and destroying objects he began to engage in constructive play with toys in the sand tray.

His relationship to his doctor also changed. Instead of staging constant battles of wills with her he now began to tell her items of news about himself, ask questions and engage her in play. The content of this related to his family and to his visions of himself grown-up. He had made a move from anal stage attitudes and activities to genital stage behaviour.

A temporary setback occurred after a minor cut on his forehead which required stitching. Treatment was ended by mutual decision. Graham was now more outgoing at school and was getting considerable satisfactions from his classroom achievements. He voiced reluctance to continue his visits to the psychiatrist because, he said, his teacher missed him when he was not at school.

4. Crisis Intervention with Children

What can we learn from treatment processes in a psychiatric setting that is of general relevance to helping children in times of stress? In psychotherapy the child is encouraged to re-enact experiences that lie either in the past or in the present but outside the treatment setting. The therapist offers himself and his play material for the child to use in reconstructing his experiences. The aims of therapy are: (1) to allow the child free expression of his feelings; (2) to help him correct his misperceptions of the environment; and (3) to provide insight, that is to help him to understand why he feels the way he does, in order to increase his mastery over his emotions.

Are these aims at all relevant to parents and other adults who look after children in times of crisis? The first two certainly are. All children in their play re-enact the stresses of their current lives. This is a spontaneous process by which children master their experiences. When a child is struggling with problems of his parents' authority over him, for example, he may well act these out in games of mothers and fathers in which he assumes the parental role and often behaves much more punitively than the real parents do. More definite crisis experiences also become incorporated into play. When a death occurs games of funerals and burial may be stimulated. To the onlooker such games often appear sadistic and callous and the impulse to intervene can be strong. It is not difficult however to resist this if one realizes that such play has a therapeutic function in that it helps the child come to terms with anxiety-arousing events.

The relief of anxiety through play has been used as a deliberate technique to help children admitted to hospital. Several paediatric units now make special provisions for the kind of play that enables children to give expression to the feelings aroused by hospitalization and treatment. Often special 'play ladies', sometimes nurses, are given the task of supervising these activities. Children are provided with dolls, furniture, toy hospital equipment, stethoscopes and bandages and, with little encouragement, they proceed to act out their hospital experiences. *They* now give painful injections to their dolls; they kill the doctor off in play; they become in imagination nurses and matrons. Such special arrangements for play on children's wards fulfil two purposes. Firstly, the child can express his feelings unhampered, without arousing criticism from others. Secondly, his play helps doctors and nurses to become aware of the individual child's reactions to his hospital experiences and of the kind of reassurance and explanation appropriate for him. Just as in release therapy after the event, so in the playing out of currently stressful experiences the child is relieved of anxiety without recourse to interpretative, insight-producing techniques.

It is axiomatic that in any situation of sudden stress, children should be allowed to bring out in talk and in play their true thoughts and feelings about the events, even if these are aggressive, sadistic and apparently callous. It is equally axiomatic that when the child reveals his misconceptions about what has happened, these should be listened to respectfully, but that at the same time he should have access to knowledge of the facts as they are.

What about the third aim of psychotherapy: to provide insight by means of interpreting to the child the meaning of his play and the origins of his feelings? Parents and other adults who know a child really well and love him, often respond to what he says with what might technically be called interpretations. They do this quite spontaneously and while doing so they are totally identified with the child. Interpretations can only be made helpfully by someone who has intimate knowledge of a person and is close to him. There are no interpretations of general validity. When a relative stranger has a shot at guessing why a particular person feels and acts the way he does, the chances of his being wrong and of his intervention being totally beside the point are very great indeed. To tell a child that his feelings really mean something that they do not mean at all is merely confusing and only adds to his distress. Moreover, if the interpretation is correct, unless the child has a close positive tie to the person who makes it, he may not be able to master the anxiety aroused by the feelings that have been uncovered and is likely to react by repressing them even further.

While children should always be helped to ventilate their feelings and to correct their misperceptions, an interpretative approach by strange adults cannot be recommended unless it is a part of planned and continuous treatment.

The deliberate provision of opportunities for children to express their feelings during admissions to hospital is a form of *crisis intervention* that can profitably be used in other situations of special stress. Crisis intervention rests on two basic assumptions. The first is that during a crisis people are particularly accessible to psychiatric help. They are at a point in their life when they naturally review their past and are ready to plan for the future; their feelings are stirred up and their defence mechanisms less rigid than during life's usual routine. The second assumption is that short-term help offered at such times will have profound effects in preventing future mental ill-health for all members of the family involved. Gerald Caplan regards crisis intervention as a major technique for preventing mental ill-health.[27] He says 'the important point for maintenance of mental health and avoidance of mental disorder is that the activities of the family or other primary group be directed to helping the person in crisis deal with his problem by some form of activity rather than avoid the problem, or restrict his activity to tension-relieving mechanisms. . . . Thus, in the crisis of bereavement due to the death of a loved person, the sufferer must actively resign himself to the impossibility of ever again satisfying his needs through interaction with the deceased. He must psychologically "bury the dead"; only after this has been done will he be free to seek gratification of these needs from alternative persons.'[28] We shall return to the subject of crisis intervention in the final chapter in relation to the optimal timing of psychiatric treatment (see Chapter 12).

THE PSYCHOLOGICAL TREATMENT OF
DEPRIVED AND DELINQUENT CHILDREN

The method of therapeutic intervention that has been outlined presupposes a framework of care and order in the child's life. Only when there is a stable home, providing affection, continuity of care and some basic social standards can a psychotherapeutic approach alone be helpful.

For a totally rejected child, for a neglected child from a family in which social standards are grossly lacking, or for a child who has lost his family and is being cared for under conditions in which he has no parent figures at all, psychotherapy as such is not appropriate. What such children need more than anything else is an adult who will assume parental responsibility. They do not need a doctor, they need a parent.

But, because of their past deprivations and experiences of stress, such children need a very special kind of parent. They need a person or group of people who will guarantee unconditional affection and support, who are prepared to forego, often for many years, the satisfactions that parents normally get from their children and who will bring to their task professional understanding not only of childhood behaviour but of their own responses both to the children in their care and to the parents whose inadequacies have brought the children to this plight. These are enormous demands and it is not surprising that the care of deprived and delinquent children in our society is often at variance with the treatment principles and techniques recommended by professional experts such as psychiatrists, educationalists and social workers. While neurotic children on the whole get competent treatment based on professionally acceptable principles, the same is not generally true for deprived and delinquent children.

1. The Needs of the Deprived Child

Psychiatrists are often consulted about children in foster care, in children's homes and in various special residential schools. Some of these children have behind them prolonged periods of maternal deprivation in infancy; many were reared by uniformed nurses in institutions governed by strict routines; many have experienced a series of separations from people to whom successively they had become attached. Such children present very special problems. Not only are they poor at forming relationships with others, not only are their capacities to express themselves in words limited and their ideas about the world in general immature for their age, they usually display marked behaviour disorders too. Aggressive outbursts, bed-wetting, soiling, stealing and running away are common among all children who find their way into foster homes or residential care. Grossly deprived children in addition often show obsessional patterns of behaviour. They may be compulsive masturbators; they may be obsessionally preoccupied with sexual topics and swear words; they may be fascinated by keys and locks; they may be fire-setters.

The basic need of such children is to have a permanent

home, yet their symptoms, distressing enough in themselves, often make them quite unacceptable to foster parents and even to some children's homes. In this situation psychiatric help must be directed both to the home and to the child. Foster parents and house-parents require at least as much professional help as ordinary parents do. But the children themselves can often benefit from individual psychotherapeutic treatment. Lavery and Stone recently stressed that grossly deprived children respond best when they are not required to enter into a close one-to-one relationship with the therapist all at once.[98] The fear of yet another broken relationship prevents such children from coming close to their doctor and every approach from the other person evokes anxiety and retreat. In a less intensely emotional situation, for example in a play group with other children, the deprived child may more readily be able to make his initial contact with his therapist. For substitute parent and therapist alike it is important to let the child decide how much he can trust the adult and how much of himself it is safe to reveal. Given a stable substitute home, able to tolerate the child's disturbed behaviour and not make excessive demands on him, deprived children can make considerable gains in personality development.

Often quite old children who have at last found a permanent home need to retrace their developmental steps, adopting for example at eight or nine years of age infantile dependent forms of behaviour. Psychological treatment aims to help the substitute parents recognize this behaviour as an attempt at self-cure, as a recapitulation of an earlier stage of development that failed to provide satisfactory experiences. Sometimes parent surrogates can then with support supply the needed satisfactions for the child; sometimes the psychotherapist is able in his treatment sessions with the child to provide the intense infantile satisfactions he craves, nursing him for example like a baby, feeding him from a bottle, making no demands on him at all. Such needs for infantile gratifications, if fulfilled, are gradually outgrown by the child. Oral behaviour may be followed by an anal stage, pleasure in messing and in testing out capacities for destruction, or by genital stage activities.

In summary, psychological treatment with such children

has two aims: (1) to provide them in the present with experiences they have missed out in the past, and (2) to allow them to correct their distrust of human relationships. It is less a matter of interpretation, of undoing defence mechanisms, than of providing stable supplies which the child can use to make good the gaps in his personality. This process takes many years. The main agents in treatment are, of course, the substitute parents and the psychiatrist's chief functions are to help them in their task and to supply directly for the child those experiences his particular substitute parents are unable to provide.

2. *Psychological Treatment of the Delinquent Child*

The basic problem of treatment for delinquent children, whose main defect is in their conscience structure, is how to help them acquire an inner set of stable standards and values. Often severely delinquent children are also deprived and the treatment problem is a dual one. Most successful treatment approaches have used group methods and these have been particularly rewarding in institutional settings. The pioneer in this field was August Aichhorn whose book *Wayward Youth*[2] was first published in 1925. It is a reflection of his genius, but also of the lack of progress in the treatment of delinquent children, that after thirty years little has been added to his original contribution.

Severely delinquent children, like deprived children, do not benefit from interpretative psychotherapy alone. They require intensive twenty-four-hour-a-day treatment. The popular notion that undisciplined, impulsive children who do not care about the consequences of their acts and are incapable of guilt feelings require merely firm and consistent discipline has given comfort to a great many people working in approved schools and in children's homes. Such institutions are with few exceptions run on disciplinarian lines and while children are in residence their behaviour is often kept in check. There is however little evidence that a regime of enforced discipline and order contributes anything to children's personality development. They accept unavoidable external restraints while they last, but they do not become identified with them and are no more able to exert inner controls than they were before.

In 1918 Aichhorn, a school teacher turned psychoanalyst, founded a home for delinquents that was run on very different lines. All children in his care had experienced gross parental deprivation in the past and had suffered from extreme severity and brutality in their upbringing. His first aim was to compensate the children for their past deprivation of love. He deliberately made the institutional environment as enjoyable as possible for children and staff alike. No demands were at first made on the boys and Aichhorn insisted that all staff members were affectionate, permissive and non-aggressive even in response to aggressive attacks from the boys.

The experience that their own aggression did not evoke retaliation was new for these children; it was unexpected and provided the essential corrective experience. When aggression was not met with counter-aggression it ceased to be satisfying and in fact often led to intense outbursts of frustration and misery, and the first inklings of a guilty conscience. Aichhorn describes a regular sequence of behaviour shown by the asocial and aggressive delinquent boy in response to this permissive environment: an increased sense of his own power, more frequent and more violent acts of aggression, followed later by tears of rage when counter-aggression was not forthcoming, then a period of sensitivity and, finally, conforming behaviour. The emotional crisis which most boys experienced, and which was often deliberately provoked by the staff, contributed to the change from delinquency and unconcern for other people to increased tolerance of frustration and affectionate relationships with others. In time this group of serious delinquents established their own standards and values in the home and all of them later became adjusted in society.

Among the children in his care Aichhorn distinguished between those who were asocial and aggressive, in constant conflict with their environment but with no inner conflicts and those in whom delinquency was merely an expression of an underlying neurosis. It was the first group of children who benefited most from the therapeutic community he created.

In a recent review of the literature on juvenile delinquency Donald West stresses the need for adequate diagnosis and for the careful selection of children for specific treatment approaches.[157] The efficacy of different treatment methods cannot be judged on the basis of results with unselected groups of delinquents.

Ernst Papanek set up a community at Wiltwyck school in New York similar to Aichhorn's. A study of his treatment results confirmed Aichhorn's finding that the therapeutic community approach was more successful in the case of delinquents whose socialization had been defective than in neurotic children with internal conflicts.[106] A comparative study of Wiltwyck boys and boys living in a typical public reformatory where discipline was rigidly enforced, demonstrated the superiority of a therapeutic community approach. Thirty-five boys from each institution, similar in age, social background and the nature of their disorder were compared on a series of personality tests. It was found that Wiltwyck boys became less anxious the longer they were at the school while reformatory boys became more anxious. Authoritarian attitudes and prejudice decreased with length of stay at Wiltwyck; prejudice increased in the reformatory. Wiltwyck children tended to view the world as good rather than evil, to be satisfied with themselves, to see their parents and other adults as loving, and to be much more closely attached to the staff of their school. In the children from the reformatory all these attitudes were reversed. They saw the world as evil rather than good; they viewed adults as punitive and they had few attachments to the staff of their school. These findings tend to bear out the ideas of Papanek who is quoted as saying: 'Punishing teaches the child only how to punish; scolding teaches him how to scold. By showing him that we understand, we teach him to understand; by helping him, we teach him to help; by cooperating, we teach him to cooperate.'

Deprived and severely delinquent children require total care. The reparatory processes necessary to make good their defects of ego and super-ego development, that is, of emotional and intellectual functioning on the one hand and of conscience structure on the other, can only occur when the child spends twenty-four hours a day in an actively therapeutic environment. Moreover, recovery from gross deprivation or distortion of the socialization process in early life takes many years.

It is not surprising that society has not yet found a way of meeting adequately the treatment needs of these children.

Neurotic children are in a different position. Psychotherapy alone is often helpful even within a relatively short time. The treatment aims here are not to provide missing supplies but to alleviate anxiety and guilt and to undo excessive defences in order that normal personality growth can once more proceed.

Robins's long-term follow-up study of children referred to a child guidance clinic has shown that children who presented with delinquency and acting-out behaviour disorders are in adult life far less well adjusted than children who presented with neurotic symptoms.[133] In particular, the delinquent child is more likely in later life to become sociopathic and alcoholic. How far a more intensive and more highly skilled treatment approach to delinquent children can reverse this trend remains to be established. Certainly few delinquents are currently given the kind of emotional experiences Aichhorn and Papanek provided for their charges.

12. Helping the Adults Who Care for the Child

In the last chapter it was pointed out that parents may need considerable help to tolerate the changes in their child that treatment brings about. Moreover when the main causes of a child's psychiatric disturbance are his parents' attitudes and behaviour, no amount of treatment directed at the child alone will succeed unless the parents can be helped to change also. It is only at adolescence, when actual and emotional dependency on the parental home is gradually given up that psychiatrists can in some cases intervene helpfully without involving parents in treatment. One of the aims of treatment then is to strengthen the child's independent views and attitudes and to help him come to terms with his parents as they are, knowing that they can no longer set the boundaries for his existence and that he will soon be able, if he wishes, to attain independence emotionally and in fact. This approach is exceptional and most psychological treatment of children involves parents deeply.

THE CHILD PSYCHIATRIC CLINIC TEAM

The traditional child psychiatric team consists of the psychiatrist, the psychologist and the psychiatric social worker (P.S.W.). *The psychologist's* special task is to assess the child's intellectual abilities, his scholastic performance and educational needs, and to act as intermediary between the clinic and the family on the one hand, and the school and other educational services on the other.

The P.S.W's area of expertise consists of an intimate knowledge of the social services and of the social factors that influence psychiatric illness. Her specific role is to form a link between the clinic and the family, and the community outside. She has a particular responsibility for socially disorganized families who may not for various reasons – not least large family size and hence the more frequent occurrence of illness in the home – be able to keep clinic appointments. By tradition, if home visits need to be made the social worker does them. *The psychiatrist's* task is to coordinate all the information obtained about a case by members of the team, and, with their help, to arrive at a diagnosis of the child's disorder and at an assessment of the parents' personalities. It is his job too to formulate a treatment plan and to take full medical responsibility for each case.

Although each profession has a specific area of expertise, in their psychological treatment roles all use a similar theoretical framework and similar therapeutic techniques. In Britain psychologists do not function as psychotherapists, unless they have, exceptionally, undergone a special training, while in the United States 'counselling' is commonly part of their recognized activities and for this they have been trained. Both psychiatrists and P.S.W.s are experts in the use of psychological treatment methods and the nature of their cooperation and the different roles they play in treatment are determined more by the needs of their patients and by administrative considerations than by their differing treatment skills. Although P.S.W.s do not generally differentiate between their psychotherapeutic activities and their other treatment interventions, preferring to give to both the global name 'casework',[162] the principles and techniques underlying their psychological treatment are exactly the same as those used by psychiatrists in psychotherapy.

WHY A TEAM APPROACH?

In making a treatment plan for a family with a psychiatrically disturbed child, the first questions one must answer are these: (1) Does the child's present disorder lie primarily within himself, that is, is there a constitutional disability or a psychoneurosis stemming from some past emotional trauma, and are the parents on the whole functioning well? (2) Are the difficulties in the main due to disrupted or neurotic child–parent interactions, both parents and child showing psychological disturbances to some degree? or (3) Is the problem primarily within the parents, the child's minor disturbances being but a sign of the parents' own treatment needs?

(1) In the first case it is often possible and even preferable for one person to undertake treatment. This may be the psychiatrist or the psychologist and sometimes the P.S.W., depending on the child's needs. For example, if the problem is basically educational, the psychologist may take on the case, discussing the child's condition and his treatment frequently with the parents. If the child suffers from brain dramage or autism, the psychiatrist may choose to undertake treatment himself because he is often in a better position than the P.S.W. to evaluate the significance of the symptoms the parents describe and to advise them on their day-to-day care of the child. Parents of handicapped children frequently need help to come to terms with their child's difficulties and this can effectively be given only by someone with psychotherapeutic skills. If the child has a psychoneurosis and his parents function relatively well, intensive psychotherapy for the child may be all that is needed.

(2) Most cases referred to a child psychiatric clinic, however, fall into the second category of children whose psychiatric disorder is the result of disturbed child–parent interactions. Here both child and parents need treatment.

(3) If the main disturbance is within the parents, if, for example, the problem is primarily a disturbed marital relationship or a neurotic reaction of a mother to her very young child, the decision will usually be to focus on the parents alone. They may be offered psychotherapy individually, or else joint interviews with husband and wife, or possibly psychotherapy in a group together with other parents. Which member of the treatment team, psychiatrist or P.S.W., undertakes this treatment will depend more on their individual training and experience than on their professional discipline.

TREATMENT FOR PARENTS

The principles underlying psychotherapy for adults are the same as for children (see pp. 195–6). Consideration of these principles explains why it is difficult for the same person to treat both parent and child separately. The child therapist identifies with the child. He sees the world from his viewpoint. When a child has experienced recurrent hostile attacks from his mother, for example, or when his mother's repeated, unsuccessful love affairs have utterly bewildered him, it is difficult for his therapist not to feel critical of this mother. Yet such feelings, even if not expressed in words, are antitherapeutic for the mother. They provide her with a mere repetition of her everyday experiences with other people. They increase her defensiveness so that her energies go into warding off hostile attacks from others and she has no chance to express her own feelings and to understand them and her behaviour better. The child's therapist is urgently motivated to have the mother be different and this does not help her at all.

Expression of previously repressed parts of the self are possible only when one feels accepted and uncriticized and is sure that whatever one reveals will not be passed on to people who do not share this attitude. Children attending a psychiatric clinic with reactive behaviour disorders are always in conflict with their parents to some degree. Their parents have been unable to accept them, or at least a part of them, uncritically. Indeed this is what has kept the disturbance going. How can a child express repressed thoughts and feelings in treatment when he knows that his therapist also has an intimate relationship with his mother? But more than this: a basic assumption of all intimate interpersonal relationships is frankness. How can the same therapist guard the secrets of one member of the couple in treatment while yet being completely frank with the other?

These two dilemmas can be resolved by having different therapists for parents and child. Therapists meet of course to exchange information, to assess progress and to decide on which area to focus in treatment. The child's therapist also has contact with the parents. He is after all treating their child and to this extent he is responsible to them. But his relationship with them is a more objective and a more formal one. Which member of the child guidance team takes on the parents and which the child depends again on the particular skills and experiences of the staff members in each clinic. The traditional arrangement is for the child psychiatrist to treat the child and for the P.S.W. to treat the parents. If a child psychotherapist is attached to the clinic he or she may take on the child and then either psychiatrist or P.S.W. will treat the parents.

An alternative solution to the dilemmas that arise when one therapist undertakes to treat both child and parents is to see them jointly as a *family group.* This may be the treatment of choice with older children especially in those cases where relationships between child and parents are so strained that, unless some immediate improvement of mutual understanding is achieved, an actual break in the family may occur.

The presence of the therapist in a neutral treatment setting allows the family members to distance themselves from their interactions with each other which, when they happen at home, involve them so completely that no control and no understanding of their own and each other's feelings are possible. Such a treatment setting also makes possible the revelation of feelings and thoughts which none had been free to tell the others before and this too increases mutual understanding.

What are the aims of psychological treatment for parents? Those parents whose disturbed attitudes and behaviour towards their children or each other spring from their own neurotic personality difficulties require a therapeutic experience that will help them to undo excessive repressions, to face unconscious conflicts within themselves and to cope with their feelings more realistically. In psychotherapy parents display their habitual patterns of interacting with other people. They also project onto the therapist feelings which stem from their own childhood relationships.

Graham's mother, for example (see Chapter 11), told the P.S.W. early in the course of treatment of her own special childhood attachment to her father and of her feelings of guilt towards her elder sister who got less affection than she did. While Mrs Smith's own marriage had been happy, her sister's had ended in divorce. Somehow Mrs Smith, who had never resolved her childhood feelings of rivalry, triumph and guilt towards her sister, felt it was up to her to make the sister's life easier. When her father became ill Mrs Smith felt obliged to help the sister in the parental shop although she resented the strains this imposed on her own family life. Without her help, she felt, the sister would not manage.

Graham's parents at first had joint interviews with the P.S.W. while the psychiatrist saw the child, and at the end of each treatment session the psychiatrist joined the P.S.W. and parents briefly. When it became clear that the mother required more help than her husband, that he in fact, had no particular neurotic problems, Mrs Smith and Graham came alone to the clinic. As the psychiatrist became more involved in Graham's treatment she suggested that she should no longer meet Mrs Smith on a regular basis. The P.S.W. at first resisted this plan, feeling that there were complexities to the case with which she might need help from the psychiatrist. She felt that she wanted the psychiatrist there to support her in her treatment of the mother. After some discussion the psychiatrist indicated that she thought the P.S.W. would manage very well on her own and in fact subsequent interviews were completed by mother and P.S.W. without the psychiatrist's presence. It was following this change of arrangements that Mrs Smith was able to make a very similar change in her own life. She too now felt it possible to leave her sister to it. She withdrew from the shop and, to her surprise and to her slight disappointment, the sister indicated that she was managing perfectly well on her own. In identifying herself with the psychiatrist and her sister with the P.S.W., Mrs Smith was able to correct her misperception of her sister as a helpless, dependent person.

The alteration in Mrs Smith's life was important not so much in itself but because it sprang from a more fundamental change in her attitudes. To have 'advised' her to stop working in the shop would not have had the same effect. For one thing she might not have been able to take this advice and would then have felt guilty not only towards her sister but towards the clinic. Even if she had been able to follow such advice, her basic conflicts would have remained untouched, and, what is more, the social worker would have put herself into a position of authority over Mrs Smith, thus reinforcing rather than reducing her defensive manoeuvres.

Some parents require to make more profound changes than this mother. But if a parent's problem is primarily a neurotic one, treatment aims to help him express in the transference relationship with the therapist those remnants of childhood feelings that give him trouble. The therapist's interventions encourage the parent to bring into treatment feelings currently experienced outside the treatment setting and feelings of long ago, to understand them and to match them against the actual relationship between parents and therapist in the 'here and now'. It is this process that provides the 'corrective experience'.

Other parents, whose personality difficulties are not neurotic, who, for example, are disturbed because their own ego and super-ego development have been defective, perhaps on the basis of gross family disruption or deprivations in childhood, may require a less interpretative, analytical approach. Here the therapist's function is often to provide very long-term support, to offer herself as someone to whom the mother or both parents can always come when in difficulties, in fact to supply a kind of substitute mothering. Often too other social agencies must be mobilized to help families who are disrupted or who have difficulty in coping with the ordinary demands of family life. Nursery school placement, for example, may be essential to provide a fatherless child with additional stimulation and contact with other adults and to free the mother for work or other activities outside the home. Fathers with poor work records may need help especially directed at this area of their functioning.

To enable parents to use other community sources of social and practical support is one of the P.S.W.s' specific responsibilities. In carrying out this task her aim is never to take over from her clients but to strengthen the parents' own capabilities and their feelings of self-worth. Every decision must in the end be theirs and it is they who must initiate every change in their life circumstances.

HELPING FOSTER PARENTS

Children who have no parents able to look after them are taken care of by local authority children's departments. Current policy is that these children should as far as possible be boarded out with foster parents especially in infancy and during the pre-school period to avoid the personality defects which can result from an institutional upbringing during the early years of life.

Foster parents play a vital part in the care of temporarily or permanently deprived children in our society. Their role is essentially a parental one but the children they look after have inevitably been exposed to unusual life stresses and often to gross social deprivation too before they reach their foster homes. Foster children are almost all emotionally disturbed to a greater or lesser degree and fostering itself must be looked on as a therapeutic undertaking. To this extent foster parents are more than parents. Their extra responsibilities are recognized and they are supported and supervized in their task by trained child-care workers attached to children's departments.

Whenever a child is fostered four sets of people are involved: the child, the foster parents, the child-care officer and the real parents. Long-term fostering generally indicates a failure in parental functioning, and even short-term fostering, necessitated by maternal illness or childbirth, may be a pointer to more widespread family pathology.[146] Inevitably parents applying for public care for their children have profound guilt feelings. Their reactions towards the children's department, the foster parents and the children themselves are irrational, a common defence in these parents being the projection of their guilt, so that instead of presenting themselves as unhappy and remorseful they become belligerent and complaining, voicing hostile criticism of the child or of the care he is getting. Such parents require skilled help in their own right. Their children need realistic explanations for their behaviour, so that they can eventually come to terms with it without having to think of their parents as 'bad'. Every child incorporates his parents: to some degree he *is* his mother and his father. To the extent that his parents seem 'bad' to him, he himself feels bad and unlovable.

Foster parents must clearly be able to manage a series of complicated relationships with other people: with the children in their care, with the child-care officer, and in many cases also with at least one of the child's own parents. This is a tall order. What is remarkable is that so many people, themselves untrained, manage this complex undertaking extremely well. It is the more remarkable because very often the motivation of a couple to offer themselves as foster parents springs directly from neurotic parts of their own personalities. It seems that fostering provides opportunities for people to sublimate a previously repressed part of themselves and in the majority of cases the process is entirely successful. But the fact that foster parents are frequently motivated by neurotic forces also has its dangers.

Mrs White was illegitimate but spent the first years of her life with her own parents. The father then deserted the family and, because the mother had to work, Mrs White was fostered, unfortunately in a series of different foster homes. The last of these was with a childless couple who became so attached to her that they asked to adopt her. The mother however opposed this and at the age of twelve Mrs White returned home. Meanwhile her mother had married and there were now other children in the family. The relationship between Mrs White and her step-father was poor and she was not really close to her mother either. She felt herself to be a constant reminder to both of them of her mother's first, illicit relationship.

Mrs White married young and although she had three sons and a daughter, Anne, she continued working part-time, latterly in a home for unmarried mothers and their babies. She described her 'special feelings for people in that situation' and the great satisfactions this work gave her. Some years ago however she heard of an illegitimate child. 'With my background I've always been interested in homeless children and I thought it would be a sister for Anne.' She accepted the girl as a foster child despite the fact that housework and looking after her already large family did not satisfy her and she was eagerly anticipating the time when she would be free to take a full-time job again.

Her feelings for the child were such that she was unable to cope with the jealousies that arose between her and her own daughter. Her real sympathies were with the foster child and Anne reacted to this with great distress. Mrs White could not tolerate the guilt feelings she had towards Anne and, unable to resolve the situation, she decided the foster child must go back to her children's home. She was identified with this child and the conflict she acted out by taking her into her home and then letting her go was between her own needs and those of her family. Her inability to reconcile these was a re-creation in adult life of her unresolved childhood conflict. *Then* she felt herself an unwanted member of her family, having to repress her own needs for the sake of her mother and step-father.

Now in adult life she adopted the very same solution. It was one that did not in fact clear up her own child's miseries. She continued to be emotionally disturbed, feeling responsible for having pushed the other child out of the house. Nor did her actions help the foster child. For her it might have been better not to have been fostered at all. This mother had yet a further pregnancy and it was at this time that she first presented to a psychiatrist with a severe neurotic illness.

It is clear that when people offer themselves as foster parents their own personalities must be assessed in great detail. One must know why it is they want to foster a deprived child and exactly what this will mean to the family as a whole. One must know too what the strengths of potential foster parents are and how prepared they will be to accept the help available to them in their new undertaking.

Perhaps Mrs White should not have been encouraged to take a foster child at all. It is possible, however, that if expert help, not only 'supervision' but treatment, from a trained social worker, such as a child-care officer, or P.S.W., or even a psychiatrist, had been available to her at the crucial time she might have coped better with the foster child and with Anne, and could have made considerable gains in her own personality adjustment. Such help is time-consuming and it can only be given by people trained in psychotherapeutic techniques. Yet time spent then could perhaps have prevented Mrs White's subsequent nervous illness and admission to hospital.

What sort of help is available to foster parents? Certainly all get supervision and support from child-care workers. In some children's departments child-care officers conduct discussion groups for foster parents in which the parents can talk about problems that arise in caring for their charges and help each other increase their understanding of the children and of their own reactions to them. Such groups have therapeutic responsibilities for foster mothers but their chief function is to enable foster parents to view their work not merely as charitable but in a professional light. The support they get from each other and from the child-care worker helps them to tolerate the emotional strains that invariably accompany their task, strains that may be due to the child's difficulties or their own unresolved conflicts, often to a combination of both. To exclude from the pool of foster parents all those who are motivated for this work by their own childhood experiences would reduce the available foster homes to a very small number indeed. But it should be recognized that in helping foster parents the professional worker must focus not only on the child's feelings and life experiences but on those of the foster parents too.

In this situation the child psychiatrist can be helpful in several ways: (1) directly, by providing psychiatric treatment for those foster children who need it and who may be referred to him from a number of sources (e.g. the child-care officer, the foster parents, the G.P., the school); (2) indirectly, by providing a consultation service for children's departments and voluntary child-care agencies and (3) by organizing professional discussion groups for staff members of fostering agencies.

(1) *Direct treatment of the child*, of course, involves the foster parents too. Like natural parents they must understand the aims of treatment and be prepared to explore and, if necessary, modify their own reactions to the child. But for deprived children the foster home is potentially more therapeutic than the psychiatrist (see Chapter 11), and his main task is to collaborate with the child-care worker in helping foster parents to increase their therapeutic effectiveness.

(2) Leon Eisenberg has described the success of a *consultation service* set up in Baltimore specifically *to help child-care agencies*.[46] Children regarded as psychiatrically disturbed were given complete diagnostic assessments which included interviews with the foster parents and with the true parents if they were still in the picture. Each case was then discussed fully by the clinic staff together with the child-care workers concerned and recommendations for future care were made. Most children had experienced gross neglect, physical ill-treatment, marital strife and frequent desertions prior to fostering. One half had had three or more placements either because of their own unacceptable behaviour or because of a crisis in their foster families. Psychiatric referral was commonly precipitated by a definite event such as an impending court appearance, suspension from school or a request from foster parents to have the child removed. Three quarters of the children seen were found

to be most suitably placed in their present foster homes although some needed very specialized foster care. A few were able to return to their own parents, some required psychiatric hospital care, and for a small number placement in a training school or in a children's home was recommended. In three quarters of the cases the clinic recommendations were put into practice and most of these children improved. The child-care workers appreciated the service greatly. It relieved them of the burden of medical responsibility for which their training did not equip them; it helped them to clarify their own ideas about their cases and it supported them in carrying out their work. They were no longer alone but had skilled psychiatric and psychological help to call on whenever the need arose.

(3) There is yet a third way in which psychiatrists can provide indirect help for foster parents. This is by holding *regular discussion groups with the staff members of fostering agencies*. Group discussions with a psychiatrist are a most effective technique for helping professional workers of all kinds who are concerned with taking care of other people. Such groups fulfil two functions: they help the participants with their day-to-day clinical problems and they provide in-service training in psychotherapeutic skills.

WHAT CAN PSYCHIATRISTS CONTRIBUTE TO OTHER
PROFESSIONAL WORKERS IN THE CHILD CARE FIELD?

All children who need to be looked after outside their own homes, for whatever reason, are children at risk. All have experienced unusual stresses and many are psychiatrically disturbed. The people who care for them are in a unique position to prevent life crises from becoming pathogenic, to prevent separation experiences from developing into deprivation, and to provide the kind of upbringing for each child that will make good his past deficiencies of care. This more than any other is the field of practical preventive psychiatry. It is not surprising that it is a major concern of the child psychiatrist although at present he is often called in only when a child is obviously ill or when an administrative crisis arises. Of course psychiatrists try to be helpful when a social agency is faced with a dilemma. But they would also welcome being consulted more often about the proper psychiatric first aid for children in the throes of emotional crises.

All people who care for children outside their own homes, whether semi-professional like foster parents, or professional like house-parents in institutions and teachers in special residential schools, require psychological skills in order to do their work effectively. Common sense and kindness are not enough. Many people who find themselves looking after other people's children have in fact had no training to help them do their work in a way that is therapeutic for the child. They are forced to rely on their own life experiences and on their personal attitudes and beliefs and these are often woefully inadequate to meet the needs of children in special risk groups. Seventy per cent of full-time care staff in children's homes have no formal qualification for their job.[117] Even professional people like teachers, doctors and nurses have not generally been taught much about psychological aspects of child care. This is not to say that no untrained person must look after children but to emphasize the need for *regular in-service training*.

The most effective way of providing this is the *professional training group*. This has a very important part to play *outside institutions* in helping social workers, child-care and probation officers, family doctors and health visitors in the psychological management of their patients in the community. The pioneer in this field is Michael Balint whose training groups for general practitioners in London have served as a model for all such endeavours.[10, 11] Regular group meetings of professional workers with a psychiatrist are an ideal setting for the discussion and clarification of interactions between doctor or social worker and patient. The mutual exploration of problem cases not only helps the participants with their ongoing work but provides a valuable extension to their training in psychological treatment methods. The reactions of his fellow-workers and a psychiatrist to his report of a problem case often enable the doctor or social worker to take a fresh look at what is happening and to structure his treatment approach more effectively.

Professional training groups also contribute greatly to the care of children *in institutions*. Here the group is composed of all staff members irrespective of status or professional background and is led by an expert in psychological treatment methods who may be a psychiatrist, a psychoanalyst or a social worker trained in group methods. The discussion focuses on the interactions between staff and children. Inevitably the children arouse feelings in the staff members: anger, frustration and anxiety, as well as affection and pleasure. Inevitably too irritations and frustrations arise between staff members, often in relation to the organization of institutional life. The group provides an opportunity to ventilate such feelings and to get relief from doing so. When frustrations are aired in the group they are unlikely to intrude into the staff members' relationships with the children. But a training group does more than provide opportunities for catharsis. When several staff members describe their individual responses to the same child, they learn to see him from a slightly different and more objective point of view. They can help each other to work out why a child evoked a particular response in them and what this means from the point of view of the child's personality development. The psychological expert's role in a training group is not primarily a didactic one. He is not there to answer questions. His main task is to facilitate free discussion and to enable all staff members to participate. He does this by being alert to the tensions within the group, by reducing anxiety if need be and especially by helping all participants to preserve their self-esteem with their colleagues. His second task is to be a role model and to put across a therapeutic attitude. He shows the group members, by example and by alerting them to their own experiences in the group, how tensions can be resolved so that they in turn can be helpful to their charges.

His third contribution is to offer interpretations of the children's behaviour if staff members are not themselves able to explain it. Such a group is not a therapeutic group. The private lives of the participants are not analysed. Their own feelings are examined only in relation to their work.[176] Although an expert leader is essential for the running of the group, its members in the end learn more from each other than from him.

A training group in an institution, for example in an

approved school or a school for maladjusted children, in a children's home or in a hospital unit for children, is often very successful indeed in increasing the therapeutic skills of its participants. It also serves to form the individual members of the unit into a truly cooperative team. Difficulties can arise, however, as a result of the hierarchical staff structure of institutions. In the group all are equally free to participate, matron and junior staff alike are called upon to give their views. This frequently arouses anxieties that the authority of senior staff members will be undermined outside the group. In a hospital setting, where the psychiatrist is part of the staff structure, such difficulties are usually overcome easily. In a non-medical setting, however, particularly one where staff members come from a number of different professional backgrounds, this may be more difficult. The success of a training group in such an institution depends very largely on the enthusiasm of its director. When he or she is identified with the aims of the group, this new teaching venture can in time have profound effects on the total atmosphere of the community. Staff members learn new methods of coping with problems, methods whose purpose is not merely to preserve the institution intact but to do so in a way that fosters personality change and the acquisition of new social skills in all its residents.

In summary, child psychiatric units can be viewed as providing three different kinds of service:

(1) *An individual diagnostic and treatment service* for all children and their families who are identified or who identify themselves as in need of help and who are referred to the psychiatrist. These are generally children who are not cared for by other social agencies. The main source of referral are general practitioners, paediatricians, school teachers and school psychologists.

(2) *A special diagnostic service for social agencies.* Here close, direct links between the psychiatric clinic and the agency are cultivated. Special problem cases are referred for full diagnostic assessment and for treatment recommendations based on the mutual discussion of each case.

(2) A programme of *regular group discussions with other professional workers* to help them deal with their current problems and to increase their therapeutic skills. Professional workers

in residential schools, children's homes and hospital units function better when they have regular help and support in their treatment of the children and in their contacts with parents. Professional workers in the community whose job it generally is to help other adults, e.g. parents and foster parents, to care for children, welcome opportunities to discuss the management of their cases.

At present child psychiatrists are used by many social agencies. The courts can ask for psychiatric reports and recommendations for delinquent children, probation officers can refer children for assessment and treatment and children's departments and voluntary agencies also have access to psychiatric clinics. But the nature of the contact between the social agency and the psychiatric department and the kind of service provided vary widely. Often the contact is a purely informal one depending on the personal relationships between individual members of staff. More often than not diagnostic assessment of a child, even a child in the care of another agency, is a prelude to the psychiatric clinic totally taking over the case. This may indeed be the right treatment for the child, but very often the professional worker already concerned with the case could, with help, have continued the treatment himself. The plea is sometimes made that the agency case worker is 'too busy' to undertake more intensive work with children or their parents. But the psychiatrist is also busy and the waiting time for treatment at most clinics is absurdly long. The fact is that not extra time but extra skill is needed to help families under stress.

Should child psychiatrists assume that they alone can develop this skill, and so devote all their time to the very skilled care of a very few families? Or should they rather use every opportunity available to help other professional workers in the child-care field increase their own therapeutic expertise? The answers to these questions depend not only on child psychiatrists. They depend as much on social workers and on how they view their roles. So long as they fight shy of dignifying their work by calling it 'treatment', they will regard the psychiatrist as in some special way fitted to deal with 'serious' cases, while they themselves feel confident only in their handling of 'ordinary cases'. But what is a 'serious' case and does the 'ordinary' case in fact require less therapeutic skill?

Unless other workers in this field, probation officers, child-care workers, health visitors, even family doctors, are prepared to use the psychiatrist not only to take difficult cases off their hands or to resolve a crisis but to help them in their day-to-day work with families, and unless psychiatrists are prepared to spend a large part of their time on providing both a diagnostic service and further training for other professions, very many families who need psychologically skilled help will not get it at all. It is not just a fancy to suggest that the child psychiatrist's ultimate, although perhaps unrealistic aim, should be to make other professional workers so skilled in psychological treatment techniques that he himself is out of a job.

References

1. Ackerman, N. W., from *The Psychodynamics of Family Life*, Basic Books Inc., Publishers, New York, 1958.
2. Aichhorn, A., *Wayward Youth*, Viking, New York, 1935 (first published 1925).
3. Andrews, G., and Harris, M., *The Syndrome of Stuttering*, Clinics in Developmental Medicine No. 17, 1964.
4. Anthony, E. J., 'An Experimental Approach to the Psychopathology of Childhood: Encopresis', *British Journal of Medical Psychology*, 1957, *30*, p. 146.
5. Anthony S., *The Child's Discovery of Death: a Study in Child Psychology*, Kegan Paul, Trench, Trubner & Co., 1940.
6. Asuni, T., 'Maladjustment and Delinquency', *Journal of Child Psychology and Psychiatry*, 1964, *3–4*, p. 219.
7. Backett, E. M., and Johnston, A. M., 'Social Pattern of Road Accidents to Children', *British Medical Journal*, 1959, *1*, p. 409.
8. Baird, D., 'The Contribution of Obstetrical Factors to Serious Physical and Mental Handicap in Children', *Journal of Obstetrics and Gynaecology*, 1959, *66*, p. 743.
9. Bakwin, H., 'The Hospital Care of Infants and Children', *Journal of Pediatrics*, 1951, *39*, p. 383.
10. Balint, M., *The Doctor, his Patient and the Illness*, Pitman Medical, 1957.
11. Balint, M. and E., *Psychotherapeutic Techniques in Medicine*, Tavistock Publications, 1961.
12. Bannister, H., and Ravden, M., 'The Problem Child and his Environment', *British Journal of Psychology*, 1944, *34*, p. 60.
13. Bannister, H., and Ravden, M., 'The Environment and the Child', *British Journal of Psychology*, 1945, *35*, p. 82.
14. Bany, M. A., and Johnson, L. V., *Classroom Group Behaviour*, Macmillan Company, New York, and Collier-Macmillan, London, 1964.
15. Bateson, G., Jackson, D. D., Haley J., and Weakland, J., 'Towards a Theory of Schizophrenia', *Behavioral Science*, 1956, *1*, p. 251.
16. Bernstein, B., 'A Socio-linguistic Approach to Social Learning', in Penguin Survey of the Social Sciences, 1965.
17. Bettelheim, B., *Love is Not Enough*, Free Press, Glencoe, Illinois, 1950.
18. Borgatta, E. F., and Fanschel, D., *Behavioral Characteristics of Children Known to Psychiatric Out-Patient Clinics*, Child Welfare League of America, 1965.
19. Boverman, H., personal communication, 1967.
20. Bowlby, J., *Maternal Care and Mental Health*, W. H. O., Monograph 2, Geneva, 1951.
21. Bowlby, J., 'Childhood Mourning and Its Implications for Psychiatry', *American Journal of Psychiatry*, 1961, *118*, p. 481.

22. Bowlby, J., Ainsworth, M., Boston, B., and Rosenbluth, D., 'The Effects of Mother–Child Separation: a Follow-up Study', *British Journal of Medical Psychology*, 1956, *29*, p. 211.

23. Branch, M. and Cash, A., *Gifted Children*, Souvenir Press, 1966.

24. Briffault, R., *The Mothers, a Study of the Origins of Sentiments and Institutions*, Vol. I, Allen and Unwin, 1927.

25. Brown, G. W., 'The Family of the Schizophrenic Patient', in Coppen, A., and Walk A., (eds.), *Recent Developments in Schizophrenia*, Headley Brothers, Ashford, Kent, 1967.

26. Burn, M., *Mr Lyward's Answer*, Hamish Hamilton, 1959.

27. Caplan, G., *Principles of Preventive Psychiatry*, Tavistock Publications, 1964.

28. ibid., p. 45.

29. Casler, L., 'The Effects of Supplementary Verbal Stimulation on a Group of Institutionalised Infants', *Journal of Child Psychology and Psychiatry*, 1965, *6*, p. 19.

30. Cattell, R. B., *The Scientific Analysis of Personality*, Penguin Books, 1965.

31. Caudill, W., and Weinstein, H., 'Maternal Care and Infant Behavior in Japanese and American Urban Middle Class Families', in Koenig, R., and Hill, R., (eds.), *Yearbook of the International Sociological Association*, 1966.

32. Central Advisory Council for Education (England), *Children and Their Primary Schools*, Vol. I, H.M.S.O., 1967.

33. Central Advisory Council for Education (England), *Children and Their Primary Schools*, Vol. II, appendix 3, H.M.S.O., 1967.

34. ibid., appendix 10.

35. Creak, M., 'Childhood Psychosis: a Review of 100 Cases', *British Journal of Psychiatry*, 1963, *109*, p. 84.

36. Dinnage, R. and Kellmer Pringle, M. L., *Residential Child Care – Facts and Fallacies*, Longmans, 1967.

37. Dinnage, R. and Kellmer Pringle, M. L., *Foster Home Care – Facts and Fallacies*, Longmans, 1967.

38. Douglas, J. W. B., *The Home and the School*, McGibbon and Kee, 1964.

39. Douglas, J. W. B., Ross, J. M. and Simpson, H. R., *All our Future*, Peter Davies, London, 1968.

40. Drillien, C. M., *The Growth and Development of the Prematurely Born Infant*, Livingstone, 1964.

41. Earle, A. M., and Earle, B. V., 'Early Maternal Deprivation and Later Psychiatric Illness', *American Journal of Orthopsychiatry*, 1961, *31*, p. 181.

42. Eilenberg, M. D., 'Remand Home Boys: 1930–1955', *British Journal of Criminology*, 1961, *2*, p. 111.

43. Eisenberg, L., 'The Strategic Deployment of the Child Psychiatrist in Preventive Psychiatry', *Journal of Child Psychology and Psychiatry*, 1961, *2*, p. 229.

44. Eisenberg, L., 'Behavioral Manifestations of Cerebral Damage in Childhood', in Birch, H. G., (ed.), *Brain Damage in Children*, Williams and Wilkins Co., New York, 1964.

45. Eisenberg, L., and Kanner, L., 'Early Infantile Autism 1943–1955', *American Journal of Orthopsychiatry*, 1956, *26*, p. 556.

46. Eisenberg, L., Marlowe, B., and Hastings, M., 'Diagnostic Services for Maladjusted Foster Children: an Orientation towards an Acute Need', *American Journal of Orthopsychiatry*, 1958, *28*, p. 750.

47. Erikson, E. H., *Childhood and Society*, Penguin Books, 1965.

48. Erikson, E. H., 'Identity and the Life Cycle', *Psychological Issues*, *I*, Monograph 1, 1959.

49. Fairweather, D. V. I., and Illesley, R., 'Obstetric and Social Origins of Mentally Handicapped Children', *British Journal of Preventive and Social Medicine*, 1960, *14*, p. 149.

50. Faris, R. E. L., and Dunham, H. W., *Mental Disorders in Urban Areas*, Chicago, 1939.

51. Field, E., *A Validation Study of Hewitt and Jenkins' Hypothesis*, Home Office Research Unit Report No. 10, H.M.S.O., 1967.

52. Freud, A., *The Psycho-Analytical Treatment of Children*, Imago Publishing Company, 1946.

53. Freud, A., *The Ego and the Mechanisms of Defence*, Hogarth Press, 1946.

54. Freud, A., 'The Role of Bodily Illness in the Mental Life of Children', *Psychoanalytic Study of the Child*, 1952, *8*, p. 69.

55. Freud, S., 'Analysis of a Phobia in a Five-year-old Boy' (1909), in *Collected Papers*, Vol. 3, Hogarth Press, 1959.

56. Freud, S., 'Mourning and Melancholia' in *The Complete Works*, Vol. 14, Hogarth Press, 1957.

57. Gay, M. J., *Children in Residential Care*, unpublished prize essay, 1967.

58. Gay, M. J., and Tonge, W. L., 'The Late Effects of Loss of Parents in Childhood', *British Journal of Psychiatry*, 1967, *113*, p. 753.

59. General Register Office, *Classification of Occupations*. H.M.S.O., 1960.

60. Glueck, S. and E., *Unraveling Juvenile Delinquency*, Harvard University Press, 1950.

61. Goldberg, E. M., and Morrison, S. L., 'Schizophrenia and Social Class', *British Journal of Psychiatry*, 1963, *109*, p. 785.

62. Goldfarb, W., 'Effects of Psychological Deprivation in Infancy and Subsequent Stimulation', *American Journal of Psychiatry*, 1946, *102*, p. 18.

63. Government White Paper, *The Child, the Family and the Young Offender*, H.M.S.O., 1965.

64. Graham, P. J., and Meadows, C. E., 'Psychiatric Disorder in the Children of West Indian Immigrants', *Journal of Child Psychology and Psychiatry*, 1967, *8*, p. 105.

65. Graham, P. and Rutter, M., 'Organic Brain Dysfunction and Child Psychiatric Disorder', *British Medical Journal*, 1968, *3*, p. 695.

66. Greer, S., 'The Relationship between Parental Loss and Attempted Suicide: a Control Study', *British Journal of Psychiatry*, 1964, *110*, p. 698.

67. Gregory, I., 'Anterospective Data Following Childhood Loss of a Parent: 1. Delinquency and High School Drop-out', *Achives of General Psychiatry*, 1965, *13*, p. 99.

68. Hare, E. H., and Shaw, G. K., *Mental Health on a New Housing Estate*, Maudsley Monographs No. 12, Oxford University Press, 1965.

69. Harlow, H. F., and Zimmerman, R. R., 'Affectional Responses in Infant Monkeys', *Science*, 1959, *130*, p. 421.

70. Hawkes, N., *Immigrant Children in British Schools*, Pall Mall Press, 1966.

71. Hersov, L. A., 'Persistent Non-attendance at School', *Journal of Child Psychology and Psychiatry*, 1961, *I*, p. 130.

72. Hersov, L. E., 'Refusal to Go to School', *Journal of Child Psychology and Psychiatry*, 1961, *1*, p. 137.

73. Hewitt, L. E., and Jenkins, R. L., *Fundamental Patterns of Maladjustment: the Dynamics of their Origin*, Michigan Child Guidance Institute, Illinois, 1946.

74. Hilgard, J. R., Newman, M. F., and Fisk, F., 'Strength of Adult Ego Following Childhood Bereavement', *American Journal of Orthopsychiatry*, 1960, *30*, p. 788.

75. Hollingshead, A. B., and Redlich, F. C., *Social Class and Mental Illness: a Community Study*, Chapman and Hall, 1958.
76. Howells, J. G., *Family Psychiatry*, Oliver and Boyd, 1963.
77. Ingram, T. T. S., 'A Characteristic Form of Overactive Behaviour in Brain Damaged Children', *Journal of Mental Science*, 1956, *102*, p. 550.
78. Ingram, T. T. S., 'Specific Developmental Disorders of Speech in Childhood', *Brain*, 1959, *82*, p. 450.
79. Isaacs, S., 'Some Notes on the Incidence of Neurotic Difficulties in Young Children', *British Journal of Educational Psychology*, 1932, *2*, p. 71.
80. Jaspers, K., *General Psychopathology*, transl. by J. Hoenig and M. Hamilton, Manchester University Press, 1963, p. 328.
81. ibid., p. 447.
82. Johnson, A. M., and Szurek, S. A., 'The Genesis of Anti-social Acting-out in Children and Adults', *Psychoanalytic Quarterly*, 1952, *21*, p. 323.
83. Johnson, W., *The Onset of Stuttering*, University of Minnesota Press, Minneapolis, 1959.
84. Kagan, J., and Moss, H. A., 'The Stability of Passive and Dependent Behavior from Childhood through Adulthood', *Child Development*, 1960, *31*, p. 577.
85. Kanner, L., 'Early Infantile Autism', *Journal of Pediatrics*, 1944, *25*, p. 211.
86. Kanner, L., 'To What Extent is Early Infantile Autism Determined by Constitutional Inadequacies?', *Research Publications of the Association for Research into Nervous and Mental Diseases*, 1954, *33*, p. 378.
87. Kellmer Pringle, M. L., 'The Incidence of Some Supposedly Adverse Family Conditions and of Left-handedness in Schools for Maladjusted Children', *British Journal of Educational Psychology*, 1961, *31*, p. 183.
88. Kellmer Pringle, M. L., *Deprivation and Education*, Longmans, 1965.
89. Kellmer Pringle, M. L., *Adoption – Facts and Fallacies*, Longmans, 1967.
90. Kidd, C. B., Giel, R., and Brown, J. B., 'The Antecedent Mental Health of Pregnant Unmarried Women', *Proceedings of the British Student Health Association*, 1964, *16*, p. 51.
91. Klein, D. C., and Lindeman, L., 'Preventive Intervention in Individual and Family Crisis Situations', in Caplan, G., (ed.), *Prevention of Mental Disorders in Children*, Tavistock Publications, 1961.
92. Klein, M., *The Psychoanalysis of Children*, Hogarth Press, for the Institute of Psychoanalysis, London, 1963.
93. Klein, M., *Narrative of a Child Analysis*, Hogarth Press, for the Institute of Psychoanalysis, 1961, with acknowledgement to the Melanie Klein Trustees.
94. Klein, M., 'The Psychoanalytic Play Technique', in Haworth, M. R., (ed.), *Child Psychotherapy*, Basic Books, 1964, pp. 119–21.
95. Kreitman, N., 'The Patient's Spouse', *British Journal of Psychiatry*, 1964, *110*, p. 159.
96. Langford, W. S., 'Physical Illness and Convalescence: Their Meaning to the Child', *Journal of Pediatrics*, 1948, *33*, p. 242.
97. Lapouse, R., and Monk, M. A., 'An Epidemiological Study of Behaviour Characteristics in Children', *American Journal of Public Health*, 1958, *48*, p. 1134.
98. Lavery, L., and Stone, F. H., 'Psychotherapy of a Deprived Child', *Journal of Child Psychology and Psychiatry*, 1965, *6*, p. 115.
99. Levy, D. M., 'Release Therapy', *American Journal of Orthopsychiatry*, 1939, *9*, p. 713.
100. Levy, D. M., 'The Infant's Earliest Memory of Inoculations: a Contribution to Public Health Procedures', *Journal of Genetic Psychology*, 1960, *96*, p. 3.

101. Levy, D. M., 'Psychic Trauma of Operations in Children and a Note on Combat Neurosis', *American Journal of Disease in Childhood*, 1945, *69*, p. 7.

102. Lewis, H., *Deprived Children*, Oxford University Press, 1954.

103. Lippitt, R., and White, R., 'The "Social Climate" of Children's Groups', in Barker, R. G., Konnin, J., and Wright, H., (eds.), *Child Behavior and Development*, McGraw-Hill, New York, 1943.

104. Lotter, V., 'Epidemiology of Autistic Conditions in Young Children: 1. Prevalence ', *Social Psychiatry*, 1966, *1*, p. 124.

105. Lowrey, L. G., 'Personality Distortion and Early Institutional Care', *American Journal of Orthopsychiatry*, 1940, *10*, p. 576.

106. McCord, W., and J., *The Psychopath*, Van Nostrand, Princeton, New Jersey, 1964.

107. McCulloch, J. W., Henderson, A. S., and Philip, A. E., 'Psychiatric Illness in Edinburgh teenagers', *Scottish Medical Journal*, 1966, *11*, p. 277.

108. MacDonald, E. K., 'Follow-up of Illegitimate Children', *The Medical Officer*, 1956, *96*, p. 361.

109. MacFarlane, J. W., Allen, L., and Honzig, P., *A Developmental Study of Behavior Problems of Normal Children between 21 Months and 14 Years*, University of California Press, Berkeley and Los Angeles, 1954.

110. McWhinnie, A. M., *Adopted Children: How They Grow Up*, Routledge and Kegan Paul, 1967.

111. Mahler, M. S., and Gosliner, B. J., 'On Symbiotic Child Psychosis: Genetic, Dynamic and Restitutive Aspects', *Psychoanalytic Study of the Child*, 1955, *10*, p. 195.

112. Marris, P., *Widows and their Families*, Routledge and Kegan Paul, 1958.

113. Ministry of Education, *Report of the Committee on Maladjusted Children*, H.M.S.O., 1955, p. 22.

114. Ministry of Health *and* Central Health Services Council, *The Welfare of Children in Hospital*, H.M.S.O., 1959.

115. Mitchel, S. and Shepherd, M., 'A Comparative Study of Children's Behaviour at Home and at School', *British Journal of Educational Psychology*, 1966, *36*, p. 248.

116. Munro, A., 'Parental Deprivation in Depressive Patients', *British Journal of Psychiatry*, 1966, *112*, p. 443.

117. National Council of Social Service, *Caring for People*, Allen and Unwin, 1967.

118. Newson, J. and E., *Infant Care in an Urban Community*, 1963, also published as *Patterns of Infant Care in an Urban Community* by Penguin Books, 1965.

119. Newson, J. and E., *Four Years old in an Urban Community*, Allen and Unwin, 1968.

120. Ounstedt, C., 'The Hyperkinetic Syndrome in Epileptic Childern', *Lancet*, 1955, *II*, p. 303.

121. Palmer, J. W., 'Smoking, Caning and Delinquency in a Secondary Modern School', *British Journal of Preventive and Social Medicine*, 1965, *19*, p. 18.

122. Parkes, C. M., 'Effects of Bereavement on Physical and Mental Health: a study of the Medical Records of Widows', *British Medical Journal*, 1964, *2*, p. 274.

123. Pasamanick, B., Rogers, M. E., and Lilienfeld, A. M., 'Pregnancy Experience and the Development of Behavior Disorders in Children', *American Journal of Psychiatry*, 1956, *112*, p. 613.

124. Piaget, J., *The Child's Conception of the World*, Routledge and Kegan Paul, 1929, p. 220.

236

125. Piaget, J., *The Language and Thought of the Child*, Kegan Paul, Trench, Trubner & Co., 1932.
126. Piaget, J., *The Moral Judgement of the Child*, Kegan Paul, Trench, Trubner & Co., 1932.
127. Pond, D. A., Ryle, A., and Hamilton, M., 'Marriage and Neurosis in a Working Class Population', *British Journal of Psychiatry*, 1963, *109*, p. 592.
128. Prugh, D. G., Staub, E. M., Sands, H. H., Kirschbaum, R. M., and Lenihan, E. A., 'A Study of the Emotional Reactions of Children and Families to Hospitalization and Illness', *American Journal of Orthopsychiatry*, 1953, *23*, p. 70.
129. *Report of the Committee on Local Authority and Allied Personal Social Services*, H.M.S.O., 1968.
130. Rheingold, H. L., 'The Modification of Social Responsiveness in Institutional Babies', *Monographs of the Society for Research in Child Development*, 1956, *21*, No. 2.
131. Rie, H. E., Boverman, H., Ozoa, N., and Grossman, B. J., 'Tutoring and Ventilation', *Clinical Pediatrics*, 1964, *3*, p. 581.
132. Robertson, J., *Young Children in Hospital*, Tavistock Publications, 1958.
133. Robins, L. N., *Deviant Children Grown Up*, Williams and Wilkins Co., Baltimore, 1966.
134. Rowley, K. G., 'Social Relations between British and Immigrant Children', *Educational Research*, 1968, *10*, p. 145.
135. Rutter, M., *Illness in Parents and Children*, M.D. thesis, University of Birmingham, 1962.
136. Rutter, M., 'Medical Aspects of the Education of Psychotic (Autistic) Children', in Weston, P.T.B., (ed.), *Some Approaches to Teaching Autistic Children*, Pergamon Press, 1965.
137. Rutter, M., 'Classification and Categorization in Child Psychiatry', *Journal of Child Psychology and Psychiatry*, 1965, *6*, p. 71.
138. Rutter, M., *Children of Sick Parents*, Maudsley Monograph No. 16, Oxford University Press, 1966.
139. Rutter, M., 'Prognosis: Psychotic Children in Adolescence and Early Adult Life', in Wing, J. K., (ed.), *Early Childhood Autism*, Pergamon Press, 1966.
140. Rutter, M., Birch, H. G., Thomas, A., and Chess, S., 'Temperamental Characteristics in Infancy and the Later Development of Behavioural Disorders', *British Journal of Psychiatry*, 1964, *110*, p. 651.
141. Rutter, M., and Graham, P., 'Psychiatric Disorder in 10- and 11-year old Children', *Proceedings of the Royal Society of Medicine*, 1966, *59*, p. 382.
142. Ryle, A., Pond, D. A., and Hamilton, M., 'The Prevalence and Patterns of Psychological Disturbance in Children of Primary Age', *Journal of Child Psychology and Psychiatry*, 1965, *6*, p. 101.
143. Schaffer, H. R., and Callender, W. M., 'Psychological Effects of Hospitalization in Infancy', *Journal of Pediatrics*, 1959, *24*, p. 528.
144. Schaffer, H. R., and Emerson, P. E., 'The Development of Social Attachments in Infancy', *Monographs of the Society for Research in Child Development*, 1964, *29*, No. 3.
145. Schaffer, H. R., 'Activity Level as a Constitutional Determinant of Infantile Reaction to Deprivation', *Child Development*, 1966, *37*, p. 595.
146. Schaffer, H. R. and E. B., *Child Care and the Family*, Occasional Papers on Social Administration, No. 25, G. Bell and Sons, 1968.
147. Scottish Education Department, *Primary Education in Scotland*, H.M.S.O., 1965.
148. Scottish Education Department *and* Scottish Home and Health Department, *Social Work and the Community*, H.M.S.O., 1966.

References

149. Scottish Home and Health Department *and* Scottish Education Department, *Children and Young Persons, Scotland*, H.M.S.O., 1964.
150. Sears, R. R., Maccoby, E. E., and Levin, H., *Patterns of Child Rearing*, Row, Peterson & Co., Illinois and New York, 1957.
151. Seglow, J., 'Introductory Paper on Adoption', read at Annual Conference of National Bureau for Co-operation in Child Care, 1968, to be published in the series *'Studies in Child Development'*, Longmans, 1969.
152. Shepherd, M., Oppenheim, A. N., and Mitchell, S., 'The Definition and Outcome of Deviant Behaviour in Childhood', *Proceedings of the Royal Society of Medicine*, 1966, *59*, p. 379.
153. Slater, E., and Woodside, M., *Patterns of Marriage: a Study of Marriage Relationships in the Urban Working Classes*, Cassell, 1951.
154. Spence, J., 'The Care of Children in Hospital', in *The Purpose and Practice of Medicine*, Oxford University Press, 1960.
155. Spence, J., Walton, W. S., Miller, F. J. W., and Court, S. D. M., *A Thousand Families in Newcastle Upon Tyne*, Oxford University Press, 1954.
156. Spitz, R. A., and Wolf, K. M., 'The Smiling Response: a Contribution to the Ontogenesis of Social Relations', *Genetic Psychology Monographs*, 1946, *34*, p. 57.
157. Spitz, R. A., 'Hospitalism', *Psychoanalytic Study of the Child*, 1945, *1*, p. 53.
158. Stanley, G. R., 'Health Education and Cigarette Smoking: an Appendix on Adolescents', *Health Bulletin*, 1966, *24*, p. 1.
159. Stein, Z., and Susser, M., 'The Families of Dull Children: Identifying Family Types and Sub-cultures', *Journal of Mental Science*, 1960, *106*, p. 1296.
160. Terman, L. M., and Oden, M. H., 'The Stanford Studies of the Gifted', in Witty, P., (ed.), *The Gifted Child*, D. and C. Heath & Co., Boston, 1951.
161. Thomas, A., Birch, H. G., Chess, S., Hertzig, M. E., and Korn, S., *Behavioral Individuality in Early Childhood*, New York University Press, 1963.
162. Timms, N., *Psychiatric Social Work in Great Britain 1939-1962*, Routledge and Kegan Paul, 1964, Chapter 5.
163. Tizard, J., 'Schooling for the Handicapped', *Special Education*, 1966, *55*, p. 4.
164. Tolstoy, L., *Anna Karenin*, transl. R. Edmonds, Penguin Books, 1954.
165. Townsend, P., *The Family Life of Old People*, Routledge and Kegan Paul, 1957, and Penguin Books, 1963.
166. Ullman, C. A., *Identification of Maladjusted School Children*, U.S. Public Health Monograph No. 7, Washington, 1952.
167. Vaughan, G. F., 'Children in Hospital', *Lancet*, 1957, *I*, p. 1117.
168. Wardle, C. J., 'Two Generations of Broken Homes in the Genesis of Conduct and Behaviour Disorders in Childhood', *British Medical Journal*, 1961, *2*, p. 349.
169. Waring, M., and Ricks, D., 'Family Patterns of Children Who Became Adult Schizophrenics', *Journal of Nervous and Mental Diseases*, 1965, *140*, p. 351.
170. Weil, A. P., 'Certain Severe Disturbances of Ego Development in Childhood', *Psychoanalytic Study of the Child*, 1953, *8*, p. 271.
171. West, D., *The Young Offender*, Duckworth and Penguin Books, 1967.
172. Whiting, J. W. M., and Child, I. L., *Child Training and Personality: a Cross Cultural Study*, Yale University Press, 1953.
173. Wickman, E. K., *Children's Behavior and Teachers' Attitudes*, The Commonwealth Fund, New York, 1928.
174. Wing, J. K., (ed.), *Early Childhood Autism*, Pergamon Press, 1966.
175. Wing, L., *Autistic Children*, National Association for Mental Health, London, 1964.

176. Wolff, S., 'Group Discussions with Nurses in a Hospital for Alcoholics', *International Journal of Nursing Studies*, 1964, *1*, p. 131.

177. Wolff, S., 'Behavioural Characteristics of Primary School Children Referred to a Psychiatric Department', *British Journal of Psychiatry*, 1967, *113*, p. 885.

178. Wolff, S., 'The Contribution of Obstetric Complications to the Etiology of Behaviour Disorders in Childhood', *Journal of Child Psychology and Psychiatry*, 1967, *8*, 57.

179. Wolff, S., and Acton, W. P., 'Characteristics of Parents of Disturbed Children', *British Journal of Psychiatry*, 1968, *114*.

180. Wolff, S., and Chess, S., 'A Behavioural Study of Schizophrenic Children', *Acta Psychiatrica Scandinavica*, 1964, *40*, p. 438.

181. Woodward, J., and Jackson, D., 'Emotional Reactions in Burned Children and Their Mothers', *British Journal of Plastic Surgery*, 1961, *13*, p. 316.

182. Yelloly, M. A., 'Factors Relating to an Adoption Decision by the Mothers of Illegitimate Infants', *Sociological Review*, 1965, *13*, p. 5.

183. Young, M., and Willmott, P., *Family and Kinship in East London*, Routledge and Kegan Paul, 1957, and Penguin Books, 1962.

184. Yudkin, S., 'Children and Death', *Lancet*, 1967, *1*, p. 37.

Index